An Imperfect Union

D0224187

WITHDRAWN
UTSA LIBRARIES

The New Europe: Interdisciplinary Perspectives
Stanley Hoffmann, Series Editor

AN IMPERFECT UNION

UNION

The Maastricht Treaty and the New Politics of European Integration

Michael J. Baun

Westview Press

A Division of HarperCollins*Publishers*

The New Europe: Interdisciplinary Perspectives

All rights reserved. Printed in the United States of America. No part of this publication may be repro-duced or transmitted in any form or by any means, electronic or mechanical, including photocopy, recording, or any information storage and retrieval system, without permission in writing from the publisher.

Copyright © 1996 by Westview Press, Inc., A Division of HarperCollins Publishers, Inc.

Published in 1996 in the United States of America by Westview Press, Inc., 5500 Central Avenue, Boulder, Colorado 80301-2877, and in the United Kingdom by Westview Press, 12 Hid's Copse Road, Cumnor Hill, Oxford OX2 9JJ

Library of Congress Cataloging-in-Publication Data
Baun, Michael J.
    An imperfect union : the Maastricht Treaty and the new politics of European integration / Michael J. Baun.
        p.   cm. — (The new Europe)
    Includes bibliographical references and index.
    ISBN 0-8133-2710-5 (hardcover). — ISBN 0-8133-2711-3 (paperback)
    1. European Union.   2. European federation.   I. Title.
    II. Series: New Europe (Boulder, Colo.)
    JN30.B38   1996
    341.24'2—dc20   95-40995
                                                                                         CIP

The paper used in this publication meets the requirements of the American National Standard for Permanence of Paper for Printed Library Materials Z39.48-1984.

10   9   8   7   6   5   4   3   2   1

Library
University of Texas
at San Antonio

Contents

Two Models for the Future, 165
Notes, 167

Preface

For the past fifty years, the countries of Western Europe have been engaged in a fascinating and important experiment. For the first time in modern history, a group of independent nation-states have sought to integrate their economies and political decisionmaking structures to ensure peace and improve their joint capacity to meet the challenges of interdependence. After being launched in the 1950s, European integration bogged down in the 1960s and 1970s, only to be dramatically reborn in the 1980s with the dynamic Single Market ("Europe 1992") project. The dramatic collapse of communism in Eastern Europe and the end of the cold war, however, have confronted the architects of European integration with an entirely new set of problems and challenges. This book examines how the European Union (EU) and its member states have responded in the immediate term to these challenges and what these challenges may mean for the longer-term development of the EU and European integration.

Nevertheless, writing about the EU is not an easy task at this particular time. One obvious reason is the difficulty inherent in writing about a current issue or topic, a problem exacerbated by the rapidly moving pace of events within Europe in recent years. However, the pace of change has slowed somewhat since the hectic period of 1989–1993, encompassing the fall of the Berlin Wall and the final ratification and adoption of the Maastricht Treaty on European Union. Even though the EU now prepares for its next major intergovernmental conference in 1996, a sequel of sorts to the Maastricht negotiations, this pending conference is unlikely to produce any dramatic developments or bold new steps in the direction of greater integration, for reasons explored in this book. With the situation in Europe and the EU having settled down in the mid-1990s, more detached and sober analysis of developments over the previous half-dozen years is now both possible and necessary.

Also making it difficult to write about the EU at this time is the turbulent state of EU studies. The relaunching of European integration in the 1980s brought about a resurgence of interest in, and debate between, the two dominant "grand" theories of integration: neofunctionalism, which emphasizes the role of supranational institutions and the dynamic of spillover, and intergovernmentalism, which stresses the centrality of nation-states and bargaining between national governments. Developments in the EU since 1989, however, including the Maastricht

Treaty and the treaty ratification crisis, have posed a severe challenge for both grand theories and have prompted the search for new or alternative explanations of integration.

In this book I do not attempt a systematically theoretical explanation of EU developments since 1989. Nevertheless, I do operate on the basis of some key theoretical assumptions. I assume, for instance, that integration takes place because it is in the interests of the EU's member states. In keeping with this fundamentally intergovernmentalist perspective, I argue that developments in the EU, and in particular the Maastricht Treaty, represent essentially the response of European governments to the new geopolitical and security imperatives created by German unification and the end of the cold war. I also work from the assumption that the interests of the largest and most influential member states are those that matter most in EU affairs. For this reason, I give particular attention to the actions of Germany and France, though recognizing a key secondary role for Britain. At the same time, however, I agree with neofunctionalism in acknowledging the importance of institutions, and I attempt to explain how perceptions of national and state interests have been shaped, and in some cases transformed, by the previous decades of integration and interdependence.

If this book has a central theoretical claim, it is that the end of the cold war and German unification have made European integration once again primarily a matter of "high politics." By this I mean that considerations of security and geopolitics, affecting both the Community's internal balance and relations among its member states and the EU's external position and role, have again become the driving force of European integration, much as they were in the early postwar years. It may well be the case that after a period of rebalancing and consolidation, "low politics" issues (i.e., economics) will once again come to predominate within the EU. Given the fundamental nature of the regional and global geopolitical changes that have taken place since 1989, however, this new high politics moment for the EU will likely last for an extended period of time.

As this book goes to press, the EU is experiencing a new period of pessimism and malaise, a continuation of its post-Maastricht crisis. Despite the new high politics focus of the EU, however, in fact precisely because of it, my own view of the prospects for European integration is much more optimistic. I continue to regard further integration as both necessary and inevitable, although it will undoubtedly take new forms and directions in the future. Thus, my own interest in, and fascination with, the EU and European integration remain undiminished in this period of "Europessimism," and I hope that this sentiment is transmitted in this book.

I wish to conclude with a brief word of thanks for all those who have made this book possible and writing it more enjoyable. This group includes my colleagues and students in the Department of Political Science at Georgia State University and in particular the department chair, Glenn Abney, who provided me with the time and financial support to work on the project. I thank the professionals at Westview Press, particularly senior editor Susan McEachern, for their interest in this book and efforts to bring it to press in a timely fashion. Finally, I thank my wife, Julia, for her loving consideration and support during the writing of this book. Being an "academic widow" is not easy, especially in a new marriage, and I appreciate her patience and forbearance tremendously.

Michael J. Baun

Acronyms

CAP	Common Agricultural Policy
CDU/CSU	Christian Democratic Union/Christian Social Union
CFSP	Common Foreign and Security Policy
CSCE	Conference on Security and Cooperation in Europe
DM, D-mark	deutsche mark
EC	European Community
ECB	European Central Bank
Ecofin	Council of Economics and Finance Ministers
ECSC	European Coal and Steel Community
ECU	European Currency Unit
EDC	European Defense Community
EEA	European Economic Area
EEC	European Economic Community
EFTA	European Free Trade Association
EMCF	European Monetary Cooperation Fund
EMI	European Monetary Institute
EMS	European Monetary System
EMU	Economic and Monetary Union
EP	European Parliament
EPC	European Political Cooperation
EPU	European Political Union
ERM	Exchange-Rate Mechanism
EU	European Union
Euratom	European Atomic Energy Community
FDP	Free Democratic Party
FRG	Federal Republic of Germany
GATT	General Agreement on Tariffs and Trade
GDP	gross domestic product
GDR	German Democratic Republic

NATO	North Atlantic Treaty Organization
SEA	Single European Act
SED	Socialist Unity Party
SPD	Social Democratic Party
WEU	Western European Union

Introduction

In 1989 Europe experienced a geopolitical earthquake of the first magnitude. With the unexpected collapse of communism and the Berlin Wall, the cold war that had divided Europe for more than four decades came suddenly to an end. For the most part, the end of that war was hailed as a victory for peace and freedom. The ceremonies commemorating the fifty-year anniversary of the end of World War II that were held in many European capitals in early May 1995 were perhaps as much a celebration of the avoidance of a third global conflagration as they were a remembrance of the final Allied victory over Nazi Germany. Nevertheless, the end of the cold war also meant an end to the long period of peace and stability that it had imposed on Europe, despite considerable political and economic costs for both sides. In the cold war's aftermath, new possibilities for disorder and conflict emerged, so much so that some neorealist scholars have even argued that Americans and Europeans would "soon miss the cold war."[1]

The end of the cold war has therefore prompted the search for new institutional bases for stability and peace to replace the old bipolar order. In this search, much attention has focused on the European Community (EC),[2] the organization of Western European states that was created in 1958, and that has since grown to include fifteen member countries. Through integration within the EC, European countries have achieved substantial economic growth and prosperity, as well as intensified political cooperation. Largely because of the EC, democracy in Western Europe has been consolidated, and war between Western European countries is now unthinkable. Thus, many on both sides of the Atlantic hope that the EC may serve as the institutional anchor for the New Europe, becoming the focal point of a new pan-European order of democracy, economic prosperity, and political security.

A major problem with this scenario, however, is that the EC itself was greatly shaped by the cold war. Among the key factors influencing the formation and development of the Community were the division of Europe into mutually exclusive superpower blocs, the existence of a common Soviet military threat, and the hegemonic U.S. security role in Europe. These geopolitical and structural conditions not only limited the potential membership of the EC and generated a common sense of identity and purpose but also helped overcome the security rivalries and conflicts that had bedeviled Western European countries in the past. In addition, the division of Germany temporarily resolved the traditional "German problem" and was an important factor promoting Franco-German reconciliation and the development of a balanced relationship between the Federal Republic of

Germany (FRG) and France. As a consequence, this tandem was able to function as the primary axis or motor of European integration throughout the postwar decades.

With the end of the cold war and German unification, however, the geopolitical context of European integration has been drastically transformed. This geopolitical revolution, in turn, poses a number of important challenges for the EC and European integration. To begin with, Eastern European countries are no longer separated from Western Europe by the "iron curtain"; consequently the enlargement of the EC into a truly pan-European organization is now on the agenda, with all of the problems for the Community this entails. At the same time, the new geopolitical environment in Europe, as well as a decreasing U.S. security presence and role, means that European states must develop new institutions for regional security and political cooperation while preventing the reemergence of nationalism and traditional interstate rivalries. Finally, the geopolitical earthquake of 1989 has significantly altered the political balance within the Community among its key member states. Most crucially of all, the end of the cold war has seen the reemergence of the so-called German problem, the traditional dilemma posed by the existence of a united and powerful Germany in the center of a politically fragmented Europe. Of particular concern in this regard is the impact of German unification on the vital Franco-German relationship. Bound up with the question of whether the EC can serve as the institutional basis for post–cold war Europe, therefore, is the equally important question of how it will adapt to these fundamental geopolitical changes.

The European Community after the cold war is the subject of this book. I examine and seek to explain developments within the EC since 1989. I argue that an immediate consequence of the end of the cold war and German unification was the effort to "deepen" integration within the existing Community, as evidenced by the 1991–1992 Maastricht Treaty.[3] However, this initial impulse toward deeper integration has since stalled in the face of mounting public opposition to further integration and continued economic uncertainty. I argue that, although not directly responsible for the treaty's ratification difficulties and the Community's post-Maastricht crisis, the geopolitical changes in Europe since 1989 may have indirectly contributed to them. I also look beyond recent developments and ask what the geopolitical realities of the New Europe mean for the future of the EC and European integration. I contend that, despite current problems, European integration will continue in the future. Nevertheless, the end of the cold war and German unification pose new difficulties and challenges for the Community and ensure that European integration in the future will follow a pattern very different from that which has characterized the EC in the recent past.

The Maastricht Treaty and Beyond

In December 1991, EC leaders met in the Dutch town of Maastricht and agreed to the Treaty on European Union. At the heart of this treaty was a plan for achieving full monetary and currency union among EC countries by 1999. The treaty also established new intergovernmental mechanisms for cooperation on foreign and security policy, as well as on immigration, police, and judicial affairs. After the formal signing in February 1992, all that remained before the Maastricht Treaty could take effect was its ratification by each of the twelve member states, which was due to be accomplished by the end of the year. The treaty's rejection by Danish voters in a June 1992 referendum, however, sparked growing opposition in other EC countries and initiated a prolonged ratification crisis. This situation was compounded by currency crises in September 1992 and July–August 1993, which greatly endangered the Maastricht plans for monetary union. Although the treaty was finally ratified and adopted in November 1993, the events of the previous seventeen months had plunged the EC (now EU) into a mood of pessimism and despair and raised new questions about the future of European integration.

Because of the treaty's central role in EC developments after 1989, the Maastricht Treaty is a primary focus of this book. I argue that, although the treaty had important roots in EC developments before 1989, particularly in preexisting plans for Economic and Monetary Union (EMU), it can also be understood as the response of European governments to the new geopolitical conditions and imperatives created by the end of the cold war and German unification. Of central importance in this regard were the revived German problem, and the belief that a united Germany had to be bonded even more firmly to the Community and Western institutions. Failing such bonding, it was feared, Germany could once again become a more dominant and threatening force in the center of Europe. It was also feared that without deeper integration, post–cold war Europe could experience growing fragmentation and the resurgence of traditional national rivalries and conflicts. Such views and concerns were held not only by many of Germany's European neighbors but by most German political elites as well. Also important, although perhaps secondary to the German question, was the widely shared belief that deeper integration was necessary to enable the Community to serve as the architectural cornerstone for the New Europe and to allow the EC to adequately address the problems and needs of postcommunist Eastern Europe. Finally, it was generally believed that greater cooperation in foreign and security policy was necessary for Europe to have a stronger role in the more pluralistic post–cold war global order.

Whether the Maastricht Treaty was able to meet these objectives is a key question that I consider in this book. I also analyze the diplomacy of the intergovernmental negotiations on monetary and political union and explain the key factors influencing the final shape and contents of the treaty. I then examine the Community's post-Maastricht crisis, which occurred after the treaty had been signed and had entered its ratification phase. I show that this crisis resulted from the confluence of two separate but interrelated developments. The first of these was the large-scale popular backlash against the treaty and European integration, as evidenced by the Danish veto and ratification problems in other member states. Popular opposition to the treaty, I argue, stemmed from economic insecurity and concerns about the loss of national sovereignty and identity as well as a variety of nationally specific factors. The anti-Maastricht backlash also revealed the existence of a huge gap between popular and elite views on the need for further integration. Whether this backlash could have been avoided by a different approach to negotiating the treaty, or through the establishment of more democratic Community structures, is a question I consider herein.

The second development contributing to the post-Maastricht crisis was turmoil in international currency markets. The currency crises of 1992 and 1993 placed the European Exchange-Rate Mechanism under considerable stress and raised serious doubts about the Maastricht timetable for achieving monetary union. The currency crises also raised new concerns about the economic consequences of Maastricht and reinforced growing public doubts about the desirability of further integration. In view of the anti-Maastricht backlash and currency upheavals, it could be argued that in concluding the Maastricht Treaty, EC leaders, motivated as they were primarily by geopolitical concerns and fear of Germany, moved too far ahead of both public opinion and economic conditions, thus helping precipitate a crisis. In this book, I examine in detail both the political and economic dimensions of the Community's post-Maastricht crisis.

With the final ratification and adoption of the Maastricht Treaty in November 1993, the European Union has entered a new phase of consolidation. I maintain that although economic uncertainty and the critical public reaction to Maastricht have imposed short-term limits to further integration, in the longer run the prospects for further integration remain good. Integration in the future, however, will be greatly influenced by the new geopolitical realities of post–cold war Europe and the challenges these realities pose, including the imperative of enlargement, the enhanced power and influence of Germany, and the need to construct new institutions for political and security cooperation. Integration will also be shaped by the continued divergence of economic conditions and interests within the Community as well as the different political wills and capacities of member states to proceed with further integration. Such economic and political diversity, in fact, will only grow as a result of Community enlargement. For these reasons, I argue, European integration in the future will likely proceed according to a "multi-speed" or "variable geometry" model, featuring different levels of cooperation among different groups of states. Indeed, the basis for such a model has already been established by previous EC institutional developments, including the two-speed provisions of the Maastricht EMU agreement. The full economic and political ramifications of such a model, however, remain as yet unclear.

France and Germany

In analyzing European integration after 1989, I give a central role to Franco-German relations. As has been frequently noted, France and Germany are the Community's two most important member states, and the Franco-German partnership has generally served as the primary axis of European integration in the postwar decades.[4] The situation has been no different since 1989. In this book I argue, in fact, that the Franco-German axis was the driving force behind the Maastricht Treaty. For each country, the Maastricht Treaty served important national interests. For France, it was a means of integrating a united Germany more firmly into European institutions, thus limiting that country's independence. Through promoting further integration, the treaty would also give France greater leverage and control over Germany, particularly in the crucial realm of monetary policy. For Germany, the Maastricht Treaty was a means of assuaging the fears of its European neighbors about German power and independence. By agreeing to EMU, Germany demonstrated both its willingness to give up national sovereignty and its continued commitment to European integration. The treaty also represented an important step in the direction of further political union. This was a goal that Germany had always sought for its own sake but that it now viewed as being even more vital in the uncertain security environment of post–cold war Europe. For both countries, the Maastricht Treaty was a way to preserve the Franco-German partnership amid the altered geopolitical conditions of the New Europe.

The dynamics of the Franco-German relationship could also be a major factor promoting the movement to a multi-speed EU in the future. Even with the final ratification of the Maastricht Treaty, many of the geopolitical and security problems created by the end of the cold war remain, as does the problem of enhanced German power and influence. For this reason, it might well be in the interest of both France and Germany to lead a core of more economically and politically prepared states into closer union in the future, with the justification that this will serve as the nucleus for an eventual pan-European union. In this manner, some of the key geopolitical and security objectives of both countries could be achieved and in a form that does not sacrifice the possible (closer union among a small group of states) on the altar of the desirable (uniform integration among all EU countries). As I discuss later in the book, a vigorous debate over the "core Europe" concept has emerged in Germany and other European countries since final ratification of the Maastricht Treaty, indicating a revived interest in the multi-speed model for further integration.

Despite its focus on France and Germany, I do not neglect the role of other countries in the post-1989 integration process; nor do I argue that other countries were unimportant. In particular, Britain was a key actor in the Maastricht Treaty negotiations and in the subsequent currency upheavals and ratification crisis. At the same time, smaller countries made their own important contributions to the politics of European integration. One cannot forget, for instance, that it was a referendum in tiny Denmark that first plunged the Community into crisis in 1992. Also important has been the role of the European Commission. In particular, commission president Jacques Delors was a primary catalyst behind the Maastricht negotiations and preceding moves toward EMU. Largely because of this, Delors and the commission were also key targets of the anti-Maastricht backlash that developed after the treaty was signed. In any account of the Maastricht Treaty and European integration after 1989, therefore, the Delors Commission would have to figure prominently, as it does in this book.[5]

Neverthless, it remains the case that very little has ever happened in the EC without Franco-German cooperation and leadership, and certainly nothing of importance has happened against the wishes of this formidable tandem. For this reason, the focus on these two countries is amply justified. In fact, I argue that, if anything, developments since 1989 have only increased the central role of the Franco-German relationship in the process of European integration.

The Maastricht Treaty and Integration Theory

With its emphasis on state interests and intergovernmental bargaining, this book clearly takes issue with functionalist and neofunctionalist theories of integration. The former argues that integration proceeds from functional cooperation between states in relatively noncontroversial "low politics" areas (i.e., economics). Cooperation in some policy areas leads, through a grassroots or bottom-up process of learning, to cooperation in others, eventually resulting in the creation of a complex web of overlapping, functionally specific international organizations. This transnational network increasingly circumscribes and erodes the functions of states, thereby diminishing the power and role of national governments. The end result of this process, as envisioned by its original proponents at least, is less the creation of a supranational superstate than the "withering away" of the national state.[6]

Neofunctionalism stresses the role of supranational institutions as the focal point of an incremental integration process. Integration occurs as national political and social-economic elites forge alliances with supranational entities to promote common policies and institutions. Through a dynamic process of "spillover," integration proceeds from relatively noncontroversial low politics to more sensitive high politics areas of policy (money, foreign policy, defense). At the same time, national political actors are increasingly persuaded "to shift their loyalties, expectations and political activities toward a new center, whose institutions possess or demand jurisdiction over the pre-existing national states."[7] Unlike functionalism, the end point for the more politically oriented theory of neofunction-alism is some form of supranational federal polity.[8]

Even though there are important differences between these two bodies of theory concerning the process and consequences of integration, they also share some basic assumptions. Both view the integration process as being incremental and driven by some version of spillover. Both also predict the eventual demise of the nation-state, although there is considerable disagreement about what will replace it. Although integration theories were greatly discredited by developments within the Community in the 1960s and 1970s, a period that saw the reassertion of national interests and stagnation in EC institutional development, neofunctionalist theories in particular enjoyed a resurgence of interest and support in the late-1980s, due largely to the renewed momentum of European integration generated by the "1992" Single Market project and the Single European Act (SEA).[9]

The approach taken in this book, however, has more in common with intergovernmentalist or realist theories of integration. These emphasize the central role of the state and national interests and argue that integration and interstate cooperation are designed to further national interests and enhance sovereignty rather than undermine it. According to proponents of this view, such has been the goal and outcome of European integration over the years.[10] By stressing the central role of geopolitics in the Maastricht Treaty process, as well as the interests and actions of the EC's key member states (particularly France and Germany), this book adopts a more traditional intergovernmentalist or realist perspective on European integration.

Among this book's major conclusions is that developments since 1989 have only increased the central role of geopolitical and security considerations in the integration process. Since the late 1940s, European integration has proceeded according to two logics: the logic of security and geopolitics and the logic of interdependence and economic necessity. Although both logics have been present and at work throughout the history of the Community, their relative importance for European integration has changed over time. In the early postwar years, security considerations, particularly the need for Franco-German reconciliation, were the primary motivation behind the formation of the European Coal and Steel Community (ECSC) and the ill-fated attempt to create the European Defense Community (EDC). By the late 1950s, however, economic interest and necessity had become the driving forces of integration, and they remained so for the next three decades. In the latter half of the 1980s, however, as fissures within the Soviet bloc began to appear, and uncertainties about U.S. intentions and policy toward Europe grew, the logic of security began to reassert itself. As this book argues, the events of 1989–1990 have made the logic of security once again the predominant driving force of European integration, and this will likely continue well into the future, until a stable new political and security order in Europe is established.[11]

Book Structure and Plan

The origins and negotiation of the Maastricht Treaty are the focus of the first four chapters of this book. Chapter 1 examines the treaty's roots in economic and political developments before 1989. Particular attention is given to the formation of the European Monetary System (EMS) in the late 1970s and the renewed momentum of European integration in the 1980s. Following the launching of the Single Market project and ratification in 1987 of the SEA, attention turned to the goal of monetary union. The motivation for this was partly economic, with monetary union being viewed as a necessary complement to the Single Market, but mainly political, with France and other EC countries seeking to gain some control over the monetary policies of Germany's dominant central bank (the Bundesbank). The Delors Plan for EMU that was approved by EC leaders in June 1989 served as the blueprint for the eventual Maastricht agreement on monetary union.

Chapter 2 examines developments in the thirteen months following the opening of the Berlin Wall. The primary focus of this chapter is the sequence of events and decisions that led to the December 1990 launching of parallel intergovernmental conferences on EMU and European Political Union (EPU). Particular attention is given to the role of the new German problem in promoting the Maastricht negotiations and to the interactions of Franco-German diplomacy. For the governments of both countries, deeper integration was a necessary counterpart to German unification. Further integration would prevent both increased German independence and renewed European fragmentation in the post–cold war era while also helping preserve the Franco-German relationship.

The next two chapters analyze the intergovernmental conferences on EMU and EPU, which culminated in the December 1991 agreement on the Maastricht Treaty. Chapter 3 examines the negotiations on EMU. After surveying the positions and interests of key member states, the chapter analyzes the bargaining over major issues affecting the nature and timing of EMU. The final outcome of the negotiations, it is argued, represents a compromise between the German demand for European monetary institutions and norms that closely replicate its own national model and the general political goal of gaining a firm German commitment to an "irreversible" EMU process.

Chapter 4 examines the conference on political union. It shows that, unlike the negotiations on EMU, the EPU talks did not proceed from any clear agenda or plan but instead involved a complex array of topics and issues. These included the development of a common foreign and defense policy, enhanced powers for the European Parliament (EP), and the extension of Community authority into new policy areas. After briefly surveying the positions of key countries and the main areas of discussion, the chapter traces the progress of EPU negotiations through successive draft treaties. In the final EPU agreement, Germany, which had been a primary exponent of greater political union and had even linked its approval of EMU to a substantive agreement on political union, was forced to accept much less than it had originally wanted. The main reason for this, it is argued, was the Kohl government's overriding desire to secure the Maastricht Treaty in order to demonstrate Germany's continued commitment to European integration.

Chapter 5 examines the Maastricht ratification crisis of 1992–1993. A key cause of this crisis, the chapter demonstrates, was the popular backlash against the Maastricht Treaty and European integration that began with the June 1992 Danish referendum and that delayed final ratification of the treaty by ten months. The chapter also examines the currency crises of September 1992 and July–August 1993. These upheavals almost destroyed the exchange-rate mechanism of the EMS and raised serious doubts about the Maastricht Treaty's ambitious timetable for EMU.

Chapter 6 examines developments in the EU since the final ratification and enactment of the Maastricht Treaty, as well as the prospects for European integration in the post-Maastricht era. After briefly analyzing the sources of the Maastricht crisis, the chapter looks at the new mood of pessimism that has gripped the EU since 1992 and the new pragmatism in EU policy that which this has engendered. The chapter then discusses some of the key issues on the agenda for the EU's next major intergovernmental conference, to be launched in 1996. It concludes with a survey of some of the major challenges confronting the EU in the post-Maastricht era.

In the Conclusion, the book's key findings about the consequences of the end of the cold war and German unification for European integration are reviewed. The book concludes with a discussion of the future prospects for European integration, in which a multi-speed or variable geometry model for the EU is seen as most likely.

Notes

1. John J. Mearsheimer, "Why We Will Soon Miss the Cold War," *Atlantic Monthly* (August 1990):35–50. This is a popularized version of an earlier article: John J. Mearsheimer, "Back to the Future: Instability in Europe After the Cold War," *International Security* 15, 1 (Summer 1990):5–56. For a direct rebuttal of Mearsheimer's neorealist argument from a neoliberal institutionalist perspective, see Richard H. Ullman, *Securing Europe* (Princeton: Princeton University Press, 1991), esp. pp. 138–153. See also Jack Snyder, "Averting Anarchy in the New Europe," *International Security* 14, 4 (Summer 1990):5–41.

2. With final ratification of the Maastricht Treaty, the European Community has been officially renamed the European Union. In this book, the term "European Community," or "EC," is used in discussion of events and developments prior to November 1, 1993, the date on which the Maastricht Treaty formally took effect. Given the nature of things, however, complete consistency in observing this rule is impossible, and in some places in this book the two terms are used interchangeably. Throughout the book, the term "Community" is used to refer to both the EC and European Union.

3. Although the basic terms of the treaty were agreed on at the December 1991 Maastricht summit, the treaty was not formally signed by national leaders until February 1992.

4. On the Franco-German relationship, see Roy Willis, *France, Germany and the New Europe,* 2d ed. (Stanford: Stanford University Press, 1968); Haig Simonian, *The Privileged Partnership: Franco-German Relations and the European Community, 1969–1984* (Oxford: Clarendon Press, 1985); Julius W. Friend, *The Linchpin: French-German Relations, 1950–1990* (New York: Praeger, 1991); Patrick McCarthy, ed., *France-Germany, 1983–93: The Struggle to Cooperate* (New York: St. Martin's Press, 1993).

5. For an analysis of the Maastricht Treaty that does give a primary role to Delors and the commission, see George Ross, *Jacques Delors and European Integration* (New York: Oxford University Press, 1995).

6. On the functionalist theory of integration, see David Mitrany, *A Working Peace System* (London: RIIA, 1944); A.J.R. Groom and Paul Taylor, *Functionalism: Theory and Practice in International Relations* (New York: Crane Roussak, 1975); Paul Taylor, *The Limits of European Integration* (London: Croom Helm, 1983); Paul Taylor, "Functionalism: The Approach of David Mitrany," in A.J.R. Groom and Paul Taylor, eds., *Frameworks for International Cooperation* (London: Pinter), 1990, pp. 125–138.

7. Ernst B. Haas, *The Uniting of Europe* (Stanford: Stanford University Press, 1958), p. 16.

8. The classic texts on neofunctionalism include ibid.; Leon Lindberg, *The Political Dynamics of European Integration* (Stanford: Stanford University Press, 1963); Leon Lindberg and Stuart Scheingold, *Europe's Would-Be Polity* (Englewood Cliffs, N.J.: Prentice-Hall, 1970). For a more recent restatement, see Jeppe Tranholm-Mikkelsen, "Neo-Functionalism: Obstinate or Obsolete? A Reappraisal in the Light of the New Dynamism of the EC," *Millennium* 20 (1991):1–22.

9. For example, see Tranholm-Mikkelsen, "Neo-Functionalism," pp. 1–22; David Mutimer, "1992 and the Political Integration of Europe: Neofunctionalism Reconsidered," *Journal of European Integration* 13 (1989):75–101.

10. On intergovernmentalist or realist theories of integration, see Andrew Moravcsik, "Negotiating the Single European Act," in Robert O. Keohane and Stanley Hoffmann, eds., *The New European Community* (Boulder: Westview Press, 1991), pp. 41–84. The resiliency of the nation-state and its central role in the EC were emphasized by Stanley Hoffmann, "Obstinate or Obsolete: The Fate of the Nation-State and the Case of Western Europe," *Daedalus* 95 (1966):862–915. For the argument that European integration has not undermined the sovereignty of nation-states but has enhanced it, see Alan Milward, *The European Rescue of the Nation-State* (Berkeley and Los Angeles: University of California Press, 1992). See also David Calleo, "Rebalancing the U.S.-European-Soviet Triangle," in Gregory Treverton, ed., *Europe and America Beyond 2000* (London: RIIA, 1989), p. 49; Stanley Hoffmann, "Reflections on the Nation-State in Western Europe Today," *Journal of Common Market Studies* 21, 1–2 (September–December 1982):21–37 (reprinted in Stanley Hoffmann, *The European Sisyphus: Essays on Europe, 1964–1994* [Boulder: Westview Press, 1995], pp. 211–226).

11. A similar argument that European integration since 1989 has been driven chiefly by security concerns is made by Ole Waever, "Identity, Integration, and Security: Solving the Sovereignty Puzzle in E.U. Studies," *Journal of International Affairs* 48, 2 (Winter 1995):389–431.

1

The European Community Before 1989

Although the Maastricht Treaty was a response by the EC and its member countries to German unification and the end of the cold war, it also had important roots in economic and political developments in the Community prior to the opening of the Berlin Wall. Of particular significance in this regard was the considerable momentum toward further integration that had been achieved in the 1980s. By November 1989, in fact, with the Community's project to create a single market well under way, the outlines for a possible agreement on monetary union (the "Delors Plan") had already been approved by national leaders, and member states had tentatively decided to convene a new intergovernmental conference to negotiate a treaty on EMU sometime in the latter half of 1990. The previous history of European integration provided a basis for the Maastricht Treaty in another important sense by establishing a set of institutions and habits that would shape the responses of EC and national leaders to the new challenges of the post–cold war world. An understanding of what happened in the EC after the opening of the Berlin Wall is impossible without knowledge of what occurred before this point. For this reason, developments in the Community prior to 1989, and especially since the late-1970s, are briefly examined in this chapter.

Origins and Historical Evolution of the EC

Although the European Community has evolved mainly as an economic organization, political and security considerations were of primary importance in its formation.[1] In the aftermath of World War II, many Europeans viewed economic and political integration as a means of ensuring that future war and conflict among the nations of Europe would be impossible. Of particular importance was the need for reconciliation between Germany and France, the two main continental powers and the primary antagonists in three European wars within the previous century. At the same time, integration and the construction of supranational institutions were seen as the best means for integrating into capitalist and democratic Western Europe the new Federal Republic of Germany, which had been formed in 1949 through the fusion of the U.S., British, and French zones of occupation. In this manner, France and the Federal Republic's other neighbors could be sure that a reconstructed and strong Germany would pose no threat to them in the future. This became a particularly important issue with the heating up of the cold war after 1949 and the consequent realization that German economic and military power was needed to bolster the Western security alliance. For the most part, these views were shared by leaders of the new Bonn republic, including its first chancellor, Konrad Adenauer. In addition, German leaders favored integration into Western structures as a means of providing external support for the development of fledgling democratic institutions at home, which otherwise lacked a strong basis in national traditions and political culture. Finally, the efforts of the European countries to integrate and forge supranational ties were strongly supported by the United States, which saw these ties as a way to strengthen the alliance against Soviet expansionism while at the same time providing a more prosperous business and trading partner across the Atlantic.

The institutional development of the present-day EC began with the establishment of the European Coal and Steel Community in 1951.[2] At this time six countries—the FRG, France, Italy, and the Benelux countries (Belgium, the Netherlands, and Luxembourg)—agreed to place their coal and steel industries under supranational control. In the immediate term this agreement provided an acceptable means for phasing out Allied control of the German coal and steel sectors exercised through the International Ruhr Authority. In the longer run, the agreement was a key step toward achieving broader political goals. Since these industries were generally considered to be the primary basis of national warmaking power, subjecting them to supranational control would make future war among member countries virtually impossible. Through the ECSC, the integration of a rebuilding Germany into the Western community of democratic states could begin, and German industrial power could be harnessed to the anti-Soviet cause. The ECSC also represented an important gesture of solidarity and reconciliation between Germany and France. Finally, it was widely viewed as the basis for further supranational integration, leading to an eventual European political union. A disappointment connected with the establishment of the ECSC was Britain's decision not to join. The London government wanted to preserve national sovereignty and British separateness from the Continent and also saw Britain's interests linked more closely to the United States and the Commonwealth system.

Even more ambitious than the ECSC was the parallel attempt to forge a European defense community. The EDC initiative, initially proposed in October 1950 by France—only months after French foreign minister Robert Schuman's May 1950 announcement of his plan for the ECSC—called for the integration of national defense forces and the creation of a common army under a unified command. This proposal was primarily a response to the recognition, in the wake of

North Korea's invasion of the South, that German rearmament as a means of bolstering Western defense against the threat of communist expansionism was both necessary and inevitable. Through the EDC, German rearmament could take place within an international framework that would make it more acceptable to France and other European countries. Since defense is a basic function of the state and a key aspect of national sovereignty, the EDC meant, in effect, a fairly significant move in the direction of political union. This, as it turned out, was too big a step for some to take. The EDC treaty was actually signed in 1952 by the six member countries of the ECSC and thereafter ratified by the national parliaments of all but France. It died in August 1954, however, when the French Assembly refused to approve it, reflecting growing sentiment in France that the treaty involved the surrender of too much national sovereignty and independence. In the wake of the EDC's failure, German rearmament was made possible through the integration of the FRG into both the North Atlantic Treaty Organization (NATO) and the Western European Union (WEU). The latter was a much looser intergovernmental organization for European defense cooperation that had originally been established in 1948; it would, however, prove to be of only limited importance until its revival in the 1980s.

The failure of the EDC convinced proponents of European union that integration could not take place through ambitious political leaps in sovereignty-sensitive areas but instead had to proceed in a more gradual or incremental fashion, beginning with cooperation in relatively less controversial and visible low politics spheres such as economics. As a result, at a June 1955 conference in Messina (Italy) the six members of the ECSC decided to expand the integration of their economies beyond the coal and steel sectors and create a Common Market through the elimination of all internal tariff barriers to trade between member countries and a customs union for trade with nonmembers. This was the essence of the 1957 Rome Treaty, which established the European Economic Community (EEC). Also signed at this time by the ECSC six was a treaty creating the European Atomic Energy Community (Euratom), which was to pool nuclear resources and technology and exercise supranational control over this emerging industry. The institutions of the EEC mirrored the tripartite structure of the ECSC and included an executive commission located in Brussels, a council of ministers representing each of the member states, and a legislative assembly—the European Parliament—located in Strasbourg. The EEC, which formally came into existence in 1958, was primarily an economic organization, but it also embodied long-term political goals, with the preamble of the Rome Treaty calling for the creation of an "ever closer union" of European states. Once again the government of Britain, opposed to the political union goals of the EEC and favoring instead a looser free trade arrangement, decided not to take part in the negotiations or sign the treaty, opting instead to remain on the outside.

For all of the EEC's importance as a step toward European union, it was essentially an exercise in "negative" integration, linking member countries through the joint elimination of barriers to the movement of goods across national borders. With the exception of a common external trade policy, the EEC entailed little in the way of "positive" integration, or the formation of true common policies and supranational institutions.[3] Generally speaking, this remained the case until the early 1990s, with the Maastricht Treaty representing a major departure from this pattern. There was one significant exception to this rule, however, and that was the Common Agricultural Policy (CAP). Formally established in 1964, although under negotiation since 1958, the CAP was a system for protecting and subsidizing agriculture and involved both a common external tariff and the central determination of prices for European farm products. It is commonly accepted that the CAP was part of the basic bargain struck between Germany and France, the Community's two largest and most important states, which allowed the formation of the EEC to take place. In return for permitting Germany's powerful manufacturing industries open access to the French domestic market, where they could compete with France's generally less efficient manufacturers, the French government gained Bonn's agreement to help support France's large and politically important agricultural sector.[4] The CAP, then, is of great significance in the historical evolution of the EC for two reasons: Not only is it a rare example of positive integration in the EC, but it is also one of the core interstate bargains underlying the foundation and existence of the Community.

With the establishment of the EEC, the European movement reached a temporary high point. In the early 1960s, the fledgling Community began to experience a number of problems that slowed down its continued evolution and inhibited progress toward further integration. Chief among these was the assertion of national interests and prerogative by France and its president, Charles de Gaulle. This dynamic began with de Gaulle's veto of Britain's first attempt at entry into the Community in 1963. In the following year, crises erupted over the question of the commission's powers and the issue of majority voting in the Council of Ministers. Basically, de Gaulle objected to any strengthening of the Community's supranational institutions, viewing this as an infringement on the fundamental sovereignty of the French state. Rather than a supranational Community, de Gaulle's vision of European union was a more loosely structured "Europe of nation-states," in which individual countries retained their basic identities and sovereignty. To resist enhanced powers for the commission, and to block the planned transition to a system of qualified majority voting within the Council of Ministers, de Gaulle seized on the opportunity presented by a dispute with Germany over CAP grain prices and in July 1965 withdrew French representatives from Community decisionmaking institutions—the so-called empty chair policy. French participation only resumed with the "Luxembourg compromise" of the following year, whereby member states would retain the right to veto Community policies that threatened what they perceived to be vital national interests. This decision, in effect, preserved the system of unanimity voting within the Community and blocked the EEC's evolution into a more supranational organization.

After the mid-1960s, the Community entered a period of relative stagnation and malaise; despite this, however, important institutional innovations were to occur in the 1970s. By 1968 the transition to the Common Market was completed. The Community also consolidated the parallel institutions of its heretofore three separate organizations—the EEC, the ECSC, and Euratom; from this point there was the single European Community, with one executive commission, a council of ministers, and the European Parliament. In 1970 the European Political Cooperation (EPC) was launched as a mechanism for foreign policy coordination among EC states. The formation of EPC was to a great extent the result of Germany's new policy of détente with Eastern Europe and the USSR (*"Ostpolitik"*) and was intended by both the Federal Republic and its neighbors to ensure against too much German independence in the future. Another new institution created in the 1970s was the European Council, the name given to the regular meetings (summits) of EC heads of government that began in 1974. The council was intended primarily to provide high-level leadership and direction for the Community. Both the European Council and EPC were established outside the EC's normal (Treaty of Rome) governmental framework, which only served to reinforce the Community's movement in an intergovernmental direction. Also in the early 1970s, the EC completed its first enlargement. After being vetoed a second time by de Gaulle in 1967, Britain finally gained entry into the EC and along with Ireland and Denmark formally joined the Community in 1973.

The European Monetary System

An important development in the history of the Maastricht Treaty was the establishment of the European Monetary System in 1978–1979.[5] This framework for monetary cooperation stabilized economic relations and enhanced integration among EC states, thereby providing the economic and institutional bases for future efforts at full monetary union. Equally important, the EMS signaled a shift in the political balance of power among EC states, particularly between France and Germany. In each of these respects, the creation of the EMS laid the groundwork for the more dramatic initiatives on European economic and monetary integration in the 1980s.

The creation of the EMS followed an earlier unsuccessful attempt by the Community to achieve monetary integration.[6] At a December 1969 summit, EC leaders, led by German chancellor Willy Brandt and French president Georges Pompidou, called for the study of further steps toward economic and monetary union. This resulted in the so-called Werner Plan, named after the chairman of the working group established by the Council of Ministers, which was submitted in October of the following year. The plan proposed a three-stage process of closer monetary cooperation leading to full EMU. In the first phase, to begin in 1971, the exchange rates of national currencies were to be brought into closer alignment. The fluctuations of intra-Community rates would be limited within fairly narrow bands, with national central banks required to intervene in currency markets to keep exchange rates within the established margins. Externally, the European currencies would jointly fluctuate within a broader band against the U.S. dollar. In the second stage, the European Monetary Cooperation Fund (EMCF) would come into existence to help manage monetary relations and provide medium-term financial assistance to countries experiencing exchange-rate difficulties. There would also be increased efforts at the coordination of national economic policies. The third stage, to be realized by 1980, would see the creation of full EMU, including the permanent fixing of exchange rates and the establishment of a regional central bank.

The ambitious plans for EMU contained in the Werner report never really got off the ground but were instead quickly overwhelmed by the consequences of international economic and monetary disorder. The initial stage of the EMU plan, the closer alignment of exchange rates within the so-called snake,[7] was originally set to begin in June 1971, but instability in the global monetary system made this move impossible, resulting in a one-year postponement. In August European monetary plans were dealt a further blow by the unilateral U.S. decision to delink the dollar from gold, effectively ending the postwar system of fixed exchange rates (the "Bretton Woods" system)[8] and preparing the way for a general floating-rate regime. EC countries tried once again in 1972 to align their currencies within the snake, but this new arrangement came under immediate stress as a consequence of continued global economic instability. The EMCF was created in 1973 as planned but was never given significant powers or resources. Instead, by the begining of 1974 European leaders had capitulated in the face of international economic disorder, and plans for EMU were officially abandoned.

The primary legacy of this first effort at European monetary cooperation was a revised version of the currency snake, which came into existence in March 1972. Initially participating in this arrangement were all nine EC member countries, plus nonmembers Sweden and Norway. Although not formal members of the system, Austria and Switzerland also chose to link their currencies to the snake. This arrangement soon proved to be unworkable, however, in the context of global monetary and economic instability. On top of the collapse of the Bretton Woods system and the ensuing U.S. policy of "benign neglect" vis-à-vis the dollar, there were also the recessionary consequences of the 1973–1974 oil shock. In response to the economic crisis, the performance and policies of European countries increasingly diverged. This was due both to the varying strengths of national economies and the different policy preferences of European governments. Germany, with Europe's strongest economy and under the guidance of its independent and stability-oriented central bank, responded with restrictive monetary and fiscal policies aimed at controlling inflation and maintaining a strong national currency (the deutsche mark, or D-mark). Other European governments, however, still under the sway of Keynesian ideas or finding it politically impossible to do otherwise, chose a different course, preferring to emphasize growth and employment through expansionary economic policies.

Divergence in national economic policies and performance was quickly reflected in the path of currency values. Because of the strength of the German economy and the conservative policies of the federal government and Bundesbank, the D-mark quickly established itself as the strongest currency in the snake and steadily gained in value. The currencies of all other European countries, however, tended to depreciate. This meant that to maintain currencies within the required fluctuation bands, other members of the exchange-rate mechanism had to emulate the low-inflation and stability-oriented policies of Germany. This was something that most governments at this time were not able or willing to do, preferring instead to keep export prices competitive and create more scope for expansionary economic policies. In addition, leaving the snake would avoid the need to deplete precious currency reserves in the effort to defend exchange rates. As a result, throughout the mid-1970s there was a gradual defection of countries from the system. Britain was the first to withdraw in 1972 and was soon followed by Italy and Ireland. In early 1974 France also decided to pull out of the snake. It attempted to rejoin in 1975, only to withdraw once again the following year. By 1977 the snake had contracted into what was essentially a D-mark bloc, the remaining group of small northern European countries being too closely integrated with the German economy to permit a floating of their currencies against the D-mark.[9]

Despite the failure of this initial attempt at EMU, by the late 1970s there was a renewed interest among European governments in monetary cooperation.[10] A key reason was continued global economic instability. Of particular concern to Europeans were the effects of unstable and, as they saw it, irresponsible U.S. monetary and economic policies. These had led to a rapid depreciation of the dollar and a fully fledged "dollar crisis," which in turn generated considerable inflationary pressures for the world economy and volatility in international currency markets. The resulting exchange-rate instability among European currencies posed a real threat to trade relations among the interdependent EC economies. In particular, the German government was concerned about the impact of U.S. monetary policy on the relationship between European currencies; while the D-mark appreciated sharply in response to the dollar crisis, other national currencies declined in value as they tended to follow the course of the dollar. This led to a growing divergence in the values of the D-mark and other European currencies, posing a severe threat to German exports in an area where Germany conducted more than half of its trade. As a result, there was a growing German interest in forming a regional zone of monetary and economic stability that would shield, to the greatest extent possible, intra-European trade relations from the disruptive effects of U.S. policies and global instability.[11]

A second major development favoring European monetary cooperation in the late 1970s was the emergence of a new transnational consensus on economic and monetary policy. Basically, there was a growing acceptance by other EC governments of the German preference for low inflation and stability over growth and maximization of employment. While the conversion to German economic and

ry norms was taking place throughout Europe, of particular importance
e change of attitude in France, where traditional growth-oriented policies
giving way to a more conservative monetarist outlook. Beginning in 1976,
er the leadership of President Valéry Giscard d'Estaing and his prime minister, Raymond Barre, the French government reversed the expansionary policies of
the previous two years, which had weakened the franc and forced it out of the
snake, and instituted a program of economic austerity. This shift in French policy,
and the conversion of French political authorities to a German-type monetary
philosophy, in turn helped pave the way for close Franco-German cooperation in
forging a new institutional framework for European monetary coordination.

The renewed effort to achieve monetary integration began in October 1977,
with proposals made by European Commission president Roy Jenkins. Jenkins
appealed specifically to Germany for leadership, citing the exemplary character of
German policies and institutional arrangements. The initial response to this plea
was generally negative among officials of the Bundesbank and Finance Ministry;
Chancellor Helmut Schmidt remained cautious and noncommittal. By early
1978, however, Schmidt had decided to move and communicated to both Jenkins
and French President d'Estaing his own ideas on European monetary cooperation. These were then endorsed by Giscard at a bilateral summit on April 2, leading to a joint Franco-German proposal on European monetary cooperation at the
EC's Copenhagen summit only several days later. After months of negotiation, a
formal agreement on establishment of the EMS was reached in December 1978 at
the European Council meeting in Bremen. In the resolution establishing the EMS,
EC leaders cited as their avowed objective the creation of a "zone of monetary stability in Europe."[12]

At the core of the EMS was the European Exchange-Rate Mechanism.[13] Under
this system of fixed exchange rates, currency values were permitted only a limited
fluctuation, within 2.25 percent of the official established rate. A wider band of 6
percent was created for the Italian lira as a concession to the relative weakness of
that country's economy. At the limits of the fluctuation bands, central banks
would be required to intervene to maintain currency values at the fixed rate.
Although all EC countries joined the EMS, not all participated in the ERM.
Greece initially did not, and Spain and Portugal delayed their membership as
well. The most notable nonparticipant in the ERM, however, was Britain, which
cited considerations of national sovereignty and differences of economic and
monetary philosophy as its reasons for remaining outside this agreement. The
British pound was to eventually enter the ERM in October 1990, with a 6 percent
band.

Among the main differences of the EMS from the earlier snake was the creation
of the European Currency Unit (ECU) as an accounting currency or credit instrument. The ECU was composed of a basket of national currencies whose value was
weighted to reflect the relative economic size and strength of the EC member
countries. The EMS also differed from the snake in terms of its enlarged credit

mechanisms. These included short- and medium-term facilities to be used for balance-of-payments problems and very-short-term facilities for the purpose of currency market interventions, each housed within the EMCF.

As originally planned, the EMS was to initiate a phase of institutional reform in 1981, thus making it into a more permanent structure. This reform would involve the transformation of the EMCF into the European Monetary Fund and the transfer to it of some national monetary reserves and authority, thus creating a form of European central bank. This phase would also involve an upgrading of the ECU and its full utilization as a reserve asset and a means of settlement. These steps were never taken, however, owing to the persistent divergence of national economic and monetary developments, as well as the continued lack of political consensus. At a December 1980 summit, Community leaders indefinitely postponed the move to the institutional stage, declaring that the transition would take place "at the appropriate time."

Unlike the snake, the EMS held together. It also proved successful, at least in terms of its stated goal of promoting economic and monetary stability. Early on there was a period of considerable fluctuation in currency values and frequent realignments of exchange rates. By the mid-1980s, however, currency values had stabilized, and realignments were rare. There was also a convergence of national inflation rates at a low level. Between 1980 and 1988, the average annual inflation rate of ERM states decreased from 12 to 3 percent.[14] The difference between the highest and lowest rates in the system, meanwhile, decreased from 13.6 percent in 1980 to only 4 percent in 1988.[15] Not all credit goes to the EMS for the decrease in inflation, however, since this was a general trend among members of the Organization for Economic Cooperation and Development during this period.

One can debate whether the institutional mechanism of the EMS or the change in domestic policy commitments is more responsible for the low inflation performance of EC countries since the early 1980s. Even if it is the latter, the constraints of the EMS have nevertheless played a key role in strengthening the low-inflation resolve of national policymakers. A further positive consequence of the EMS is the strengthening of habits of cooperation in monetary and economic affairs within the Community. Since 1983 there has been a growing tendency toward collective action in the setting of exchange rates and monetary targets among EMS countries, which has helped prepare the ground for further steps toward economic and monetary union.[16]

On the negative side of the ledger, economic growth rates in EMS countries declined or remained stagnant thoroughout the 1980s, especially in comparison to countries outside the system, such as the United States and Japan. Europe's slow economic growth in the 1980s has led to the charge that the EMS has a built-in deflationary or antigrowth bias.[17] A key reason for this bias, some argue, is that the EMS is an "asymmetrical" system dominated by German monetary policy priorities. The main source of this asymmetry is Germany's relative strength, deriving from the overall weight of its economy, its persistently low levels of inflation, and the international role and importance of the D-mark. Under the system, Germany dominates EMS monetary policy, yet is under no obligation to intervene in currency markets or otherwise act to defend fixed exchange rates, this task falling instead to weaker countries. Instead, the Bundesbank is free to focus exclusively on national economic conditions and interests in making its policy decisions. At the same time, Germany dominates the system's external monetary policy, focusing on the dollar-mark relationship and pulling other countries within the EMS along with it. The result has been, according to one analyst, an "implicit division of labor in terms of exchange-rate interventions between different central banks."[18] In addition to economic objections to the EMS, its asymmetrical nature has also been the source of considerable political resentment and unease among other European governments.

For Germany, however, the EMS experience has been almost wholly positive. To begin with, the EMS has not interfered with Bundesbank monetary sovereignty, as was originally feared by the bank and its supporters, but has instead imposed few constraints on German policies.[19] Nor has the EMS proved to be inflationary, another original concern of German monetary and financial authorities. Rather than importing inflation from other European countries, Germany has instead exported monetary stability through the system to other EMS participants. The Bundesbank itself has lauded the accomplishments of the EMS in promoting exchange-rate stability, citing the ERM in 1989 "as an example of successful [international] cooperation" at a time of turbulence in international monetary relations.[20] Exchange-rate stability, in turn, has generated substantial trade advantages for Germany, as indicated by a booming trade surplus with other EMS countries.[21] Competitive advantages for German industry have also been created by a persistent undervaluation of the D-mark within the system, due to the inability of currency readjustments to fully compensate for continued differentials in the inflation rates of Germany and other member countries.[22] As a result, by the late 1980s Germany was generating close to three-quarters of its overall trade surplus in exchanges with other EC states, even though these accounted for only one-half of total German trade.[23] If one includes non-EC countries that are nevertheless closely linked to the D-mark, the "zone of stability" created by the EMS represents about two-thirds of all German trade. In many respects, then, the EMS has given Germany the best of both worlds, enhancing its economic power and advantage without imposing much in the way of responsibility or constraints.

Despite the costs of the EMS in terms of reduced growth and employment, and its obvious asymmetry in favor of Germany, other European countries have remained in the system, largely because they felt they had little choice. According to one student of European monetary politics, authorities in countries such as France and Italy were gradually forced to recognize and bow to the severe external constraints on national policies that stemmed from increased international economic and financial interdependence.[24] Under these conditions, the negative consequences of pursuing inflationary or expansionary policies that were out of step with the rest of the world economy were simply too great, as France was to find out in 1981–1983. Given this fact, these traditionally high-inflation countries hoped that tying their currencies to the D-mark would provide the external discipline needed to bring their own monetary and economic policies into line with international realities. Beyond this reason is the European factor: Since the EMS had become a visible symbol of Europe and progress toward European integration, in countries such as France and Italy the debate about participation in the EMS became "synonymous with the debate over abandoning other spheres of cooperation in Europe."[25] To leave the EMS, in other words, was to leave Europe. Nevertheless, by the late 1980s resentment about the asymmetry of the EMS had grown. Rather than prompting considerations of withdrawal, however, this resentment strengthened the determination of other EC countries to dilute German monetary dominance and regain some control over monetary policy by transferring authority in this realm to European-level institutions.

The formation of the EMS was also significant for other reasons. For one thing, it signaled the renewal of the Franco-German partnership as the motor of European integration. Indeed, this was reportedly a key objective of Chancellor Schmidt in promoting the EMS initiative.[26] Nevertheless, the primary driving force behind the creation of the EMS was Germany. This role was a reflection of Germany's increased economic and political power, as well as its growing self-confidence as a European and international actor. According to one observer, "The EMS was arguably the first major act of German leadership in the history of the European Community."[27] Therefore, even though the Franco-German partnership still functioned, Germany was now in many ways the lead partner. At the same time, Germany's position of dominance within the Community was only further reinforced by the functioning of the EMS. The political consequences of this altered balance of power would be a key factor in subsequent efforts to promote monetary union in the 1980s and 1990s.

Europe Relaunched: The 1992 Project and SEA

Despite the establishment of the EMS, the Community found itself in the early 1980s afflicted by a deep sense of malaise. Popularly referred to as "Europessimism," this mood of despair was generated by both the perception of stagnation in the development of EC institutions and the reality of economic recession and growing unemployment throughout the Community. Also contributing to this mood was the widely held view that, in competitive terms, Europe was steadily falling behind the more dynamic economies of Japan, the United States, and the East Asian "newly industrializing countries," especially in the cutting edge realms of high technology. In an effort to counter this mood of Europessimism, and simultaneously impart new dynamism to both the European economy and the project of regional integration, EC leaders united in the mid-1980s around the idea of completing the Community's internal market via the "Europe 1992" project.

The decision to launch the 1992, or "Single Market," project resulted from a number of factors.[28] Of central importance was the convergence of national economic philosophies and policies around monetarist, market-oriented ideals. To some extent, this convergence was promoted by the discipline and constraints exerted by the German-dominated EMS. A key moment in this regard came in 1983 when the Socialist government of French president François Mitterrand was forced to abandon its inflationary, growth-oriented economic policies in order to remain within the exchange-rate framework of the EMS.[29] France's Socialist government was among the last converts to a more market-oriented philosophy, however, and most European governments had by this point come to accept the argument of "Eurosclerosis," which held that economic growth and competitiveness in Europe were being hampered by excessive government regulation and control of the economy. For this reason, these governments were prepared to accept the liberalizing and deregulatory prescriptions of the Single Market project.

In addition to this general consensus on economic policy, the Single Market project was also favored by the political interests of the Community's key member states. A primary lesson that the French government drew from its forced reversal of policy in 1983 was that in an era of increased economic and financial interdependence, national economic goals could not be achieved in isolation but instead had to be pursued through international and regional cooperation. As a result, the Mitterrand government turned away from nationalistic approaches to economic policy and increasingly focused its attention on European policies and institutions. This French reorientation toward Europe would prove to be a key development preparing the way for new steps toward further EC integration.[30]

The Single Market initiative was also favored by the German government. Beyond Germany's economic interests in a more open European market, the 1992 project also coincided with the foreign policy goals of Germany's new Christian Democratic chancellor, Helmut Kohl. A convinced Europeanist in the tradition of Konrad Adenauer, Kohl was also a strong proponent of close Franco-German relations. He thus made renewal of this crucial bilateral partnership a central objective after taking office in 1982. While he favored this goal for its own sake, Kohl also viewed it as the cornerstone of a revitalized *Westpolitik,* which he viewed as necessary to counterbalance the groundbreaking initiatives in Eastern Europe of previous Social Democratic governments. Kohl's Europeanist views converged nicely with the new European orientation of the Mitterrand government after 1983. As a result, under the leadership of the unlikely collaboration of the Socialist Mitterrand and the Christian Democrat Kohl, the Franco-German axis was revived in the 1980s and became a key factor promoting new initiatives for further integration.

Also facilitating the Single Market project were the positive attitude and role of the British government. The idea of liberalizing the internal European market, with implications for deregulation and elimination of government controls on economic activity, was tremendously appealing to the neoliberal government of Prime Minster Margaret Thatcher. Liberalization also accorded with traditional British preferences for a Community that was more an open free-trading area than an exclusionary political union. Viewing Europe 1992 as an exercise in market-oriented negative integration, the Thatcher government was fully supportive of the project, a position that diverged considerably from the usual British intransigence regarding new initiatives on European integration.

Another key factor in the relaunch of European integration in the 1980s was the active and skillful leadership of the president of the European Commission, Jacques Delors.[31] As a French Socialist and former finance minister under President Mitterrand, Delors reflected the new Europeanist orientation of the Paris government after 1983. He went considerably beyond this, however, in his federalist ambitions for a more politically integrated Europe. On assuming the office of commission president in 1985, Delors immediately seized on the Single Market idea as the vehicle for advancing his goal of European union, and he played a key role in facilitating intergovernmental agreement on the 1992 project and accompanying institutional reform. Given the considerable amount of consensus among national governments on the Single Market idea by this point, this facilitation was perhaps not so difficult. His greatest challenge would come in later attempts to move the Community toward the more controversial and problematic objectives of monetary and political union.

The 1992 project was initially spelled out in a 1985 commission report prepared under the direction of Britain's Lord Cockfield.[32] The report proposed some three hundred measures aimed at eliminating remaining national barriers to the free movement of goods, services, capital, and labor within the Community by the end of 1992. Although the removal of formal tariffs on trade between EC countries had been achieved with the establishment of the Common Market after 1958, a significant number and variety of nontariff restrictions on transborder economic activity continued to exist and had increased in number and importance since the mid-1970s because of the protective responses of national governments to economic crisis and recession. As a result, the emergence of a true single market in Europe had been frustrated. The continued fragmentation of the EC economy in turn was widely regarded as something seriously limiting the efficiency, competitiveness, and growth potential of European firms while at the same time contributing to an overall perception of economic stagnation and decline in the Community.

The commission's proposals for liberalizing the internal market were subsequently endorsed by national leaders at a June 1985 Milan summit. Nevertheless, it was apparent that the goals of the 1992 project could not be realized under current Community decisionmaking procedures. Since the move to majority voting had been frustrated by the resistance of de Gaulle in 1965–1966, decisionmaking in the Council of Ministers had been by consensus, with individual countries retaining a veto right in matters affecting vital national interests. The rule of unanimity would quickly frustrate attempts to pass legislation necessary for the Single Market project, given the variety of national, sectoral, and other interests affected by the proposed measures. What was needed, therefore, was the reform of EC decisionmaking procedures.

Such reform was achieved through the Single European Act, which was approved by EC leaders and ratified by national parliaments in 1986 and came into effect in 1987.[33] The SEA committed member countries to the goal of completing the internal market by January 1993. It also amended the 1957 Rome Treaty to provide for qualified majority voting within the Council of Ministers on matters pertaining to the Single Market project. In addition, the SEA expanded Community authority in some policy areas related to the Single Market, such as environment and competition policy, and increased the European Parliament's voice in the legislative process somewhat. Most significantly, however, by removing the unanimity rule for all EC legislation, the SEA made possible the realization of the 1992 project.

The 1992 project and SEA breathed new life into what many had believed was a moribund or stagnating European Community. In material terms, creation of the single market was widely expected to have significant benefits. By removing barriers to cross-border economic activity, European companies would enjoy greater economies of scale and become much more efficient and profitable, thus enabling them to compete more effectively with U.S. and Japanese multinationals. The 1992 project would also result in increased economic growth and employment. The most well-known study of these effects is the commission's own "Cecchini report." This concluded that even without accompanying government measures to stimulate demand, the completion of the internal market should lead, in the medium term, to a 4.5 percent increase in Community gross domestic product (GDP) and the creation of 1.8 million new jobs. With accompanying expansionary measures, these gains could be as much as 7.5 percent in GDP and 5.7 million jobs.[34] Perhaps even more important than the economic benefits of the 1992 project, however, was the psychological boost it gave the Community, thus helping it overcome the mood of Europessimism that had predominated in the early 1980s. Instead, by the end of the decade the EC was on the move again, and the project of European integration appeared to be back on track with plenty of momentum. The renewed movement toward European integration provoked both admiration and concern among the EC's trading partners, which feared the possibility of an economically powerful but protectionist "Fortress Europe," while within Europe this renewal prompted consideration of further steps toward economic and political union.

The Delors Plan for Monetary Union

By 1988, with the Single Market project well under way, attention had begun to focus on the next steps for EC integration. The most important of these was monetary union. For many, this was the logical sequence to the 1992 project since the existence of different national currencies and monetary policies was a significant barrier to economic activity across borders. To some extent, there had already been a convergence of national monetary policies and a stabilization of exchange rates since the creation of the EMS in 1979. Even so, recent studies had shown that the cost of economic transactions across borders was increased simply through the need to exchange currencies.[35] For this reason, the sentiment had grown within the business and economic communities, and among some political leaders, that, if Europe was ever to achieve true economic integration and enjoy the efficiency and dynamism that would result from a single market, complete monetary union was necessary.[36] In addition, central bankers and national governments recognized that in a unified Community market without any exchange or capital controls—something that would become a reality with the 1992 project—the conduct of strictly "national" monetary policy would become difficult, if not impossible.

For many, monetary union was simply a logical and necessary complement to the 1992 project, but for others it was a major step toward the ultimate goal of a politically united or federal Europe. Commission president Delors, among others, belonged in this camp.[37] Nevertheless, despite the considerable level of integration and the pooling of sovereignty that had already been achieved, the EC remained a grouping of independent nation-states, and conventional national interests would be the primary driving force behind the new initiative for monetary union.[38]

The main source of interest in monetary union for many EC countries was the asymmetrical nature of the EMS and the economic and monetary dominance it allowed Germany. This was a sore point for France, which had been forced to bow to German monetary priorities and abandon expansionary economic policies in the early 1980s to stay within the ERM. From this moment a key goal of the French government had been to undermine German monetary hegemony through the transfer of Bundesbank authority to European institutions.[39] Since within European institutions Paris would presumably have some voice, it would thereby regain a certain degree of control over monetary policy. At the very least, the French government wanted to ensure that in the future German monetary authorities would act more responsibly by being compelled to take European, not simply German, economic needs and interests into consideration when making their policies. These views were shared by most other EC countries, except Britain, which still remained outside the exchange-rate mechanism of the EMS and in general opposed any further moves toward monetary integration as a threat to national sovereignty.

As might be expected, Germany was more ambivalent about the idea of monetary union. Among German monetary and financial authorities, there was widespread opposition to such plans. In addition to objecting that the EMU would undermine Bundesbank sovereignty, these authorities felt that monetary union was simply not workable given the still considerable divergence of economic conditions among EC countries. Any precipitous moves toward monetary union, they believed, would only be inflationary while threatening the hard-won achievements of German monetary stability. Similar concerns had been voiced about the EMS. By now, however, German monetary authorities had become strong supporters of the EMS and the monetary status quo.[40] German political authorities were also skeptical about the economic consequences of monetary union but were willing to consider it for other reasons, including an ideological commitment to the goal of European union and a desire to maintain positive relations with France.[41]

As a result, a new initiative on monetary union was launched in January 1988 with the French government's proposal for the creation of a European central bank, an idea that also had the strong support of Delors.[42] Although the German government was initially cool to the idea of a European central bank, it was willing to discuss improved mechanisms for monetary cooperation with France, mainly as a means to achieve other policy objectives. In particular, the Kohl government was seeking more bilateral cooperation on foreign and defense policy to counter the growing instability and uncertainty in Eastern Europe and a perceived decline in the U.S. commitment to European security. In reaction, French officials indicated a willingness to discuss greater defense cooperation but only on the condition that Germany make a similar commitment in the area of economic and monetary policy. The result was a policy trade-off, which led to the signing on January 22, 1988, of agreements establishing two bilateral councils, one for economic policy and one for defense and security cooperation.[43] In addition, the French made it known that they wanted further steps toward the creation of European monetary institutions.

Considerable suspicion about the new bilateral Economic and Finance Council was expressed by Bundesbank authorities, who feared that it could exert political pressure on the Bundesbank for more expansionary monetary policies, thereby undercutting its anti-inflationary mandate and threatening its institutional autonomy. Bundesbank officials were also unhappy with having been left out of the decisionmaking process; they had not been notified by government authorities about the full nature and potential consequences of the council until only hours before the agreement was signed. This, they felt, was much too reminiscent of the Bundesbank's exclusion from the secretive discussions between Chancellor Schmidt and President d'Estaing in early 1978 that had laid the basis for the EMS. The Bundesbank claimed that the decision to create the council was yet another example of the federal government making faulty economic policy decisions for essentially political reasons. Most worrisome for the Bundesbank, however, was the possibility that the council might be a precursor of further steps toward European monetary union and the creation of a regional central bank, something to which German monetary authorities remained adamantly opposed.[44]

Despite Bundesbank objections, discussion of European monetary union continued. At a June 1988 EC summit in Hannover, national leaders established a commission to study ideas on monetary union and make concrete proposals for achieving it. This group, chaired by Delors, consisted of the central bank governors of each of the EC countries and three independent experts. In April 1989 the commission made public the results of its work. The "Delors Plan" for EMU envisaged a three-stage process leading to full monetary union. In the first stage, which was set to begin on July 1, 1990, closer coordination of national monetary policies would begin, and all controls on transborder capital movements within the Community would be terminated. By this point as well, those EC countries still outside the ERM—at that time Britain, Spain, Portugal, and Greece—would become members of the system. In stage two, for which no starting date was proposed, the margin of fluctuation for national currencies within the ERM would be tightened, and a European system of central banks—the precursor of a single regional bank—would be established. In addition, EC authorities would begin to formulate economic targets for member countries and set rules on such matters as the size and financing of budget deficits. In the third stage, a single currency would be created and managed by the European central bank, and the EC would assume greater powers to direct the economic and financial policies of member states.[45]

The contents of the Delors Plan were endorsed by EC leaders at a June 1989 summit in Madrid, although Britain's Prime Minister Thatcher expressed strong reservations. In addition to approving the July 1, 1990, date for the beginning of stage one, leaders decided to convene a special intergovernmental conference to discuss the implementation of EMU and the necessary revisions to the Treaty of Rome. Although no specific date was set, the general consensus was that this conference should begin sometime in the second half of 1990, after stage one had been initiated. A final decision on the starting date for the conference, it was agreed, would be made at a December EC summit in Strasbourg.[46] In addition, the Strasbourg summit would consider the controversial proposal for a Community "Social Charter" aimed at guaranteeing the rights of workers in the European Single Market. This charter had been strongly pushed by labor unions as a necessary counterpart to the 1992 project and had also been endorsed by Delors and many national governments. As with EMU, however, the strongest opposition to the Social Charter came from the Thatcher government.

Although the German government publicly supported the Delors Plan and the goal of monetary union, opinion among political and economic elites was highly divided.[47] The chief supporter of monetary union in the federal government was Foreign Minister Hans-Dietrich Genscher, who saw it as important for improving

Franco-German relations and realizing the broader goal of European political union. In a speech delivered on May 5 in Davos (Switzerland), Genscher indicated his belief that full monetary and currency union could be achieved by 1995, much sooner than was commonly assumed. At any rate, he urged EC leaders to approve a firm timetable for EMU at their upcoming December summit. A close friend of French foreign minister Roland Dumas, Genscher also declared that any disagreements in negotiations over the nature of monetary union—such as the independent status of the European central bank—could be easily worked out, since the issue was "in the end one between Bonn and Paris."[48] Also sympathetic to the idea of monetary union was Chancellor Kohl, who, like Genscher, was motivated by deeply felt Europeanist views. In addition the main opposition party in Germany, the Social Democratic Party (SPD), was generally supportive of the goal of monetary union.[49]

Not surprisingly, the biggest critic of monetary union was the Bundesbank.[50] This despite the fact that its president, Karl-Otto Pöhl, had been on the Delors commission and played a prominent role in drafting the final report. In general, the Bundesbank believed that a common central bank and monetary policy for Europe should only follow the achievement of greater economic convergence (at low, German levels of inflation) among EC countries. Beyond this, the bank emphasized that to be acceptable, a future European central bank would have to be closely modeled on the Bundesbank; that is, it must be politically independent, possess total control of monetary policy, and have a statutory mandate to keep inflation low. It also went without saying that a common European currency would have to be every bit as strong and stable as the D-mark.[51] The view that EMU should only take place according to the German model and standards was also accepted by the supporters of monetary union in Germany; the differences centered mainly on the question of how soon monetary union might be possible. On the whole, the skepticism of the Bundesbank about monetary union was shared by much of the German business and financial community.

There was also opposition to monetary union within the governing coalition parties in Germany. This included the chairman of Genscher's own Free Democratic Party (FDP), Count Otto Lambsdorff, who shared many of the objections of the Bundesbank and German financial authorities. At the same time, within Kohl's own party there was concern that government support for EMU might be politically unwise since it would play into the hands of emerging right-wing parties by giving them further ammunition for their claims that the Kohl government was not assertive enough of German national interests. Despite the existence of such strong doubts about monetary union, however, these were not generally expressed in public because in the mainstream parties of Germany, even among opponents of monetary union, there was a keen desire not to be perceived as "bad Europeans."[52]

The EC Before November 1989

By fall 1989, the European Community had generated considerable momentum toward deeper economic, and possibly political, integration. In ten years of existence, the EMS had proved to be a success in terms of keeping currency exchange-rates stable, promoting lower levels of inflation, and fostering new habits of cooperation among the governments and economic authorities of EC countries. This success had prepared the ground for further steps toward economic integration. In the mid-1980s, the Community had decided to complete the construction of its internal market, and by 1989 the Europe 1992 project was well under way. With the launching of the Single Market project, attention was focused on plans for monetary and currency union, with an intergovernmental conference on EMU tentatively scheduled to begin in late 1990. As a result of these developments, the mood of Europessimism that had pervaded the Community in the early 1980s had been swept away, and there was considerable optimism about the future of European integration.[53] It was against this background that the opening of the Berlin Wall and the revolution in Eastern Europe took place. These developments would not only put in doubt the progress toward EC integration that had been made to this point but would also present the Community and its member countries with a new set of challenges for the future. It is to the new political situation in Europe after November 1989 and its consequences for the EC and European integration, that we now turn.

Notes

1. There are a number of excellent histories of the European Community, from which this section of the chapter draws heavily. These include John Pinder, *European Community: The Building of a Union* (New York: Oxford University Press, 1991); Derek W. Urwin, *The Community of Europe: A History of European Integration Since 1945* (London: Longman, 1991); Desmond Dinan, *Ever Closer Union? An Introduction to the European Community* (Boulder: Lynne Rienner, 1994), esp. Chaps. 1–6.

2. The Treaty of Paris establishing the ECSC was signed in April 1951. After being ratified by the national parliaments of each of the signatory countries, the ECSC came into effect in July 1952.

3. On the distinction between negative and positive integration, see John Pinder, "Positive Integration and Negative Integration: Some Problems of Economic Union in the EEC," *The World Today* 24 (1968):88–110.

4. See, for instance, Wolfram F. Hanrieder, *Germany, America, Europe: Forty Years of German Foreign Policy* (New Haven: Yale University Press, 1989), p. 16.

5. For an account of the ten-year process leading from the creation of the EMS to the Maastricht Treaty in 1991, with an emphasis on technical and policy issues, see Tommaso Padoa-Schioppa, *The Road to Monetary Union in Europe: The Emperor, the Kings, and the Genies* (Oxford: Clarendon Press, 1994).

6. For an account of the EC's first attempt at EMU, see Loukas Tsoukalis, *The Politics and Economics of European Monetary Integration* (London: Allen & Unwin, 1977).

7. The snake was a mechanism for maintaining narrower margins of exchange-rate fluctuations among European currencies, while European currencies as a block would float against the U.S. dollar.

8. The Bretton Woods system was established in 1944 as a key part of the U.S.-dominated postwar global order and was based on the U.S. dollar and U.S. economic and financial strength. The dollar was linked to gold and convertible at $35 per ounce, while other national currencies were fixed to the dollar at predetermined rates. Under this "adjustable peg" system of fixed exchange rates the value of national currencies could be moved up or down, but in practice exchange rates remained fairly rigid. Although the Bretton Woods system was certainly not perfect and was rife with internal contradictions and structural flaws that eventually led to its demise, it nevertheless provided for almost twenty-five years a fairly stable institutional framework for international monetary relations, keeping exchange rates relatively constant and creating an atmosphere conducive to the expansion of global trade and economic interdependence.

9. Marcello De Cecco, "The European Monetary System and National Interests," in Paolo Guerrieri and Piercarlo Padoan, eds., *The Political Economy of European Integration* (New York: Harvester Wheatsheaf, 1989), p. 88.

10. For a detailed study of the events leading to the creation of the EMS, with a particular emphasis on the politics, see Peter Ludlow, *The Making of the European Monetary System* (London: Butterworth, 1982).

11. Hanrieder, *Germany, America, Europe,* pp. 299–306.

12. "Resolution of the European Council of 5 December 1978 on the Establishment of the European Monetary System (EMS) and Related Matters," reprinted in Ludlow, *The Making of the European Monetary System,* pp. 303–308.

13. For a more complete description of the institutional structure and operation of the EMS, see John T. Woolley, "Policy Credibility and European Monetary Institutions," in Alberta Sbragia, ed., *Euro-Politics* (Washington, D.C.: Brookings Institution, 1992), pp. 185–190.

14. W. R. Smyser, *The Economy of United Germany: Colossus at the Crossroads,* 2d ed. (New York: St. Martin's Press, 1993), p. 268.

15. Elke Thiel, "Changing Patterns of Monetary Interdependence," in William Wallace, ed., *The Dynamics of European Integration* (London: Pinter, 1990), p. 76.

16. Woolley, "Policy Credibility and European Monetary Institutions," pp. 187–188.

17. Loukas Tsoukalis, "The Political Economy of the European Monetary System," in Guerrieri and Padoan, eds., *The Political Economy of European Integration,* pp. 59–61.

18. Ibid., p. 65.

19. Ibid., p. 70.

20. Deutsche Bundesbank, "Exchange Rate Movements Within the European Monetary System," *Monthly Report of the Deutsche Bundesbank* 41, 11 (November 1989):28.

21. By 1988 Germany's trade surplus with other EMS countries had reached DM 46 billion, eight times greater than what it was in 1983. *Economist,* June 3, 1989, p. 17.

22. Tsoukalis, "The Political Economy of the European Monetary System," p. 70.

23. Deutsche Bundesbank, "Exchange Rate Movements," p. 34.

24. John Goodman, "Monetary Politics in France, Italy, and Germany: 1973–85," in Guerrieri and Padoan, eds., *The Political Economy of European Integration,* p. 176.

25. Jeffry Sachs and Charles Wyplosz, "The Economic Consequences of President Mitterrand," *Economic Policy* 2 (April 1986):294–295; quoted by Woolley, "Policy Credibility and European Monetary Institutions," p. 168.

26. On Schmidt's reasons for promoting the EMS, see Ludlow, *The Making of the European Monetary System,* pp. 63–87.

27. Ibid., p. 290.

28. On the sources and explanation of the 1992 project, see Wayne Sandholtz and John Zysman, "1992: Recasting the European Bargain," *World Politics* 42, 1 (October 1989):95–128; Andrew Moravcsik, "Negotiating the Single European Act: National Interests and Conventional Statecraft in the European Community," *International Organization* 45, 1 (Winter 1991):19–56; David R. Cameron, "The 1992 Initiative: Causes and Consequences," in Sbragia, ed., *Euro-Politics,* pp. 23–74.

29. On this decision, see Julius W. Friend, *Seven Years in France: François Mitterrand and the Unintended Revolution* (Boulder: Westview Press, 1989), pp. 64–69.

30. On the French government's reversal of policy and its consequences for the EC, see Patrick McCarthy, "France Looks at Germany, or How to Become German (and European) While Remaining French," in Patrick McCarthy, ed., *France-Germany, 1983–1993: The Struggle to Cooperate* (New York: St. Martin's Press, 1993), pp. 52–55.

31. On the role played by Delors in the 1980s revival of European integration, see George Ross, *Jacques Delors and European Integration* (New York: Oxford University Press, 1995), esp. pp. 26–50.

32. Commission of the European Communities, "Completing the Internal Market: White Paper from the Commission to the European Council" (Luxembourg: EC, 1985).

33. On the SEA, see Moravcsik, "Negotiating the Single European Act." See also Cameron, "The 1992 Initiative." For formal documentation, see *Bulletin of the European Communities,* Supplement 2/86 (Luxembourg: Office for Official Publications of the European Communities, 1986).

34. "The Economics of 1992" (Brussels: European Commission, 1988). The report derives its name from the Italian economist Paolo Cecchini, who chaired the group of experts who carried out the study. The report was later published as Paolo Cecchini, *The European Challenge 1992: The Benefits of a Single Market* (Aldershot, England: Wildwood House, 1988).

35. See, for instance, the results of a 1988 Belgian study. For a person starting out in Belgium with a given amount of money and traveling to ten other EC countries, the requirement of changing currencies consumed 47 percent of the cash. *Economist,* July 16, 1988, p. 44.

36. On this view, see the studies cited in Michael Emerson et al., *One Market, One Money* (New York: Oxford University Press, 1992).

37. On Delors's view of monetary union and its relationship to the ultimate goal of European political union, see Ross, *Jacques Delors and European Integration,* pp. 42–43.

38. For a discussion of national interests and views regarding monetary union in the late 1980s, see Loukas Tsoukalis, *The New European Economy: The Politics and Economics of Integration* (New York: Oxford University Press, 1991), pp. 189–190.

39. On French motives for EMU, see David M. Andrews, "The Global Origins of the Maastricht Treaty on EMU: Closing the Window of Opportunity," in Alan W. Cafruny and Glenda G. Rosenthal, eds., *The State of the European Community*, vol. 2, *The Maastricht Debates and Beyond* (Boulder: Lynne Rienner, 1993), pp. 108–110.

40. *Economist*, February 13, 1988, pp. 76–77.

41. Dana H. Allin, "Germany Looks at France," in McCarthy, ed., *France-Germany, 1983–1993*, p. 33.

42. *Economist*, January 30, 1988, p. 35.

43. *Economist*, February 13, 1988, pp. 76–79; March 5, 1988, p. 14. The creation of both councils was timed to celebrate the twenty-fifth anniversary of the Elysée Treaty. On the decision to create the Security and Defense Council, see Philip H. Gordon, *France, Germany, and the Western Alliance* (Boulder: Westview Press, 1995), p. 23.

44. *Economist*, February 13, 1988, pp. 76–79.

45. Committee for the Study of Economic and Monetary Union, "Report on Economic and Monetary Union in the European Community" (Brussels: EC Publications, 1989). For a summary of the Delors Commission report, see *Economist*, April 22, 1989, pp. 45–46. See also Tsoukalis, *The New European Economy*, pp. 190–191.

46. *Economist*, July 1, 1989, pp. 37–38.

47. On the divisions among German economic and political elites on EMU, see Andrews, "The Global Origins of the Maastricht Treaty on EMU," p. 111; Wayne Sandholtz, "Monetary Bargains: The Treaty on EMU," in Cafruny and Rosenthal, eds., *The State of the European Community*, p. 131.

48. *Economist*, May 13, 1989, p. 53.

49. *Economist*, July 8, 1989, pp. 37–38.

50. For a discussion of the Bundesbank's views on EMU, see Smyser, *The Economy of United Germany*, pp. 274–277.

51. *Financial Times*, July 1, 1989, p. 1.

52. *Economist*, July 8, 1989, pp. 37–38.

53. For a comprehensive assessment of the EC's progress in mid-1989, see "1992 Under Construction: A Survey," *Economist*, July 8, 1989.

2

After the Wall: The Road to Rome

The revolutionary events of 1989, including the dramatic opening of the Berlin Wall and the subsequent rush to German unification, posed a tremendous challenge to the European Community. Because of these developments, many within the Community were fearful that plans for further integration and, in particular, monetary union might be sidetracked or delayed. In fact, the exact opposite happened; the political changes in Germany and Eastern Europe served instead to accelerate the pace of EC integration. As a result, in December 1990 national leaders met in Rome to officially launch parallel intergovernmental conferences on monetary and political union. These would conclude one year later with agreement at Maastricht on the Treaty on European Union. In this chapter the new political situation in Europe after 1989 and its impact on the European Community are examined.

The Revolution in Eastern Europe

The collapse of the communist order in Eastern Europe came with shocking and unexpected suddenness.[1] In many respects, the epicenter of this geopolitical earthquake was Poland, where throughout the 1980s the communist government had been engaged in a protracted struggle with the opposition Solidarity movement. By the beginning of 1989, with the national economy near collapse and the political system's legitimacy approaching zero, Poland's president, Wojciech Jaruzelski, had agreed to begin roundtable negotiations with Solidarity. These resulted in an agreement to hold restricted elections for Parliament in June, with the promise of wholly free elections by 1993. The overwhelming victory of Solidarity at the polls in June, however, brought the opposition into power much sooner than anticipated, and by September Poland had Eastern Europe's first noncommunist government in four decades.

In Hungary, where a more liberal economic path had been pursued for years, serious efforts at political reform had begun in the spring of 1988 with the replacement of János Kádár by Károly Grósz as leader of the Communist Party. Plans were also made for the introduction of a multiparty system over a period of several years, a schedule that was to be greatly accelerated by the press of events. In June 1989 popular support for political change was dramatically symbolized by the high-profile reburial of Imre Nagy, the Hungarian leader who had been executed after the failed 1956 uprising against Soviet domination. By late summer of 1989, the Communist Party had radically revised its official doctrine and renounced its leading role in society. In October the party formally dissolved itself and announced its transformation into a more liberal socialist party.

A key event in the 1989 revolution came on May 4 when the Hungarian government began to open its border with Austria, thereby symbolically dismantling the iron curtain. This action had major unintended consequences. By late summer, thousands of East German citizens were attempting passage to the West through Hungary and through West German embassies in Budapest, Prague, and Warsaw. In September, in a historic breach of solidarity among communist bloc countries, the Hungarian government decided to allow the East Germans gathered at the embassy in Budapest to proceed to the West. Shortly thereafter, the Polish and Czech governments made similar decisions. Thus began a steady stream of East Germans escaping to Western Europe, mainly to the Federal Republic. This outflow continued throughout the fall, and by the first week in November the total number of East German refugees was approaching fifty thousand.

By mid-autumn the communist regime in East Berlin was in trouble, increasingly shaken by the uncontrolled flight of its citizens to the West and the growth of mass antigovernment demonstrations. By the middle of October, hundreds of thousands of people were gathering in the squares of Leipzig, Dresden, and Berlin to protest against the communist system and to demand more freedom and democracy. Nevertheless, the hard-line government of Erich Honecker refused to make concessions and instead considered using force to quell the demonstrations and restore order.

A major turning point came in early October during the celebration of the fortieth anniversary of the German Democratic Republic (GDR). While visiting East Berlin for the ceremonies, Soviet president Mikhail Gorbachev voiced his support for reform and indicated that Moscow would not oppose a change in the country's political leadership. Within days the Politburo of the Socialist Unity Party (SED) announced its readiness to begin discussions with the opposition. Then on October 18, Honecker was ousted from the SED leadership and replaced by the more reform-minded Egon Krenz. This move proved insufficient to satisfy popular demands for change, however, and more drastic measures soon became necessary. On November 7 the government of Minister-President Willi Stoph resigned, to be followed the next day by the entire Politburo. A new government was subsequently formed under Hans Modrow, a former mayor of Dresden and a respected reformer within the SED.

The decisive date in the demise of East Germany, and perhaps the entire communist system, was November 9. On the evening of this historic day, in response to the government's announcement that East Germans could henceforth travel freely to the West, the gates of the Berlin Wall were thrown open, and the forty-year division of Germany effectively came to an end. The decision to open the wall was a last-gasp effort to preserve the East German state. However, it only served to hasten its demise, as the exodus of East Germans to the West increased, and the chants of protesters evolved from *"Wir sind das Volk"* (We are the people) to *"Wir sind ein Volk"* (We are one people). From this moment, it became obvious to many that formal unification of the two German states was inevitable, although it would not occur until nearly one year later (October 2, 1990).[2]

The New German Question

The dramatic events of 1989 were a cause for much joy and celebration in Europe and throughout the world, but they generated uncertainty within the Community and raised new questions about the future of European integration. A primary reason for this uncertainty was the reemergence of the so-called German question. As in the past, this concerned the identity and role of a powerful Germany in the center of a politically divided Europe. The inability to resolve this problem after German unification in the mid-nineteenth century had resulted in three major wars within a span of seventy years, culminating in the tremendous death and destruction of World War II. During the cold war, a temporary resolution of this problem was achieved through the division of Germany into two separate states, each tightly bound into competing superpower blocs. Throughout the cold war, Bonn's Western allies steadfastly proclaimed their support for the goal of German unification while never believing this was a realistic possibility. Now, however, the likelihood of unification reopened a question that many had hoped was finally resolved.[3]

Reactions to the prospect of German unification varied considerably. Among some Europeans, it reawakened old fears of German domination and exploitation. There were also concerns that a united Germany could become more nationalistic and independent in the future, perhaps even turning away from the Community and other Western institutions and seeking instead to rebuild its traditional sphere of influence in Central and Eastern Europe. Most Europeans, however, were much more optimistic about the future orientation and role of a united Germany. This optimism was based on a number of different factors, including the extent of West Germany's integration into European and international institutions and the demonstrated strength and stability of its democracy. Many also felt that Germany had drawn the proper lessons from its disastrous past experiences with nationalism and aggressive unilateralism and that it had thoroughly assimilated the values of "positive interdependence." Some, in fact, even characterized Germany as a "post-national state."[4]

Regardless of whether one was optimistic or pessimistic, the Community was now faced with the challenge of dealing with the power and weight of a (soon-to-be) united Germany, which would be the pivotal country of the New Europe. With 80 million citizens, Germany would be the Community's largest country, roughly 40 percent more populous than France and with a labor force larger than that of France and Italy combined. It would also possess Europe's most powerful and dynamic economy, generating by itself nearly 30 percent of Community gross national product. To put things even more in perspective, the economy of a united Germany would be almost as large as the economies of France and Britain combined. Given the country's economic weight and geographical location in the center of Europe, not to mention its deep historical and cultural ties to many of the countries in this region, Germany was also in the best position to benefit, both politically and economically, from the end of the cold war and the opening up of Eastern Europe.

The responses of national governments to developments in Germany varied greatly. Perhaps more than any other European country, France stood to lose from German unification and the end of the cold war. Not only would a united Germany be significantly larger than France, but also many of the constraints on German sovereignty and independence that had benefited France in the past would no longer exist. At the same time, the end of the cold war had devalued France's military power relative to Germany's economic strength; in the New Europe, it was argued by some, the D-mark would be more powerful than the bomb.[5] The end of the cold war also meant an eastward shift in Europe's political center of gravity, moving Germany to the center of the New Europe and leaving France in danger of being shoved to its periphery.[6]

To compensate for these developments, France resorted to its traditional postwar strategy of "embracing-enmeshing" Germany through deeper European integration.[7] Further integration, French leaders felt, would both limit the independence of a united Germany and allow France to retain some influence and control over its powerful neighbor. In particular, the goal of monetary union now became a matter of geopolitical urgency for France. The French government also opposed an early enlargement of the Community into Eastern Europe, which some now advocated, fearing that this would only inhibit further integration and leave the EC nothing more than a glorified trading bloc. Such a Community, Paris believed, would be more easily dominated by Germany, while within it France's own national standing and influence would be greatly diminished.

The British government was perhaps the most openly hostile to the idea of German unification. Prime Minister Thatcher was highly suspicious of German power and intentions. At a December 1989 luncheon, Thatcher insisted that nothing good could ever come of the Germans and questioned the soundness of those who disagreed.[8] Following the opening of the wall, Thatcher made an unsuccessful attempt to forge an alliance with France to block unification and to counter German power through a revival of the Anglo-French "entente cordiale."[9] After briefly flirting with this possibility, Mitterrand opted instead for the strategy of integrating a united Germany more firmly into the Community.

Partly for fear of German hegemony, the British government was strongly opposed to further EC integration. While many within the Community worried about the growth of German independence as a consequence of unification and the end of the cold war, Britain was more concerned about German dominance exerted through European institutions. In contrast to France and most other EC governments, therefore, London viewed a "widening" of the Community and its transformation into a looser intergovernmental confederation as the best response to German unification. The British government's fear of German dominance in a more integrated Community was perhaps best expressed, although exaggeratedly, in a July 1990 statement of Trade and Industry Minister Nicholas Ridley that EMU and plans for further integration were simply "a German racket designed to take over the whole of Europe."[10]

Germany, for its part, insisted that unification would not diminish its enthusiasm for European integration. According to one close adviser of Chancellor Kohl, "The *Staatsräson* of a united Germany is its integration in Europe."[11] Similarly, Kohl's chief foreign policy adviser, Horst Teltschik, argued that only through further integration and cession of national sovereignty would a united Germany "find its identity in Europe."[12] This sentiment was echoed in Foreign Minister Genscher's restatement of Thomas Mann's now-famous dictum, that what the Federal Republic wanted was "a European Germany and not a German Europe."[13] Genscher also claimed that Germany had drawn the proper lessons from its history, and that it now rejected "the power politics of the past" in favor of the new "politics of responsibility."[14]

The German government was keenly aware of the suspicions and fears of its neighbors. Because of these fears, it realized that unification could occur only within the context of deeper EC integration. Bonn's need to convince EC partners of its continued commitment to European integration, as well as a desire to maintain the crucial partnership with France, would impose severe constraints on German policy, however. According to Teltschik, after the opening of the Berlin Wall the Kohl government found itself "in the situation of having to approve practically every French initiative for Europe."[15] As Chancellor Kohl himself recognized, agreement to further integration and, in particular, EMU would be the price Germany had to pay for Europe's acceptance of unification.[16]

Initial Responses

Even before the opening of the Berlin Wall, many within the Community were becoming fearful that the upheavals in Germany and Eastern Europe might delay or overwhelm plans for further integration. In response, some EC leaders had begun to urge an acceleration of EC integration. This was necessary, they argued, to more firmly anchor Germany in the West and give the Community the institutional capacity it needed to deal with the challenges of post–cold war Europe. Among the primary advocates of this view was commission president Delors, who in an October 17, 1989, speech in Bruges (Belgium) declared that the construction of a federal Europe was "the only satisfactory and acceptable response to the German question."[17] Also favoring more rapid integration was French president Mitterrand. In an address to the European Parliament on October 25, Mitterrand argued that developments in Germany and Eastern Europe made it both urgent and necessary to "reinforce" the institutional structures of the Community.[18]

Of particular importance to both men was the establishing of a firm timetable for monetary union. By fall 1989, the question of a starting date for the EMU conference had become a major subject of controversy within the Community. Both Mitterrand and Delors favored convening the conference as soon as possible after the beginning of stage one (the removal of capital controls), which was due to take place on July 1, 1990. In practical terms, this meant beginning the EMU conference in the early fall, perhaps in September. In the European Parliament speech, in fact, the French president declared that he would propose an early starting date for the conference at the upcoming Strasbourg summit.[19]

The German government remained divided and uncertain about a starting date for the EMU conference. The Bundesbank and Finance Ministry argued for delaying EMU negotiations, contending that more preparatory work needed to be done and that for now priority should be given to implementing stage one and completing the Single Market project. There were also domestic political reasons for adopting a more cautious approach. New federal elections were scheduled for December 1990, and many within the governing coalition parties felt that beginning an EMU conference before this point would provide far right parties with a potent campaign issue, allowing them to argue that the Kohl government was selling out German national interests by negotiating to give away monetary sovereignty and the beloved D-mark. Taking the opposite position was Foreign Minister Genscher, who argued that agreeing to firm dates for the conference would assuage the fears of other countries that Germany was losing interest in EMU and European integration. In the midst of this conflicting advice, the chancellor himself remained noncommital.[20]

Concerns about Germany's commitment to EMU were further heightened by the dramatic opening of the Berlin Wall on November 9. In the days and weeks that followed, Chancellor Kohl and other German leaders tried to counter such fears by making repeated assertions of loyalty to the Community and expressing continued support for further integration. In a November 16 address to the federal parliament (Bundestag), Kohl declared that the prospect of unification would not diminish German enthusiasm for the EC, and that to slow the pace of European integration at this time would indeed be a "fatal error."[21] The chancellor also underlined Bonn's continued commitment to the Community at a special European Council meeting in Paris on November 18, declaring that further integration was "now more than ever of prime importance."[22] In a November 22 speech to the European Parliament, Kohl stressed that the unification of Germany had to be closely linked to further European integration.[23]

Despite these professions of commitment to European integration, Germany's EC partners were stunned by Kohl's announcement on November 28 of "A Ten-Point Program for Overcoming the Division of Germany and Europe." At the center of this plan was the development of "confederative structures between the two states in Germany with a view to creating a federation." Nevertheless, the plan carefully linked German unification to the broader process of European integration, proclaiming that "the future architecture of Germany must fit into the architecture of Europe as a whole." The proposal lauded the accomplishments of the EC and claimed that the Community needed to be further strengthened so that it might serve as "the foundation for truly comprehensive European union."[24]

Even though the sentiments expressed in Kohl's plan were for the most part unobjectionable, other EC governments were surprised by its suddenness and upset by the fact that they had not been consulted beforehand. Thus, it only confirmed their already substantial fears that Bonn's pronouncements of commitment to the EC were essentially rhetorical and that Germany was becoming increasingly independent of and less sensitive to the interests of its neighbors. Despite the generally positive public reaction of EC governments to the ten-point plan, considerable dismay was expressed in private. At a NATO meeting in Brussels on December 4, several European governments voiced strong complaints to U.S. president George Bush about Germany's actions.[25]

The announcement of the ten-point plan, and the critical reaction to it, further soured the mood prior to the EC summit scheduled for December 8 in Strasbourg. Since the opening of the wall, Germany's position on the timetable for EMU negotiations had become increasingly viewed as a test of its commitment to European integration. Attention now focused on Strasbourg, with President Mitterrand and others making it known that they expected a positive gesture from Bonn at this meeting. Just prior to the summit, one Paris official stated, "Up to now, West Germany, France and the European Commisssion have been the engines of integration. We are going to have to see how the Germans behave. But if they don't push ahead, there will be a terrible backlash in Europe [against Germany]."[26]

Controversy was further inflamed by a letter that Kohl sent to Mitterrand just days before the summit. In the letter, Kohl stressed Germany's desire for more EC integration and declared that national leaders had to send a clear message at Strasbourg of their intention to complete the internal market and prepare for full monetary union. Nevertheless, he argued against setting a firm date for beginning the EMU conference. Kohl also called for EC political-institutional reform, arguing that the European Parliament should be strengthened to make the Community more democratic. He concluded the letter by suggesting that any new amendments to the Rome Treaty should come into effect by 1994, the year of the next scheduled elections to the Parliament.[27]

The chancellor's letter was viewed by German officials as a conciliatory gesture to France—which had been especially miffed over not being consulted prior to Kohl's announcement of his ten-point plan—and as an important signal that Bonn was not neglecting European integration.[28] Nevertheless, it had exactly the opposite effect. In the letter, Kohl had argued against setting a firm date for beginning the EMU conference and proposed a slower timetable for monetary union than was favored by France. Moreover, he now appeared to be linking progress on EMU to political-institutional reform and a stronger European Parliament, something to which France was very opposed.[29]

In response to the Kohl letter, a stunned Paris warned the German government of a crisis in bilateral relations. It also claimed that any wavering on monetary union would be interpreted by other countries as a sign of decreased German commitment to the Community and a signal that Bonn was more interested in pursuing unification than European integration. Although there was some sympathy for the goal of political-institutional reform among other EC leaders, the German proposals on this front were generally viewed as a ploy to delay talks on monetary union. President Delors, for instance, while supporting the German call for a stronger European Parliament ("One cannot have economic and monetary union without institutional reform and a democratic counterweight"), argued that such institutional changes "must not be made a precondition" for negotiations on monetary union. Expressing his fear that the Strasbourg summit might end in bitterness, Delors warned of "serious crises" for the Community if national leaders were not able to reach agreement on the starting date for an EMU conference.[30]

The German letter produced a flurry of consultations among French, German, and EC officials, with Bonn striving to downplay the rift with Paris over EMU. The German government reaffirmed its continued support for the goal of monetary union and argued that it had no intention of slowing down the integration process. All it wanted, Bonn declared, was to delay the beginning of the conference for a few months, until after the December 1990 federal elections. This, it claimed, would not significantly diminish the movement toward monetary union.[31]

In the end, just hours before the opening of the summit, a compromise was reached. Bonn accepted the French demand that an EMU conference begin in the second half of 1990, while Paris conceded the German request to delay it until after the federal elections in early December. As a result, they agreed that the conference would be formally opened at the European Council meeting scheduled for mid-December in Rome, with actual negotiations beginning in early 1991.[32] In addition to delaying the EMU conference until after the federal elections, Germany gained a further concession by extracting from France and other countries a postsummit statement endorsing the idea of a single German state as long as unification took place within the framework of European integration. Bonn considered this endorsement vital for domestic political reasons since it would help offset claims that the Kohl government was getting little in return for agreeing to talks on monetary union. Through this trade-off, "the risk . . . of a rupture" in Franco-German relations, as Mitterrand put it, "was avoided."[33] The German government was also pleased with the outcome of the meeting, which Kohl personally described as "extraordinarily successful."[34]

The Franco-German Rift

The compromise achieved by EC leaders at Strasbourg did not end the tensions between Bonn and its neighbors. Despite the conciliatory rhetoric after the summit, a rift between Germany and France had already appeared. In a visit to Bonn in early November, just prior to the opening of the wall, President Mitterrand had publicly voiced his support for an eventual unification of the two German states, bravely proclaiming, "I am not afraid of reunification."[35] In the weeks that followed, however, his actions increasingly belied his words. By early December, the rapidly accelerating collapse of the GDR and the growing demands of East Germans for integration with the West (*"Wir sind ein Volk," "Deutschland, einig Vaterland"* [Germany, one fatherland]) made it apparent that momentum toward unification was building. In the face of these developments, Paris increasingly sought to delay the inevitable. In early December, immediately prior to the Strasbourg summit, Mitterrand traveled to the Soviet Union on a trip that in Bonn reawoke old fears of a Franco-Russian alliance against Germany. Speaking in Kiev on December 6, Mitterrand pointedly warned Bonn not to force the pace of unification, arguing that to do so could upset the political balance in Europe and have negative consequences for the European Community. Further EC integration, he argued, should precede "changing borders" (i.e., unification).[36] While on this trip, Mitterrand also asked President Gorbachev to do what he could to prevent unification from taking place.[37]

In the following weeks, the French campaign to inhibit or delay unification continued. In speeches delivered in mid-December, both Mitterrand and Foreign Minister Dumas expressed grave concern about the pace of developments in Germany. They also emphasized the inviolability of the Polish border with East Germany, thus indicating that this issue would be used as a lever to brake the momentum toward unification.[38] On December 16, Mitterrand voiced his concerns about Germany to President Bush during a meeting on the Caribbean island of Martinique.[39]

These and other French actions annoyed Bonn greatly, as did the open questioning of German intentions and loyalties by Paris.[40] Perhaps most galling was the French president's visit to East Germany in late December, parallel to Chancellor Kohl's first trip to the GDR after the wall's opening. In a speech delivered in Leipzig, Mitterrand repeated his warnings about rapid unification, asserting that, although he supported the right of the German people to self-determination, such decisions also had to "take the European balance into account."[41] Not only the message but also the fact of the visit itself greatly upset officials in Bonn, who correctly saw it—the first visit to communist East Germany by a Western head of state—as an attempt to shore up a rapidly crumbling GDR and thus delay unification. The Kohl government had expressed its concerns about the trip to Paris beforehand, but to no avail. For this reason, in the words of one top adviser to the chancellor, the trip was viewed by the German government as an "unfriendly" act.[42] As such, it accentuated a growing deterioration of relations between France and Germany.

An initial step toward reconciliation came on January 4, 1990, with a meeting between Kohl and Mitterrand at the French president's country home in Latché. At this session, Mitterrand voiced his concerns about the implications of German developments for European integration and emphasized the undesirability of a neutral united Germany. He gave particular emphasis, however, to the effects of unification on internal Soviet politics, repeating what Gorbachev had told him during the December visit to Moscow: that "the day German unification is announced, a two line communique will announce that a marshal is seated in my chair."[43] Nevertheless, Mitterrand once again stated his support for unification if that was what the German people wanted. Kohl responded by reaffirming Bonn's commitment to the EC and stated his determination to preserve the Franco-German partnership as the foundation of European integration. He also proclaimed his sensitivity to the concerns of Germany's neighbors and repeated his pledge to embed unification within a broader framework of European institutions. According to one key aide of the chancellor, the meeting was viewed by Bonn as a crucial one for Franco-German ties and as necessary to keep intact the close relationship between Kohl and the French leader. From the German perspective, at least, the meeting appeared to be a success.[44]

In a speech delivered in Paris on January 17, Chancellor Kohl made a further attempt to assuage French concerns. He restated his view that unification would not detract from Germany's commitment to further EC integration and repeated such by-now-familiar slogans as "The future architecture of Germany must be integrated in the future architecture of all of Europe," and "The German house must be built under a European roof." Kohl also stated that, in addition to EMU, Bonn would like to see greater political union, including more cooperation on foreign policy. To this end, he proposed that France and Germany "should be the engine of even closer foreign policy cooperation among European Community countries regarding Eastern Europe."[45]

Improvement of relations between Bonn and Paris was made difficult, however, by the growing momentum of developments in Germany. Following roundtable discussions with opposition groups that had begun in December, the East Berlin government had decided to hold free elections for a new parliament in May 1990. It quickly became apparent, however, that this was not soon enough, and in mid-January, in response to increased upheaval and growing popular demands for change, the Modrow government decided to move up the date of elections to March 18. Moreover, it was accepted by most observers that the first freely elected government in East Germany would begin unification talks with Bonn immediately after taking office. On January 30, a major external hurdle to unification was removed when President Gorbachev, prior to a meeting with Modrow in Moscow, declared that no one any longer challenged in principle "the unification of the Germans."[46] On the following day, Prime Minister Modrow unveiled his own plans for gradual unification with the FRG.

By early February, it was clear that political order in East Germany was rapidly collapsing and that the situation there could become dangerously unstable. A major problem was the continued flight of Easterners across the border to West Germany, which now averaged close to two thousand persons every day. In response to this situation, Chancellor Kohl decided to seize the initiative and push for rapid economic and political unification of the two German states. On February 6, he suggested intergovernmental negotiations on the early establishment of a "monetary and economic community."[47] This proposal was followed by the creation, on February 13, of a joint commission to study the terms of German economic and monetary union.[48] Also on February 13, the foreign ministers of the United States, Soviet Union, France, and Britain announced that the two German states would confer jointly with the four allied powers on the external aspects of German unity in the so-called two-plus-four talks. Thus, by mid-February the only question remaining was not whether German unification would occur but when and under what terms.[49]

The prospects for improved Franco-German relations appeared enhanced by an amicable meeting between Mitterrand and Kohl on February 18 in Paris. At this time, the French president underlined his acceptance of German unity and even indicated approval of plans for German monetary union. In addition, both leaders agreed that the process of European integration needed to be pushed forward. For his part, Kohl reemphasized the importance he placed on the Franco-German partnership and on his close working relationship with Mitterrand.[50]

Shortly after this meeting, however, relations between the two governments began to sour considerably. A key reason was the issue of Germany's border with Poland. In the February meeting with Kohl, Mitterrand had stressed the need for formal recognition by Germany of the Oder-Neisse line—East Germany's current boundary—as its permanent border with Poland and argued that this had to be a precondition for unification. This demand was repeated two weeks later in a speech delivered by Foreign Minister Dumas in Berlin. Then on March 9, Mitterrand appeared at a joint press conference in Paris with Poland's President Jaruzelski and Prime Minister Tadeusz Mazowiecki, at which he declared his support for Poland's demand to be represented at the two-plus-four talks in discussions over the border issue, something to which the Germans were strongly opposed. At the same time, Mitterrand termed as "inadequate" the Bundestag resolution of the previous day, which had declared the inviolability of the Polish border but put off a formal recognition until after parliamentary elections in a unified Germany. This position set France apart from both the United States and Britain, which had indicated their satisfaction with the resolution.[51]

To German officials, it was clear that the French government intended to act as the representative of Polish interests among the Western powers and that French support of Poland's border demands was being used as a ploy to delay unification.[52] If this were not enough, the Kohl government was miffed at what it regarded as French intervention in the election campaign in East Germany. In early March, Mitterrand had received Oskar Lafontaine, the candidate for chancellor of the opposition SPD in the upcoming federal elections. This was viewed by the Kohl government as an attempt to bolster the SPD's chances in the East German elections and an open indication that Mitterrand preferred a Social Democratic government in Bonn to Kohl's Christian Democratic Union/Christian Social Union (CDU/CSU)–led coalition, particularly as the SPD favored a more gradual and cautious approach to unification than the Kohl government.[53]

Despite the rift with France, Bonn continued its efforts to assuage the concerns of other countries about unification. In early March, Kohl made a hastily arranged trip to Brussels to consult with officials from other European countries. At this meeting, the chancellor assured representatives of other governments that they would not be excluded from discussions on German unification, thus responding to complaints from several countries that they had not been properly consulted about plans for German monetary union. Kohl also stated that his "vital interest is that developments [in Germany] should be synchronized with our friends and allies." In this regard, he called attention to the fact that Bonn had been a key proponent of holding a special EC summit in late April in Dublin, which was to focus on the issue of German unification and its consequences for the Community.[54]

By the middle of March, there were signs that Franco-German relations were on the mend. A key turning point was the stunning victory of the Christian Democrats in the March 18 East German elections, which was generally perceived as an endorsement of Kohl's "go-fast" approach to unification. After this point the French government changed its strategy toward Germany. Whereas previously Paris had hoped to slow the pace of unification, it now became convinced that a single German state was inevitable. As a result, France abandoned its efforts to delay unification and turned its attention instead to integrating a united Germany more firmly into the Community. This change in policy was indicated by statements of Foreign Minister Dumas on March 20, in which he urged Bonn to absorb the GDR and complete the unification process as quickly as possible so that it could focus on the Community and European integration. The real challenge now, Dumas claimed, was "to advance further, faster and more deeply toward building Europe" as a political, as well as an economic, entity.[55] At the same time, Kohl's victory in the East German elections enabled the chancellor to now focus greater attention on the EC and improved cooperation with France.

The Dublin Summits and EPU

With Franco-German relations now repaired, the European locomotive could get back on track. After the Strasbourg summit, attention had shifted to the topic of political union. The Kohl government favored this shift, having urged new steps in this direction in numerous statements since November. Also supporting further political union was commission president Delors. Unlike the chancellor, however, Delors was reluctant to link the discussion of political union to EMU negotiations, believing that this could inhibit or delay agreement on the more important subject of monetary union. To avoid this possibility, Delors argued that a second intergovernmental conference on political integration should be delayed until after the conclusion of EMU talks. If there was simply one conference with an enlarged agenda, Delors argued, then "nothing proper will come out of it."[56] Delors repeated his proposal for a separate conference on political union in a January 17 speech to the European Parliament.[57] By February, however, Delors had changed his mind; now he reluctantly agreed that the two intergovernmental conferences could be held simultaneously.[58]

By late March, the momentum on political union had begun to build. On March 23, only five days after the decisive elections in the GDR, Chancellor Kohl traveled to Brussels to brief the commission on developments in Germany. Prior to his visit, Delors had called on the the German leader to make "a political gesture to confirm West Germany's full involvement in European construction, especially in political unity."[59] On this score the chancellor obliged, stressing while in Brussels Bonn's continued support for EC integration and restating the by now well-worn phrase that "we want to be German Europeans and European Germans." He also reemphasized Bonn's support for EMU, arguing that developments in Germany made rapid progress toward this goal even more urgent. In addition, Kohl gave his support to the Delors proposal for a second conference on political union.[60]

Kohl restated these views the following week during a visit to London. While in London, the chancellor also declared that at the upcoming Dublin summit he would push not only for progress on EMU but also for further political union. Standing before a clearly disgruntled Thatcher, Kohl stated that his primary goal was "the political unification of Europe."[61]

The Thatcher government excepted, there was by now growing support within the Community for a new conference on political union. On March 20, the Belgian government had submitted a memorandum to other member states outlining plans for additional political union. Among other things, this document proposed further powers for the European Parliament and commission, as well as closer cooperation among EC countries on foreign policy and security affairs.[62] Also announcing support for a conference on political union at this time was the Italian government.[63] In early April, Prime Minister Charles Haughey of Ireland, the current president of the European Council, announced that the Dublin summit might agree to establish a high-level working group to study proposals for EC political reform, which in turn could pave the way for a second intergovernmental conference on political union. He also indicated that discussion of political union would focus on the plan submitted in March by the Belgian government.[64]

In the meantime, talks continued on monetary union. On April 6, the French and German finance ministers met in Paris to announce wide-ranging agreement on EMU. They reemphasized the determination of their governments to press forward with EMU negotiations and declared that EMU would not be slowed down by German economic and monetary integration. They thus appeared to reject the claims of Bundesbank officials that it would be impossible to create two monetary unions simultaneously, as well as the warning of Bundesbank president Pöhl against making monetary union decisions for mainly "symbolic" political reasons.[65] Instead, German finance minister Theo Waigel stated his conviction "that the European aspect of monetary union can be accelerated by the inter-German movements."[66]

A key step forward came on April 19 with the announcement by Mitterrand and Kohl of a new joint initiative on political union. In a letter to the European Council, the two leaders declared that the pace of both monetary and political union needed to be accelerated to match the rapid movement toward German unification. "In view of the profound transformations in Europe, of the establishment of the internal market and of the achievement of Economic and Monetary Union," the message read, "we think it necessary to accelerate the political construction of the 12-member Europe." For this reason, the letter argued, a second intergovernmental conference on political union should be launched, to be held parallel to the one on EMU that was to begin in December. Both conferences should conclude their work within a year, and final agreements on both monetary and political union, after ratification by national parliaments, should take effect at the beginning of 1993. The letter stated that the political union discussions should focus on the following goals: reinforcing the democratic legitimacy of the European Union; making EC institutions more effective; ensuring the unity and coherence of the union's economic, monetary, and political actions; and defining and putting into effect a common foreign and defense policy. The two leaders urged that preparatory work on the conference begin immediately so that a preliminary report from EC foreign ministers could be presented at the next regularly scheduled EC summit in June.[67]

The surprising Franco-German initiative was the result of several weeks of secretive discussions, with the primary impetus coming from Bonn.[68] Chancellor Kohl had desired a broad agreement with Mitterrand on EC matters before the Dublin summit and had also been concerned about the state of bilateral relations after the tensions over German unification. The joint proposal on political union, therefore, was intended to both repair strained Franco-German ties and send a message to other EC leaders that the Bonn-Paris axis was functioning once again. France, for its part, welcomed the initiative as evidence that the German government remained committed to EC integration, despite being absorbed in the problems of unification.[69]

At the EC foreign ministers meeting in London on April 21, Germany's Genscher and France's Dumas jointly urged the Community to seize the moment and make a "quantum leap" toward political union. "In light of what is happening in Europe," they argued, "the moment is particularly opportune to advance the Community in this direction."[70] Several days later, Kohl and Mitterrand concluded their two-day presummit consultations in Paris with an announcement that they would press together at Dublin for a firm decision to proceed with the discussion of political-institutional reform. They also hoped to set a specific timetable for a second intergovernmental conference on political union. "We are pressing for a decisive breakthrough toward European unity," Kohl proclaimed. "A dream is being realized, to see German unity and European unity being built together."[71]

By the opening of the Dublin summit, the issue of political union had risen to the top of the Community agenda. Going into the summit, the Franco-German initiative had gained the backing of most other EC countries, including Italy, Spain, Portugal, Belgium, and the Netherlands. Along with France, they viewed deepening the Community as the best means of coping with a united Germany.[72] Opposition to political union also existed, however, chiefly among the British and Danish governments. The British government was critical of the lack of clarity about the concept of political union, and at the summit itself Prime Minister Thatcher would remark that even Kohl and Mitterrand did not know what they meant by this term.[73] Some concern was also voiced by Delors; although he favored the goal of political union, Delors felt that it should not be allowed to hinder progress toward EMU. Because of this, and because he favored more preparatory work, he continued to urge caution over the timing of a second intergovernmental conference.[74]

On April 28, EC leaders met in Dublin and instructed their foreign ministers to produce a concrete set of proposals on political union. This was to be done by the next regularly scheduled European Council meeting in June, thus allowing a second intergovernmental conference on European Political Union to be approved at this time. This conference would also begin in December, and its work would be conducted parallel to the negotiations on EMU. EC leaders also decided that the results of both conferences should be ratified by national parliaments by the end of 1992 so that they could take effect at the beginning of 1993.[75]

In Dublin Chancellor Kohl profiled himself as a champion of European union. Having spoken beforehand of the inevitability of a "federal Europe," he now boldly proclaimed that Germany was prepared "to abandon certain [national] competences" and transfer them to EC institutions. Kohl also seemed to have learned a lesson from the negative reaction of his European partners to previous unilateral moves, promising to keep other governments regularly informed of developments in Germany. Through such words and actions, he appeared to have finally convinced other EC leaders of the sincerity of Bonn's repeated claims that German unity and European integration were "two sides of the same coin." As his reward, the summit approved a statement warmly welcoming German unity. In it

EC leaders claimed, "We are confident that German unification . . . will be a positive factor in the development of Europe as a whole and of the Community in particular."[76]

The Dublin summit represented a great success for the Bonn government and a personal victory for Kohl. The chancellor himself termed the outcome of the meeting a "super result" and he expressed a tremendous sense of gratitude toward his EC partners for their acceptance of, and support for, German unification. In the German press, the summit was hailed as a triumph for the chancellor and as "Helmut Kohl's day." The press also claimed that the summit results made "it apparent that the federal government, after an initial ineptness, has done remarkable work during the past few months in easing concerns [about German unification]."[77]

The decisions of the April summit were formalized at a June 25–26 meeting of the European Council, which was also held in Dublin. Following this meeting, a satisfied Kohl asserted that these decisions provided yet more evidence of how German unification, rather than inhibiting EC integration, was a factor that was pushing European union forward.[78]

New Uncertainties

Despite the optimism generated by the Dublin summits, the road to Rome was not to be entirely smooth. One potential stumbling block was Britain's resistance to EMU. Just prior to the June summit, British Treasury secretary John Major had suggested, as an alternative to the European central bank and single currency envisioned by the Delors Plan, the creation of a parallel European currency. This "hard ECU" would be managed by a European monetary fund, which would be something much less than a central bank, and would never be devalued within the EMS against other currencies. As such, the hard ECU would compete in the market against national currencies, allowing economic actors (individuals, firms, governments) the choice of which currency to hold and use. If a European monetary and currency union was to eventually emerge, then this would be the result of market forces rather than a conscious decision by EC governments to create one.[79] The British hard ECU plan was greeted with considerable derision by other national governments, however, and failed to stop the movement toward EMU negotiations on the basis of the Delors Plan.[80]

A far more serious problem was posed by renewed uncertainty about Germany's commitment to EMU. These doubts stemmed mainly from increasingly vocal criticism of the Community's EMU plans by the Bundesbank and German financial authorities.[81] The Bundesbank had long been skeptical about EMU and had consistently urged a more cautious, or "go-slow," approach. It was particularly upset, however, about not being consulted by the Kohl government prior to the April Dublin summit, at which EC leaders decided that an EMU agreement should come into force by the start of 1993. Ever since this point, the Bundesbank had actively campaigned against a faster timetable for EMU, arguing that the difficulties of German monetary union indicated the need for caution and that a much greater economic convergence of EC countries was necessary before further steps toward monetary integration could be considered. In advocating a more cautious approach on EMU, the Bundesbank also had an important ally in the Finance Ministry.

In summer 1990, the go-slow front began to assert its views more strongly. At a June 11 meeting of EC finance and monetary officials, German finance minister Waigel pressed for a lengthy transition period to full EMU. During this period, he argued, "the foundation for a permanent stability of exchange rates" could be created, before national sovereignty over monetary policy was transferred to supranational authorities. He argued further that before a stable monetary union could be instituted, much greater economic convergence among EC countries had to be achieved. Also at this meeting, Bundesbank president Pöhl suggested the possibility of a "two-speed" approach to EMU. Accordingly, full integration could initially take place among a small group of countries that had already achieved substantial economic convergence, with other countries being allowed to join this advanced "core" once they were ready.[82]

In arguing for a two-speed, or more gradual, approach to EMU, the Bundesbank could make reference to the problematic experience of German monetary union. After hearing Kohl's initial proposals in February, Pöhl had termed the idea of an early economic merger of the two Germanys "fantastical."[83] Nevertheless, the Bundesbank's objections were overridden by the political considerations of the federal government, and on May 18 an interstate treaty on German economic and monetary union was signed. Under the terms of this agreement, full monetary and currency union came into effect on July 1, 1990. From this point, the D-mark became the official currency of the GDR, and the Bundesbank took over full authority for monetary policy in East Germany.[84]

By late summer, some of the negative consequences of German monetary integration were becoming apparent. These included increased unemployment and the need for substantial transfer payments to East Germany, resulting in inflationary pressures and a growing federal budget deficit. Feeling justified in the earlier criticism that German monetary union had been overly hasty, the Bundesbank was now prepared to use this as an argument for slowing down EMU. In a speech in late August, Pöhl pointed to the German experience as an example of the consequences of monetary union between countries that had not yet achieved a sufficient level of economic convergence. Current EMU plans, he argued, would have Germany sacrificing its D-mark "on the European altar without knowing what we would get in return." Instead, he once again urged a more limited two-speed approach, with less prepared EC countries remaining behind.[85]

At a meeting in Rome in early September, EC finance ministers discussed the commission's proposal that stage two of EMU should begin in January 1993. This plan had the support of France and Italy but it was opposed by Bonn. Finance

Minister Waigel argued against setting any firm dates for the future stages of EMU, declaring that the timing of the next moves should depend on the progress made by EC states toward economic convergence. To this end, Waigel, who was supported on this point by the Netherlands and Luxembourg, urged the setting of strict convergence targets in such areas as inflation, interest rates, and budget deficits; only when these were met by a sufficient number of countries should the next phase of monetary integration be allowed to begin.[86]

A more cautious German stance was also in evidence at the Franco-German summit in Munich on September 17–18. In discussions with Mitterrand, Kohl reflected the concerns of those in Germany who wanted to go slower on EMU. As a result, the meeting produced a statement that backed away from the April summit decision, declaring only that an EMU agreement should be ratified by national parliaments by January 1993 and leaving open when it might actually come into effect.[87] Visibly upset with Bonn's backtracking on EMU, Mitterrand responded by retreating from an earlier commitment to build a mixed Franco-German army division, a project that was much favored by the Kohl government. He also reaffirmed previously announced plans to withdraw French forces from Germany, ignoring Bonn's plea that they stay.[88] On the whole, the atmosphere at the Munich summit was frosty, indicating a renewed chill in bilateral relations just two weeks prior to the formal unification of Germany.[89]

On September 19, the Bundesbank's policymaking council, in a move that was highly unusual for this normally secretive body, made public a paper that listed the conditions to be met before EMU would be possible. These included the following:

1. A future European central bank would have to be closely modeled on the Bundesbank, with complete independence from political authority and a statutory commitment to fighting inflation.
2. There should be no firm timetable for realizing full monetary union.
3. Greater strides toward economic convergence among individual countries were necessary before establishment of a European central bank could be considered.
4. Inflation had to be effectively eliminated from all participating countries before the final stage of monetary union could take effect.

The paper concluded with a warning to the federal government that it should "advocate these principles strongly at the intergovernmental conference."[90]

As a result of these and other statements by German authorities, by late September a growing uncertainty had surfaced among many Europeans about the extent of Germany's support for monetary union.[91] In response, Delors publicly took Bonn to task, admitting that his attempt to set firm dates for EMU was a "way of testing Germany's commitment to economic and monetary union" and arguing that firm dates were needed "because we have to bind Germany into

Europe irreversibly."[92] Delors went on to pose the question "Do the Germans really want economic and monetary union?" "Quite frankly, I often wonder."[93]

Delors's comments were directed mainly at the German chancellor, who was known to be wavering in the middle between the go-slow advice of monetary and financial authorities and the view of the Foreign Ministry that Germany should agree to more rapid integration. Delors and other European leaders knew there was little chance of changing the views of the Bundesbank and the Finance Ministry. What they hoped for, however, was that objections from these sources would be overridden by Kohl in favor of improved foreign relations and the goal of European union.[94]

The Rome Summit and IGCs

Against the background of increased tensions over monetary union, German unification proceeded rapidly to conclusion. On August 31, the two German governments signed a second interstate treaty, this one establishing the legal, social, and political bases for unification. The final external hurdle was removed with the conclusion on September 12 of the two-plus-four talks, thus signifying full acceptance by the World War II victor powers of German unification.[95] Formal unity was then achieved on October 3. On this day, Chancellor Kohl and other German leaders thanked the Western allies and the Soviet Union and repeated their assurances that a united Germany would be a positive factor in the peaceful development of Europe. One day prior, the EC Commission had issued a declaration officially welcoming German unification. It also expressed confidence that unification would strengthen the Community and that a united Germany would serve as a catalyst for further European integration.[96]

With Germany now formally unified, EC leaders turned their attention once again to the issue of monetary union. In particular, there was the question of a timetable for EMU, on which considerable disagreement remained. A major breakthrough on this issue was achieved at a special European Council meeting held on October 27–28 in Rome. Just prior to the meeting, Kohl communicated to Italian prime minister Giulio Andreotti—the current European Council president and summit host—that he was now ready to set a date for the beginning of stage two. He also indicated that because of an uncertain domestic political climate—with new federal elections taking place in early December and growing economic problems stemming from unification—he could not guarantee that he would be in a position to make a similar commitment in December. This implied a window of opportunity for agreement, which Andreotti and other EC leaders decided to quickly seize.[97]

As a result, national leaders agreed—with the notable exception of Britain's Thatcher—that stage two should begin on January 1, 1994, provided certain conditions were met. These were rather minimal, consisting mainly of the completion of the 1992 single market project, the beginning of a process to make national central banks independent by the start of stage three, and limitations on the fiscal policies of member states. The summit also decided that a European monetary institution would be established at the beginning of stage two and that stage three would begin within three years of the launching of the second phase. These decisions left numerous important questions unanswered, including the exact powers and responsibilities of the European central bank during stage two. Nevertheless, the general parameters of an EMU treaty had now been set. Most important, there were now fairly firm dates for the future stages of EMU.[98]

The decisions of the October summit helped prepare the way for the launching of the intergovernmental conferences in Rome. Another key step came several weeks later when on December 6 Kohl and Mitterrand sent a joint letter to the Italian presidency calling for action on European political union. The letter proposed the establishment of a "truly common foreign and security policy, which could in time lead to a common defense." In the future, according to the letter, foreign policy decisions should be made by the European Council on a qualified majority basis. The letter also suggested that the nine-member WEU be formally linked to the EC and become the "European pillar" or defense component of NATO. In addition, the proposal called for enhanced powers for the European Parliament, the creation of a common "European citizenship," and the expansion of EC authority in new policy areas, including environmental protection, health, social policy, energy, and consumer protection. It also called for the creation of a new intergovernmental body to deal with border control issues such as visas, immigration, political asylum, drug trafficking, and terrorism.[99]

With the outline for an EMU agreement already in place, and with a set of more concrete proposals on political union now in hand, national leaders met in Rome on December 14–15 to formally launch the intergovernmental conferences on EMU and EPU.[100] This was a significant moment for many in the Community. For proponents of European union, such as Delors, it meant that integration had not been slowed down by the momentous developments in Germany and Eastern Europe; if anything, it appeared to have been accelerated. For France, the conferences held out the prospect for binding a united Germany more firmly to the Community, thus ensuring that it would not become more independent in the future. For Germany, the Rome summit marked the passage of a turbulent year; somehow, over the previous thirteen months, Bonn had managed to successfully balance the often competing demands of unification and EC integration. Now, having played a major role in bringing the two conferences about, Chancellor Kohl and his government could reasonably hope that many of the doubts about Germany's commitment to European integration had finally been erased.

Notes

1. For accounts of the 1989 revolution in Eastern Europe, see David S. Mason, *Revolution in East-Central Europe: The Rise and Fall of Communism and the Cold War*

(Boulder: Westview Press, 1992); Gale Stokes, *The Walls Came Tumbling Down: The Collapse of Communism in Eastern Europe* (New York: Oxford University Press, 1993); Joseph Rothschild, *Return to Diversity: A Political History of East Central Europe Since WWII*, 2d ed. (New York: Oxford University Press, 1993), pp. 226–262; and Michael Roskin, *The Rebirth of East Europe*, 2d ed., Englewood Cliffs, N.J.: Prentice-Hall, 1994), pp. 126–147.

2. For detailed accounts of the collapse of the East German state, see Konrad H. Jarausch, *The Rush to German Unity* (New York: Oxford University Press, 1994); A. James McAdams, *Germany Divided: From the Wall to Reunification* (Princeton: Princeton University Press, 1993), pp. 175–206; Mary Fulbrook, *The Divided Nation* (New York: Oxford University Press, 1992), pp. 318–345.

3. On the historic German question, see David Calleo, *The German Problem Reconsidered* (New York: Cambridge University Press, 1978); Harold James, *A German Identity, 1770–1990* (New York: Routledge, 1989). For a more recent discussion, see Timothy Garton Ash, *In Europe's Name: Germany and the Divided Continent* (New York: Random House, 1993), esp. pp. 378–410. See also Renate Fritsch-Bournazel, "The United States of Germany and the New Europe," Occasional Paper no. 70 (Bologna: Johns Hopkins University, Bologna Center Research Institute, January 1992).

4. On reactions to German unification, see Andrei S. Markovits and Simon Reich, "Should Europe Fear the Germans?" *German Politics and Society* 23 (Summer 1991):1–20; Harold James and Marla Stone, eds., *When the Wall Came Down: Reactions to German Unification* (New York: Routledge, 1992); Dirk Verheyen and Christian Søe, eds., *The Germans and Their Neighbors* (Boulder: Westview Press, 1993). For French reactions in particular, see Ingo Kolboom, *Vom geteilten zum vereinigten Deutschland* (Bonn: Europa-Union Verlag, 1991), pp. 9–12. For examples of the optimistic view, with an emphasis on Germany's role as a postnational state, see Elizabeth Pond, "Germany in the New Europe," *Foreign Affairs* 71 (Spring 1992):114–130; Robert Gerald Livingston, "United Germany: Bigger and Better," *Foreign Policy* 87 (Summer 1992):157–174.

5. This shift in the relative importance of national power assets was recognized even before the events of 1989. See, for instance, Dominique Moïsi, "Die Mark und die Bombe," *Die Zeit*, December 9, 1988; cited in Ole Waever, "Three Competing Europes: German, French, Russian," *International Affairs* 66, 3 (July 1990):487.

6. On France's position in post–cold war Europe, see Ronald Tiersky, "France in the New Europe," *Foreign Affairs* 71, 2 (Spring 1992):131–146. For a discussion of the strains on Franco-German relations caused by the end of the cold war and German unification, see Philip H. Gordon, *France, Germany, and the Western Alliance* (Boulder: Westview Press, 1995), pp. 32–34.

7. On this strategy, see Patrick McCarthy, "Condemned to Partnership: The Franco-German Relationship, 1944–1983," in Patrick McCarthy, ed., *France-Germany, 1983–1993: The Struggle to Cooperate* (New York: St. Martin's Press, 1993), pp. 1–25; Patrick McCarthy, "France Looks at Germany, or How to Become German (and European) While Remaining French," in McCarthy, ed., *France-Germany, 1983–1993*, pp. 51–72.

8. *Times* (London), July 16, 1990, p. 2; cited in David Garnham, "European Defense Cooperation: The 1990s and Beyond," in Dale L. Smith and James Lee Ray, eds., *The 1992 Project and the Future of European Integration* (New York: M. E. Sharpe, 1993), p. 204. On Thatcher's personal views, see Margaret Thatcher, *The Downing Street Years* (New York: HarperCollins, 1993), pp. 759–763, 789–815.

9. Garnham, "European Defense Cooperation," pp. 204–205.

10. *Spectator,* July 14, 1990, pp. 19–21.

11. Wolfgang Bergsdorf; quote cited in Ash, *In Europe's Name,* p. 385.

12. Horst Teltschik, "Vom 'politischen Zwerg' zur 'Weltmacht'—Nachdenken über Deutschlands neue Rolle in Europa," *Die Welt,* September 22, 1990; quoted in Hugh Miall, *Shaping a New European Order* (London: RIIA, 1994), p. 85.

13. *New York Times,* February 14, 1990, p. A10.

14. *New York Times,* May 27, 1990, p. A25.

15. Horst Teltschik, *329 Tage: Innenansichten der Einigung* (Berlin: Siedler, 1991), p. 61.

16. On German European policy after the wall, see Gerd Langguth, "Deutschland, die EG, und die Architektur Europas," *Aussenpolitik* 42 (1991):136–145; Reinhard Stuth, "Deutschlands neue Rolle im sich wandelnden Europa," *Aussenpolitik* 43 (January 1992):22–32.

17. *Economist,* October 21, 1989, p. 50.

18. *Economist,* October 28, 1989, p. 58.

19. Ibid.

20. *Economist,* November 4, 1989, pp. 58–59; November 11, 1989, p. 56.

21. *New York Times,* November 17, 1989, p. A14.

22. *New York Times,* November 19, 1989, p. A28; November 21, 1989, p. A8; *The Week in Germany,* November 24, 1989, p. 1.

23. *The Week in Germany,* November 24, 1989, p. 2; *New York Times,* December 1, 1989, p. A21.

24. "A Ten-Point Program for Overcoming the Division of Germany and Europe" (Official Translation), *Statements and Speeches* 12, 25 (New York: German Information Center, December 19, 1989), esp. points 5–7, pp. 5–6.

25. *New York Times,* December 6, 1989, p. A16.

26. *New York Times,* December 8, 1989, p. D5.

27. Teltschik, *329 Tage,* pp. 68–69; *Financial Times,* December 7, 1989, p. 2.

28. Teltschik, *329 Tage,* p. 54.

29. *Financial Times,* December 7, 1989, p. 2; *New York Times,* December 8, 1989, p. D5.

30. *Financial Times,* December 8, 1989, p. 24.

31. *New York Times,* December 8, 1989, p. D5; *Financial Times,* December 8, 1989, p. 24.

32. *Financial Times,* December 9, 1989, p. 1; *New York Times,* December 9, 1989, p. A1; *The Week in Germany,* December 15, 1989, p. 5.

33. *New York Times,* December 10, 1989, p. A32; December 11, 1989, pp. D1–2; *Financial Times,* December 11, 1989, p. 3.

34. Teltschik, *329 Tage,* p. 72.

35. *New York Times,* December 1, 1989, p. A1.

36. *New York Times,* December 7, 1989, p. A21.

37. Julius W. Friend, *The Linchpin: Franco-German Relations, 1950–1990* (New York: Praeger, 1991), p. 82.

38. Teltschik, *329 Tage,* pp. 75–76.

39. Ibid., p. 86.

40. On German views of Mitterrand's policy toward unification, see Robert Picht, "Deutsch-französische Beziehungen nach dem Fall der Mauer," in Robert Picht and Wolfgang Wessels, eds., *Motor für Europa? Deutsch-französische Bilateralismus und europäische Integration* (Bonn: Europa-Union Verlag, 1990), pp. 47–68.

41. *New York Times,* December 22, 1989, p. A12.

42. Teltschik, *329 Tage,* p. 95; also Tiersky, "France in the New Europe," p. 132.

43. Quoted in Friend, *The Linchpin,* p. 81.

44. Teltschik, *329 Tage,* pp. 97–100.

45. *New York Times,* January 18, 1990, p. A9.

46. *The Week in Germany,* February 2, 1990, p. 1.

47. Deutsche Bundesbank, "The Monetary Union with the German Democratic Republic," *Monthly Report of the Deutsche Bundesbank* 42, 7 (July 1990):14.

48. *Economist,* February 17, 1990, p. 73.

49. Fulbrook, *The Divided Nation,* p. 336.

50. Teltschik, *329 Tage,* pp. 150–151.

51. Ibid.

52. Ibid., pp. 164–172.

53. Friend, *The Linchpin,* p. 84.

54. *New York Times,* March 9, 1990, p. A10.

55. *New York Times,* March 14, 1990, p. A17.

56. *Financial Times,* December 13, 1989, p. 2; *Economist,* December 16, 1989, p. 51.

57. George Ross, *Jacques Delors and European Integration* (New York: Oxford University Press, 1995), p. 89.

58. *Economist,* February 24, 1990, pp. 45–46.

59. Ibid.

60. *The Week in Germany,* March 30, 1990, p. 1.

61. *New York Times,* March 31, 1990, p. A6.

62. For the text of this document, see "Belgian Memorandum on Institutional Relaunch"; reprinted in Finn Laursen and Sophie Vanhoonacker, eds., *The Intergovernmental Conference on Political Union: Institutional Reforms, New Policies, and International Identity of the European Community* (Dordrecht, The Netherlands: Martinus Nijhoff, 1992), pp. 269–275.

63. Finn Laursen, Sophie Vanhoonacker, and Robert Wester, "Overview of the Negotiations," in Laursen and Vanhoonacker, eds., *The Intergovernmental Conference on Political Union,* p. 5.

64. *Financial Times,* April 11, 1990, p. 2; *Economist,* April 21, 1990, p. 56.

65. *Financial Times,* April 7, 1990, p. 2.

66. Ibid.

67. *Financial Times,* April 20, 1990, p. 1. The text of the Kohl-Mitterrand letter is reprinted in Laursen and Vanhoonacker, eds., *The Intergovernmental Conference on Political Union,* p. 276.

68. Teltschik, *329 Tage,* pp. 175–176.

69. *Financial Times,* April 20, 1990, p. 4; Teltschik, *329 Tage,* pp. 175–176.

70. *Financial Times,* April 23, 1990, p. 24.

71. *Financial Times,* April 27, 1990, p. 1.

72. *New York Times,* April 25, 1990, p. A14.

73. Geoffrey Edwards and Simon Nutall, "Common Foreign and Security Policy," in Andrew Duff, John Pinder, and Roy Price, eds., *Maastricht and Beyond: Building the European Union* (London: Routledge, 1994), p. 87.

74. *Financial Times,* April 27, 1990, p. 1. On Delors's reservations, see Robert Wester, "The European Commission and European Political Union," in Laursen and

Vanhoonacker, eds., *The Intergovernmental Conference on Political Union*, p. 206.

75. *New York Times*, April 28, 1990, p. A5; April 29, 1990, p. A16; *Financial Times*, April 30, 1990, pp. 1, 2. See also Laursen, Vanhoonacker, and Wester, "Overview of the Negotiations," p. 6.

76. *New York Times*, April 28, 1990, p. A5; April 29, 1990, p. A16; *Financial Times*, April 30, 1990, pp. 1, 2.

77. *The Week in Germany*, May 4, 1990, pp. 2, 3; Teltschik, *329 Tage*, p. 212. The press quotations are from the April 30 edition of the Düsseldorf newspaper *Handelsblatt*.

78. *The Week in Germany*, June 29, 1990, p. 2; Laursen, Vanhoonacker, and Wester, "Overview of the Negotiations," p. 8.

79. *Economist*, June 23, 1990, p. 48.

80. *Economist*, June 30, 1990, p. 17. On the British hard ECU plan, see also Loukas Tsoukalis, *The New European Economy: The Politics and Economics of Integration* (New York: Oxford University Press, 1991), p. 197.

81. On Bundesbank opposition to EMU in 1990, see W. R. Smyser, *The Economy of United Germany: Colossus at the Crossroads*, 2d ed. (New York: St. Martin's Press, 1993), pp. 274–278.

82. *The Week in Germany*, June 15, 1990, p. 5.

83. *Economist*, February 17, 1990, p. 73.

84. On the history and terms of German monetary union, see Deutsche Bundesbank, "The Monetary Union with the German Democratic Republic," pp. 13–28. See also "The New Germany" (Survey), *Economist*, June 30, 1990, pp. 10–12.

85. *Economist*, July 7, 1990, p. 25; September 1, 1990, p. 48; September 15, 1990, pp. 61–62.

86. *Economist*, September 15, 1990, pp. 61–62.

87. *Financial Times*, October 29, 1990 ("Survey on Germany"), p. 12.

88. Friend, *The Linchpin*, pp. 87–88; *Financial Times*, September 27, 1990. The French government had announced in July 1990 that it would withdraw French forces from Germany because they were no longer needed and "no longer had a legitimate legal or political justification" (Gordon, *France, Germany, and the Western Alliance*, p. 45).

89. *Economist*, October 6, 1990, p. 53.

90. *Financial Times*, October 29, 1990 ("Survey on Germany"), p. 12. For an analysis of the September 1990 Bundesbank statement, see Wilhelm Nölling, *Monetary Policy in Europe After Maastricht* (New York: St. Martin's Press, 1993), pp. 163–165.

91. *Economist*, September 22, 1990, p. 60.

92. *Economist*, September 29, 1990, p. 58.

93. *New York Times*, October 1, 1990, p. D8.

94. *Economist*, September 15, 1990, pp. 61–62; October 20, 1990, pp. 60–61.

95. On the history of the two-plus-four talks, see Stephen F. Szabo, *The Diplomacy of German Unification* (New York: St. Martin's Press, 1993).

96. *The Week in Germany*, October 5, 1990, p. 4.

97. *Economist*, November 3, 1990, p. 55.

98. Ibid., pp. 55–59; *Financial Times*, October 29, 1990, p. 1. For the text of the conclusions of the October 1990 European Council pertaining to EMU, see Tommaso Padoa-Schioppa, *The Road to Monetary Union: The Emperor, the Kings, and the Genies* (Oxford: Clarendon Press, 1994), pp. 255–257.

99. *New York Times,* December 8, 1990, p. A3; *Financial Times,* December 8–9, 1990, pp. 1, 22; *The Week in Germany,* December 14, 1990, p. 1. The text of the Kohl-Mitterrand letter is reprinted in Laursen and Vanhoonacker, eds., *The Intergovernmental Conference on Political Union,* pp. 313–314.

100. For reports on the Rome summit, see *Financial Times,* November 17, 1990, pp. 1–2.

3

Negotiating Maastricht: Economic and Monetary Union

The EMU conference began with the broad outlines of an agreement already in place. These were contained in a draft treaty produced by the commission in December that was based on the decisions of the October EC summit. It called for a three-stage EMU process according to a fairly set timetable. Stage one was already under way, having begun with the elimination of capital and exchange controls on July 1, 1990. The second stage, which would involve the creation of a new European monetary institution that would eventually become the European Central Bank (ECB), would begin on January 1, 1994. Within three years of this date, the third stage would begin. This stage would feature the establishment of a European central bank that would manage a single European currency, tentatively named the ECU.[1] The institutional structure and rules of operation of the ECB had also, by this point, largely been agreed on. In most respects, this bank would closely resemble the German Bundesbank, with independence from government control, a primary mandate to limit inflation, and sole authority over monetary policy.

Nevertheless, much remained to be negotiated. The key issues to be decided over the course of the following year would be (1) the exact nature of stage two, including the powers and duties of the new European monetary institution during this transitional period; (2) the nature of the final transition to stage three, including the questions of when and how this would occur and which countries, and under what terms, would be allowed to join full EMU; and (3) the nature of stage three itself, including the role of EC authorities in the making of national budgetary and fiscal policies and the question of a common currency. Also to be resolved was the problem of British opposition to monetary union and the possible veto by Britain of an EMU agreement.

Nevertheless, these problems were not thought to be insurmountable, and the conference began with considerable optimism. In fact, it was generally thought that work on EMU was so far along that a treaty could be completed by late spring.[2] Unfortunately, this belief was too optimistic, and final agreement was reached only on the eve of the December Maastricht summit and only after a last-minute flurry of high-level consultations, trade-offs, and concessions by key countries.

National Positions on EMU

The positions of national governments going into the EMU conference were pretty well established.[3] For France and most other EC countries, the primary objective of EMU was to subsume German monetary power under the authority of European institutions. Although this objective was originally a means of gaining control over German monetary policy, and thereby recouping some degree of national monetary sovereignty, after 1989 the objective had a different purpose: to more firmly integrate a united Germany into the Community, and thus limit that nation's future independence and dominance. The main goal for these countries in the conference, therefore, was agreement on a firm timetable for monetary union and an irreversible commitment by Germany to EMU. In this, they had an important ally in the commission and its president, Jacques Delors.

The German government also desired an agreement on EMU, mainly because it wanted to assuage the fears of other Europeans about a united Germany and demonstrate its continued commitment to European integration. Nevertheless, Bonn was not about to give up monetary sovereignty and the D-mark without ensuring that EMU would take place according to German standards. These included a European central bank that would be modeled on the Bundesbank and a common currency that would be every bit as stable as the D-mark. For Germany, these terms were not negotiable, and they represented a consensus view within the country's political and economic establishment.

This is not to say that serious differences of opinion about EMU did not exist within Germany. On one side of this issue were the Bundesbank and Finance Ministry, which advocated a more cautious approach to EMU. If EMU was to take place at all, they argued, then it should proceed on a two-speed basis, with monetary union first occurring only among those countries that had achieved a sufficient level of economic convergence. In addition, German monetary and financial authorities wanted to avoid a transition to EMU in which the responsibilities of national and European authorities were blurred.[4] The skepticism of the Bundesbank and Finance Ministry about EMU was also shared by much of the German financial and business community. On the other side of the issue was the Foreign Ministry, whose primary concern was the external political ramifications of EMU. Because the Foreign Ministry wanted to convince other European governments of Bonn's continued commitment to European integration, the ministry favored Germany's agreement to an accelerated timetable for EMU. Foreign political considerations were also of great importance to Chancellor Kohl, who viewed EMU as a necessary counterpart to German unification.

The primary opponent of EMU among national governments was Britain, which viewed it as a gross infringement of national sovereignty and a step in the direction of a federal Europe. Under Prime Minister Thatcher, Britain had remained outside of the exchange-rate mechanism of the EMS until October 1990. Thatcher herself was finally forced to resign in November of that year, with her intransigent position on European integration being a key factor in her downfall. Her successor as Conservative Party head and prime minister, John Major, promised to increase Britain's involvement in the Community and did not appear as adamantly opposed to EMU as Thatcher. Nevertheless, the British government did not give up its basic skepticism about monetary union and went into the negotiations with the intention of limiting or delaying any EMU agreement.

In addition, the poorer EC members, especially Spain, Portugal, Greece, Ireland, and, to some extent, Italy, had a specific set of interests, particularly how to avoid being left behind in a two-speed EMU. This configuration would confer on them a "second-class" status, when most of them had originally coveted EC membership as a means of modernizing and catching up with the more economically advanced countries of northern Europe. A second goal was to secure additional financial and economic assistance as part of an EMU agreement so that they could compete in a more economically integrated Community. This goal was also in keeping with established patterns of intra-Community baragaining: Since the 1970s the governments of poorer countries had successfully demanded compensation, in the form of regional and structural policy assistance, as the price for their agreement to further EC integration.

The European Central Bank

The one area of EMU negotiations in which there was relatively little controversy concerned the structure of a future European central bank. In fact, agreement on this had largely been achieved prior to the beginning of the conference. Basically, it had been decided that the ECB would be modeled on the German Bundesbank. This outcome reflected not only Germany's direct influence and bargaining leverage but also the predominance in Europe of German monetary norms and values. If the meaning of hegemony is the exercise of dominance through the voluntary acceptance by other countries of the rules and norms of behavior established by another, then Germany's role in European monetary affairs at this point in time can be accurately termed "hegemonic."[5]

Intergovernmental discussions about a European central bank had begun in the fall of 1989 when EC finance ministers charged national central bank chiefs with developing a set of statutes for the future ECB. These statutes were to be ready for an EMU conference in late 1990.[6] In early December, the committee of central bankers met in Basel (Switzerland), where they endorsed a list of German demands on EMU, including priority for the goal of fighting inflation and the independence of a future ECB from government influence. Also at this meeting the head of the Bundesbank, Karl-Otto Pöhl, was chosen to chair the committee. Under Pöhl's leadership, the committee began the process of drafting the statutes.[7]

By fall 1990, the committee had completed its work. The draft statutes for the European central bank were unveiled on November 13, revealing an institution that was modeled closely on the Bundesbank. Among other things, the ECB would have a statutory mandate to limit inflation. It would also have complete and unambiguous control over monetary policy, not sharing this with any other government or public authority. And it would be independent from government influence. Although the ECB would be required to report annually to the European Council and the European Parliament, it would otherwise be free from any political control or direction. The governing council of the ECB would consist of six executive directors, appointed by the European Council for eight-year terms, and the twelve governors of national central banks, who would be prohibited from taking instructions from their own governments. For this reason, the political independence of national central banks would be a necessary precondition for the establishment and effective functioning of the ECB.[8]

The draft statutes laid the basis for a European central bank that, in Pöhl's view, would be even more independent and powerful than the Bundesbank. In German law the Bundesbank is required, insofar as this does not conflict with its primary task of keeping inflation low, "to support the general economic policy of the Federal government." This support includes the legally specified goals of economic growth, high employment, and balanced foreign trade, in addition to that of price stability. In principle, at least, this mandate provides some scope for political pressure on German monetary authorities by government policymakers. The wording of the draft statutes, in contrast, provided an even narrower policy mandate, requiring only that—once again without prejudice to the primary goal of price stability—the ECB support the general, and as yet undefined, economic policy of the Community. At the same time, the draft statutes contained no provisions allowing government authorities to delay central bank decisions, whereas in Germany the federal government can block Bundesbank decisions for up to two weeks if it sees fit.[9]

Despite the existence of the draft statutes, a number of important details concerning the organization and operation of the future European central bank remained to be hammered out. Among these was the nature of the relationship between the ECB's executive directors and the national central bank governors, including the relative authority of the former over the latter. There was also the issue of the political autonomy of national central banks. According to the draft statutes, national central bank governors sitting on the ECB council would be prohibited from taking instructions from their own governments. To ensure this, German monetary authorities argued that before the ECB could be established, national laws should be changed to guarantee the political independence of central banks. The governments of other EC countries balked. As a result, this particular German demand would become a key point of contention in the EMU negotiations.[10]

Another dispute concerned the role of the ECB in exchange-rate policy. German monetary authorities, reflecting national cultural values and preferences,[11] insisted that internal price stability should be a higher priority for a future ECB than external exchange-rate stability. Many economically weaker EC countries, with their focus on maximizing economic growth and employment, disagreed. They favored instead a policy aimed at keeping European currencies at a stable or competitive level against non-European currencies, such as the U.S. dollar and Japanese yen. As a means of ensuring that price stability would not be subordinated to other policy goals, German authorities insisted that the ECB have independent control of exchange-rate policy, including decisions over currency market intervention. Other countries, however—including France, Italy, and Britain—argued for more control over exchange-rate policy by governments through the EC's Council of Economics and Finance Ministers (Ecofin). At a meeting on March 31, 1990, EC finance ministers reached a compromise, deciding that Ecofin would set the general parameters of exchange-rate policy, while the ECB would be left to make decisions on day-to-day currency management and intervention.[12] Nevertheless, this was a fairly vague formulation, and the dispute over exchange-rate policy would continue throughout the EMU negotiations.

Finally, there was the issue of where to locate the ECB. German authorities favored placing the new institution in Germany; they favored the Bundesbank's home city of Frankfurt. This location, they argued, would give the new ECB more credibility in the eyes of the international financial community. At the same time, locating the ECB in Germany would help overcome domestic opposition to giving up monetary sovereignty and the D-mark. Other EC countries, as might be expected, had different ideas about the ECB's location. Citing London's traditional role as a center of global banking and finance, the British government favored locating the new European central bank there. This request struck many as odd, given Britain's generally intransigent position on EMU. France, argued for Paris or Strasbourg, fearing that a German location would only further reinforce German dominance in the monetary realm. A number of compromise proposals for sites in smaller countries also emerged, including Luxembourg and Amsterdam.[13] In the end, a decision on where to locate the European central bank was put off until after the signing of an EMU agreement.

The Nature of Stage Two

A key point of dispute in EMU negotiations was the nature of the stage two transition to full monetary union. This dispute concerned, above all else, two questions: At what point in stage two would a European central bank be established? What exactly would be the powers and responsibilities of this institution during this phase, especially vis-à-vis national authorities? The agreement reached at the October 1990 EC summit called for the establishment of a new European monetary institution, with the beginning of phase two on January 1, 1994, and a decision on launching the final stage of EMU to be made within three years. Beyond that rather vague commitment, however, much remained to be settled.

The central German interest on this issue was to ensure against any loss of Bundesbank sovereignty during stage two, before full monetary powers and responsibility could be assumed by a stability-oriented European central bank. For this reason, Germany was insistent that control over monetary policy remain "indivisible" during stage two; that is, it wanted to ensure that there was no split authority between a European institution and national central banks. Mainly, German negotiators did not want any European challenger to the authority of the Bundesbank until a European central bank, designed according to German specifications, could take over full and unambiguous control of monetary policy in stage three. To achieve this status, the Germans wanted to wait until the very end of stage two before setting up the ECB. To satisfy the agreement made in October that a new monetary institution would come into existence at the beginning of stage two, the Germans proposed that the committee of central bankers be transformed into a "council" that could be given some responsibilities for helping coordinate national policies.[14]

The German position contrasted sharply with the provisions of the commission's draft EMU treaty, which established the ECB at the beginning of the second stage and gave it more substantial powers to manage the monetary policies of member states. Only the Netherlands and Britain supported the German position on this issue, the former because it shared Germany's concern for the autonomy of national monetary authorities during phase two, the latter because it remained opposed to EMU in principle and was seeking to preserve national monetary sovereignty. One way of doing so was to make phase two look as little different as possible from phase one. On this matter, at least, an alliance between Bonn and London was possible. All other EC countries, however, backed the commission, mainly because they wished to regain, as quickly as possible, some degree of influence over regional monetary policy. With an embryonic ECB at the beginning of phase two that had some interventionist powers in the policies of national authorities, including those of the Bundesbank, this goal would be partially realized.[15]

Some confusion about the German position on stage two was created in early 1991 by contradictory statements from different government actors. In February Germany presented to the conference a draft treaty on monetary union that called for the establishment of the ECB at the very end of stage two. This document was written by the Finance Ministry and approved by the Bundesbank and supposedly had been cleared by the Foreign Ministry and the Chancellor's Office.[16] If it was true that the draft treaty had been approved by both offices, then this indicated that the room for bargaining might be limited since in the past the

Foreign Ministry and the chancellor had taken a more moderate position on EMU than monetary and financial authorities in the interest of political compromise. More uncertainty was created, therefore, when in March Foreign Minister Genscher issued a joint statement with his French counterpart, Dumas, in which he pledged Germany's support for establishing the ECB at the beginning of stage two.[17] This statement came only one month after Chancellor Kohl had publicly agreed with Prime Minister Major that a European central bank should not be created until the end of stage two.[18]

An attempt at compromise on this issue was made in June when the government of Luxembourg—current holder of the EC's rotating presidency—submitted a new draft treaty on EMU to Community leaders at their biannual summit. The document adopted the German proposal that at the beginning of stage two in 1994 the committee of central bankers would transform itself into a council that would seek only to coordinate national policies. As a concession to other countries, the new central bank would be established in 1996, one year before the possible transition to stage three. Initially, however, the bank would limit itself to preparations for taking up its full duties in the final stage of EMU.[19] Nevertheless, the Luxembourg summit did not reach any firm agreements on this or other key issues pertaining to EMU and instead postponed any major decisions until the December European Council meeting in Maastricht.

In preparation for the December summit, the government of the Netherlands, which had taken over the EC presidency in July, tried its own hand at forging a compromise. On September 9, the Dutch government presented to a meeting of EC finance ministers a new draft EMU treaty. This document mirrored the earlier Luxembourg draft and basically reflected the German—and the Dutch—desire for clarity on who would control monetary policy during the stage two transitional phase. The draft treaty called for establishment of a European monetary institute (EMI) in 1994 at the very beginning of stage two. The EMI would be a grouping of national central bank governors that would serve as the precursor of an eventual ECB. However, rather than being an embryonic central bank with significant powers, as favored by the French and Italian governments, the EMI would not have any control over monetary policy. This would instead remain exclusively in the hands of national central banks.[20] The Dutch proposal was basically adopted by EC finance ministers at a September 21 meeting[21] and was subsequently incorporated into a revised draft EMU treaty that was presented in late October.

Nevertheless, the issue of the stage two transition was not yet resolved. In the final weeks leading up to the Maastricht conference, a sharp disagreement erupted between France and Germany over the status and powers of the EMI during stage two. Basically, France desired a strong EMI, while Germany did not. To bolster the EMI by giving it more political weight, and to permit more political influence over its decisions, France wanted the EMI to have a president and a vice president who were appointed by EC governments from outside the committee of central bankers. France also wanted to give the EMI its own capital reserves and an independent role in foreign-exchange intervention. Germany wanted the EMI to be simply another version of the central bank committee, with no outside executives. Furthermore, Germany preferred that the EMI operate only as a think-tank or consultative body and that it have no foreign-exchange reserves or currency-market intervention duties. The bottom line, once again, was that Germany wanted to avoid any overlap of authority between the EMI and Bundesbank during stage two, as well as any diminution of Bundesbank sovereignty. This overlap, of course, is precisely what France hoped to achieve with its proposals.[22]

A compromise on this matter was finally reached by EC finance ministers in early December. They agreed that the EMI would consist of the twelve national central bank governors plus a vice president who was one of their own and a president whom they nominated and EC governments approved. The EMI would have only limited foreign-exchange reserves, which would be voluntarily transferred to it by national central banks, and its intervention activities would be constrained by the need for consultation with national authorities.[23]

The Transition to Stage Three

Perhaps the key question to be decided during the EMU negotiations was the nature and timing of the final transition to stage three, or full monetary union. There were two major issues here. The first of these concerned how the final transition would take place: When would the decision be made to move to stage three? Who would make it and on what basis? Which countries would be allowed to join full EMU, and on the basis of what criteria? The second concerned the commitment of Germany to EMU. Basically, France and other countries wanted an EMU treaty that contained a German commitment to monetary union that was irreversible and that set a specific date by which full EMU would go into effect.

On the first of these issues, Germany's main interest was ensuring that a future EMU would not endanger the monetary stability it had enjoyed in the past under the Bundesbank and its policies. For this reason, the Germans favored an EMU that involved only those countries that were fully ready for it. In particular, Germany feared that the incorporation of weaker, deficit-prone countries in EMU would lead to political pressures for more relaxed monetary policies by the ECB and expensive EC bailouts. The Germans, therefore, insisted that only those countries that were fully prepared to join EMU—in terms of economic performance and stability—should be allowed to do so. Those that were not could join later, once they had made the necessary improvements in their economic position.

The German preference for a two-speed approach to EMU began to surface in the summer of 1990 with statements made by Bundesbank president Pöhl and other government authorities.[24] By the end of the summer, the negative consequences of German monetary union were becoming apparent, and the

Bundesbank held these up as an example of the problems that could result from an overly hasty EMU among countries that had not yet achieved a sufficient level of economic convergence.[25] The demand for a two-speed approach and more economic convergence as a precondition for EMU was also contained in the September 19, 1990, policy statement by the Bundesbank. In this document, the Bundesbank set the virtual elimination of inflation as a basic criterion to be met before countries could be judged ready for EMU.[26] By the opening of EMU negotiations, even though the federal government had accepted the basic EMU timetable of stage two beginning in 1994 and the launching of stage three in the next three years, German authorities had considerable doubts about whether full monetary union could involve all EC countries together.

In contrast to Germany, most other EC countries, along with the commission, favored a single-speed approach to EMU. One reason for this position was the fear that a monetary union among a smaller group of countries—especially if it did not involve Britain—would be more easily dominated by Germany, whereas in a larger EMU German economic and political power could be more effectively balanced. Poorer countries were also concerned that a two-speed EMU would create an unbridgeable gap between rich and poor member states and that poor countries would be relegated to a permanent second-class, or periphery, status as a consequence. Britain, which was not necessarily opposed to the concept of a multi-speed approach to EMU, took a different stance, proposing instead that individual countries have the right to remain outside EMU if they so desired. In seeking to gain an "opt-out" right as part of an EMU agreement, however, the British government did not want to be singled out but rather wanted this right to be given to all countries equally.

Proposals on the final transition to EMU were contained in the Luxembourg draft treaty presented in June. According to this document, by the end of 1996 the commission and national central banks would report to the Council of Finance Ministers on the progress made by member states toward economic convergence. Left unspecified, however, were the exact criteria for deciding whether sufficient convergence had occurred. After the Ecofin session, a summit meeting of EC heads of government would decide if the Community was ready for stage three and, if so, would set a firm date. The goal for beginning stage three suggested by the draft treaty was 1998. Although it did not go into detail about other aspects of the final passage to stage three, the Luxembourg draft did leave open the possibility of a two-speed movement to monetary union and an opt-out clause for countries such as Britain that, for domestic political reasons, might wish to remain outside of EMU.[27]

In summer 1991, German monetary authorities began emphasizing the issue of economic convergence and their preference for a two-speed approach to monetary union. Throughout the first half of the year, the Bundesbank had continued to stress the problems created by German monetary union as an illustration of the danger of an EMU without sufficient convergence.[28] As if to underline this point, Pöhl—who was to announce in May his intention to step down as Bundesbank president—had proclaimed in March that German monetary union was a "disaster."[29] As an institutional basis for a two-speed EMU, Germany proposed at a July meeting of EC finance ministers the creation and coexistence of two separate European monetary institutions. A regional central bank would be created among those countries that were able to proceed with full EMU, and a council of central bank governors would manage the relationship between the new European currency and the currencies of weaker EC countries and help them prepare for eventual EMU membership.[30]

The German preference for a two-speed approach to EMU and strict economic convergence criteria was heavily criticized by Delors. He argued that in the first group of countries that moved to EMU there might be too few states to counterbalance German power, thereby making the group effectively a D-mark bloc. At the same time, strict convergence criteria and a lengthy transition period to EMU might frustrate weaker countries and end up subverting the entire effort.[31]

Despite such criticism, the two-speed approach was embodied in the draft treaty prepared by the Netherlands that was discussed by EC finance ministers in early September. Under this plan, any six countries that met certain economic standards—low levels of inflation and interest rates, exchange-rate stability, and low budget deficits—could proceed on their own to full monetary union and create among themselves a common central bank. Nonqualifying countries would be left behind and allowed to join later, but only if the first group agreed. The Dutch proposal was received favorably only by the Germans, with the majority of other countries preferring a decision by all twelve EC states to go forward with EMU together. In the end, the Germans bowed to the wishes of others and agreed that the final decision on EMU should be made by all EC countries in common. The German delegation did win support, however, for its demands that countries meet strict convergence criteria before they could join the monetary union.[32]

At a meeting on September 21, EC finance ministers made further progress toward an agreement on the final passage to stage three. They decided that before the end of 1996 the new EMI and the commission would report on the Community's readiness for stage three. This judgment would be based on an assessment of the progress toward economic convergence made by EC countries. If a majority of member states met convergence standards for inflation and interest rates, exchange-rate stability, and budget deficits, the Community would be judged ready for the final step to EMU. The Council of Finance Ministers would then decide whether, and when, phase three should start, with the final decision made by unanimous vote in the European Council. Questions concerning the actual implementation of EMU, including at what rate currencies should be fixed and special arrangements for weaker countries, would then be made by Ecofin on a majority vote basis. The forging of a consensus at this meeting was facilitated by the conciliatory posture of the German delegation, led by Finance Minister Waigel. The Germans not only softened their position on a two-speed move to

EMU, agreeing that the final decision should be taken by the Community as a whole, but they also indicated a more relaxed view on the convergence issue, allowing—to the consternation of the Bundesbank—that political considerations should be permitted to play some role in interpretation of the established criteria.[33]

Left unresolved by this meeting was the matter of an opt-out clause for individual countries. This issue concerned, most notably, Britain's desire not to be forced to make an irrevocable commitment to monetary union at the upcoming Maastricht summit. Citing the constitutional principle of parliamentary sovereignty, the British argued that any final decision to enter EMU had first to be debated and approved by the House of Commons and therefore could not be taken until a much later date.[34]

The opt-out issue was tackled in the revised draft EMU treaty presented by the Dutch government in late October. The draft specified that Britain, or any other country whose parliament "does not feel able to approve the irrevocable fixing of its currency," would be allowed to remain outside of the monetary union. The incorporation of a generalized opt-out clause pleased Britain, which did not want to be singled out in the treaty for its reluctance to move forward with EMU at the same pace as the rest of the Community. The clause upset other EC countries, however, which feared that a generalized opt-out clause could potentially be used by Germany to back out of a commitment to monetary union. In response to this concern, the Dutch draft had called for other countries to sign a declaration in which they promised not to use the opt-out clause themselves, a move that most observers regarded as plainly inadequate to lock in Germany.[35]

With the Maastricht conference on the horizon, it was apparent to many in the Community that they had yet to achieve their most important goal: that of gaining a firm German commitment to an irreversible process of European monetary union. France and Italy, with the support of Delors, wanted to achieve at Maastricht an irrevocable decision for EMU that would set a firm timetable and lock in Germany once and for all. The generalized opt-out clause contained in the Dutch draft treaty could stand in the way of this goal; Germany could use the clause to pull out of its commitment to EMU. As a result, by early December all EC governments, with the exception of London, had agreed with the commission that any opt-out clause in the final treaty should be restricted to Britain alone.[36]

Attention also focused on the voting procedures for the final transition to EMU. The Dutch draft had specified that a unanimous vote by the European Council would be necessary to launch stage three. The French and Italians, however, wanted a much firmer guarantee that monetary union would come about even if some countries objected or even if all were not economically ready. For this reason, the Italians and French favored a vote by qualified majority as sufficient to initiate stage three. The Germans wanted to ensure strict adherence to the precondition of economic convergence before stage three could begin and saw the requirement of a unanimous vote as a means of guaranteeing adherence. In addition, the Bundesbank was opposed to setting any firm timetable or deadline for the final move to full EMU, fearing that the need to meet a deadline could provide an excuse for political authorities to overrule the convergence criteria. On both of these issues, however, the Kohl government eventually proved willing to compromise.[37]

EC Fiscal and Budgetary Authority

Another key issue to be resolved in the EMU negotiations concerned the nature of the final stage of monetary union. By early 1991, a broad agreement existed among EC governments on most points in this regard. In stage three of EMU, a single currency would be managed by a European central bank that would look much like the Bundesbank, with complete control over monetary policy, a statutory obligation to fight inflation, and independence from political authority. Considerable disagreement remained, however, over the extent to which EC authorities would be able to exert control over the budgetary and fiscal policies of member governments after monetary union.

Germany's position on this issue was governed by its fundamental fear of inflation and loss of monetary stability. The German concern was that excessive deficits run by the governments of economically weaker countries would generate political pressure on the ECB for a more relaxed monetary policy. These deficits could also, Germany feared, create the political necessity for expensive Community bailouts that would prove inflationary and undermine monetary stability. At the same time, most of this money would come from Germany since it was the EC's wealthiest member and the largest contributor to its budget. For these reasons, Germany insisted that the EC have the power to impose sanctions or financial penalties on member states that ignored Community recommendations and maintained excessive budget deficits. In this demand Germany was supported by the Netherlands.[38]

There was also considerable sympathy among other Community countries for EC fiscal and budgetary controls. Weaker countries such as Italy and Greece, which traditionally ran high budget deficits and often found it difficult for domestic political reasons to rein in public spending, were anxious to gain external support for more restrictive national policies. France also favored EC controls over national fiscal policies, but for different reasons altogether than Germany or the deficit countries. France saw EC controls as part of a broader Community macroeconomic policy, which could be used to offset the restrictive monetary policies of a stability-oriented European central bank and promote higher levels of growth and employment. The main opponent of EC budgetary and fiscal controls was Britain, which saw these as yet further interference with national sovereignty.

Nevertheless, although there was general support for the idea of central controls over national budgetary and fiscal policies in stage three, there were considerable differences over the exact nature of these. Germany favored tougher and more binding controls, arguing that Brussels should have the power to impose sanctions on profligate governments. Other EC countries, however—especially the ones that might actually be affected by Community intervention—desired much looser constraints and no penalties, favoring instead only public reprimands for deficit countries. Also favoring a softer line was the commission, whose position on this issue had changed somewhat. The original Delors Plan had called for centrally set binding rules on budget deficits, but a March 1991 commission paper on EMU had backtracked, calling only for "binding procedures" instead.[39]

The Luxembourg draft treaty that was submitted in June sought to bridge these differences. According to the document, in stage three the Council of Finance Ministers could decide by a majority vote if a particular country had an "excessive" budget deficit and recommend policy changes. If these recommendations were ignored, Ecofin could publicly reprimand the offending government. As a last resort, Brussels could impose sanctions, although these were not specified in the draft treaty.[40]

Disagreement over the subject of EC controls in stage three persisted into the fall. The issue was largely passed over in the draft treaty presented by the Dutch government in early September. It was also left unresolved by the meeting of EC finance ministers later in the month, which reached agreements on a number of other important issues related to EMU. By this point, there was broad consensus on the need for EC monitoring of the fiscal and budgetary policies of member states once the final stage of monetary union began. EC members also agreed that Ecofin should be able to recommend changes in national policies for governments that ran excessive budget deficits. Where opinion continued to diverge, however, was on the question of what Community authorities should have the power to do if these recommendations were ignored. Germany and some other EC states, including France and the Netherlands, insisted on the need for EC sanctions on countries that borrowed too much or ran excessive budget deficits. This power was opposed by Britain and Italy, as well as Delors.[41]

An attempt to resolve this issue was made in the revised draft treaty presented by the Dutch government at the end of October. This draft attempted to specify what an excessive budget deficit and public debt might be for EMU countries, choosing to define these as an annual deficit exceeding 3 percent of GDP and a public debt amounting to more than 60 percent of GDP. The revision also sketched out possible sanctions, including fines and the possibility of being cut off from EC loans and new regional aid.[42]

While welcomed by Germany, the tough sanctions proposed in the Dutch draft were opposed by the commission and many other countries. After much wrangling, a compromise that favored a more moderate position was reached just before the Maastricht summit. To begin with, the attempt to define what constituted an excessive budget deficit or public debt was dropped. Rather than financial penalties and sanctions, EC members decided to rely on public reprimands of guilty countries and warnings about the health of bonds issued by profligate governments—for Delors, "the sternest penalty one can think of."[43] Nevertheless, the possibility of financial sanctions—including the loss of EC loans and the requirement of placing non-interest-bearing deposits with the Community—was retained.[44]

The Cohesion Fund

On the eve of the Maastricht summit, an EMU agreement was threatened by the demands of Spain and other poorer EC countries for economic and financial compensation as the price for their approval of a treaty. Among other things, these countries were concerned about the economic costs of EMU. Within a monetary union, or even permanently fixed exchange rates, poor countries would not be able to compensate for economic and competitive weakness by lowering the value of their currencies. Nor would they be able to resort to capital and exchange controls. Monetary union, then, would take away some key instruments traditionally used by poor countries to stimulate economic growth and development. At the same time, however, these countries did not want to be left behind and discriminated against in a two-speed EMU but wanted to proceed together with the more economically advanced states.

One possible solution to this dilemma was a more limited and flexible form of monetary cooperation, such as that represented by the British hard ECU plan. In late August 1990, Spain's finance minister, Carlos Solchaga, had produced an alternative version of monetary integration that resembled somewhat the earlier British plan. Solchaga's plan would allow weaker countries to retain their own currencies and monetary policies and thus a greater capacity to manipulate their economies to promote growth and competitiveness.[45] As was the case with the British plan, however, this scheme was rejected by other EC countries.

A second solution to the problems of poor countries was a longer stage two. This solution would delay the final leap into full monetary union and give economically weaker countries more of a chance to catch up with their wealthier EC partners. This idea was supported by Spain and other poor member states in the early months of the negotiations. Other EC countries, however, were not in favor of a protracted transitional phase. Germany wanted a shorter stage two, at least for the more advanced or core countries. A longer transitional phase, Germany believed, would only create more confusion over the relative duties and responsibilities of national and European monetary authorities and thereby create potential threats to Bundesbank sovereignty before full monetary duties could be handed over to an independent regional institution. As a result, by summer 1991 the possibility of a drawn-out stage two had been largely disregarded.[46]

The only real remaining possibility for poor EC countries to influence the shape of an EMU agreement was to demand economic compensation in return for their assent to a monetary union treaty. This compensation would take place through increased transfers of wealth from rich to poor European countries, mainly in the form of regional and structural assistance. Although demands for increased compensation had been made from the outset of negotiations, they had been consistently opposed by the wealthier countries that would have to foot the bill. These demands had also been largely ignored by the commission, which had advised the poor countries to postpone their demands until the regularly scheduled negotiations on the EC budget planned for early 1993.[47]

By summer 1991, however, the poor countries, led by Spain, began to more earnestly assert their demands for economic compensation. The Spanish government threatened to withhold its support for an EMU treaty; given the need for unanimity among the twelve for an agreement to be approved by the European Council, such a move would effectively scuttle the treaty. Specifically, what Spain and other poor countries wanted were increases in Community regional and structural policy funds, a restructuring of EC budgetary and taxation policies to the advantage of poorer countries, and alterations in EC common policies that would direct even more spending toward poor countries. Spain also demanded the creation of a new "Cohesion Fund" that would channel money for economic development to EC countries with a per capita GDP below 90 percent of the Community average.[48]

These demands were largely ignored by the richer countries. Germany, in particular, was opposed to such demands, flatly rejecting the creation of a new Cohesion Fund. In November a meeting of EC foreign ministers rebuffed outright the Spanish demands. What the wealthier countries offered instead was a declaration at the Maastricht summit that the request for more financial compensation would be carefully considered the following year as part of the normal EC budgetary process.[49] Angered by the rejection, Spain responded by threatening a veto at Maastricht, prompting a special round of negotiations between Community authorities and Madrid.[50] Going into the summit, Spain declared that its goal was to achieve a legally binding pledge by wealthy EC countries to increase flows of financial aid to the poorer countries. According to Prime Minister Felipe González, "If we don't arrive at a satisfactory agreement [on the financial compenation issue], we will not accept the results [of the treaty negotiations]."[51] Other EC countries, however, saw the veto threat as a bluff, pointing out that Spain knew that such a move would doom a new EC funding package in the following year.[52]

The Maastricht EMU Treaty

Final agreement on many issues related to EMU was not reached until a flurry of intergovernmental negotiations, in some cases at the very highest levels, took place in the days immediately prior to the Maastricht summit. In some instances, compromises were hammered out at the summit itself. The main impetus for agreement was the widely shared belief that, if the Community did not act now to forge an agreement that would permanently integrate Germany, it would be missing a historic opportunity that might never come again.[53] Exemplary of these concerns were the views of Andre Szasz, deputy president of the Dutch central bank, who declared in late November that Maastricht represented possibly the last chance to firmly bind a united Germany to Western Europe. Failing this, he claimed, Germany would become more of a Central European power, with interests that increasingly diverged from the rest of the Community. For this reason, he argued, "if we do not grasp this opportunity there may not be another one."[54] Such sentiments were shared by German leaders. According to Chancellor Kohl, failure to reach agreement on EMU and political union at Maastricht would be "catastrophic" and would set back the cause of European integration "for more than a generation."[55]

Spurred by a commonly felt sense of urgency, Community leaders met on December 9–10 and produced an EMU agreement that established a firm timetable for the introduction of full monetary union.[56] Under the treaty, stage two of EMU would come into effect on January 1, 1994. This stage would entail the narrowing of exchange-rate fluctuations and the establishment of an EMI that would coordinate the monetary policies of member states and oversee the preparations for full EMU. In a key concession to German demands, Community leaders decided that national central banks would become independent of political authority by the end of stage two. Also at the end of this stage, the EMI would formally become the European Central Bank.

A first opportunity for the transition to full monetary union would come in 1996 if by then a majority of EC countries met a set of strict criteria for economic performance. These included a level of inflation within 1.5 percent and interest rates within 2 percent of those in the three lowest countries; a budget deficit of less than 3 percent and a public debt of less than 60 percent of national GDP; and no devaluation of the national currency within the ERM for the previous two years. If enough countries met these standards, a two-thirds vote in the European Council would be sufficient to approve the transition to stage three, to begin in January 1997. Failing this, EMU would automatically come into existence in 1999 with the participation of all countries meeting the economic criteria, even if these countries constituted less than a majority.

The agreement to an automatic final deadline for EMU was reached at the Maastricht summit itself and had not been included in the final Dutch draft treaty.[57] Such a deadline had been strongly pushed by France and was accepted by Chancellor Kohl over the objections of his advisers. Kohl wanted to ensure Germany's commitment to an irreversible EMU process, which he felt was a necessary counterpart to German unification. At the summit, Kohl also agreed to some flexibility in interpreting the economic convergence criteria by allowing the consideration of trends in budgetary and fiscal performance.[58]

In response to its hesitancy to commit to monetary union, Britain was given an opt-out clause that allowed it to seek the formal approval of Parliament before making a final decision to join EMU. This decision resulted from behind-the-scenes bargaining between the two governments, with Germany's Kohl agreeing to support the British request for opt-outs on monetary and social policy in return for London's support for the German position on the EC's diplomatic recognition of Slovenia and Croatia.[59]

The EMU treaty specified an ECB that was largely modeled on Germany's Bundesbank. The new institution would have complete independence from political authority, being required only to report regularly to the Council of Finance Ministers and the European Parliament. It would also have a statutory duty to promote price stability—although, without prejudice to this primary responsibility, the ECB would also be expected to support general EC economic policy objectives, such as high levels of growth and employment. The external exchange-rate policy for the common currency would be set by Ecofin, but in consultation with the bank.

On the subject of fiscal and budgetary controls in stage three, EC leaders decided that Ecofin would have the right to make policy recommendations to governments whose budget deficits were excessive. If profligate governments failed to respond to public warnings, EC authorities could take a number of possible actions. These included warnings attached to new bonds issued by the guilty government, a cutoff of EC credits, and even fines.

Left undecided by the treaty was whether national currencies would be replaced by a true common European currency—whatever it might be called—or whether the final stage of monetary union should be marked only by the permanent fixing of exchange rates, thus allowing the continued existence of national currencies. The Germans, concerned about giving up the beloved D-mark—and negative popular reaction to doing so—favored the latter option, while most other EC countries leaned toward the former. For this reason, the treaty simply indicated that the printing of a common currency by the European Central Bank would begin some months after the formal initiation of stage three. Also put off until a later date was a decision on the location of the EMI and ECB.

In the final analysis, the EMU agreement reached at Maastricht represented a major victory for those countries concerned about the strength and future orientation of a united Germany. It was, in particular, a victory for France, which was desperately searching for ways to tie down and bind in its more powerful neighbor. With the Maastricht Treaty, France and other EC countries basically got what they had wanted: a firm German commitment to a seemingly irreversible process of monetary union, with a strict timetable and a certain amount of automaticity. With ratification by all member states, full EMU would come into being by 1999 at the very latest, thereby bringing about the transfer of the Bundesbank's monetary authority to European institutions.

The German government could also claim victory, however. It was able to ensure that a future European monetary regime would essentially replicate the German model. As a result, Bonn could argue that EMU would entail little risk of the loss of monetary stability. Germany also gained acceptance of the need for economic convergence as the basis for EMU and of strict adherence to economic criteria as a measure of such convergence. Of crucial importance, implicit in the Maastricht Treaty was the provision for a two-speed movement to monetary union in the event that all EC countries did not meet the specified convergence criteria. Perhaps even more important than the technical details of the EMU treaty, though, was its political significance. The Kohl government could argue, because of its agreement to EMU and role in bringing the treaty about, that a united Germany had demonstrated its commitment to the Community and European integration. In a December 13 address to the Bundestag, Kohl claimed that as a result of the Maastricht Treaty,

> we [the federal government] have now achieved one of the central goals of Germany's European policy. Maastricht is proof of the fact that a united Germany is actively fulfilling its responsibilities in and for Europe, and is standing by what we have always said: that German unification and European unity are two sides of the same coin. We are particularly close to France in our shared vision of a Europe that is growing closer together not only economically but politically as well.[60]

One area in which the German government could not claim victory, however, was the progress made toward European political union. Athough the Kohl government had made accomplishments on political union a precondition for Germany's agreement to EMU, in the end it had to accept far less than originally desired. It is to the negotiations on political union that we now turn.

Notes

1. *Economist,* December 22, 1990, pp. 62–63; *Financial Times,* December 17, 1990, pp. 1–2.

2. Ibid.

3. On the positions of national governments on EMU and on the EMU negotiations, see Wayne Sandholtz, "Monetary Bargains: The Treaty on EMU," in Alan W. Cafruny and Glenda G. Rosenthal, eds., *The State of the European Community,* vol. 2, *The Maastricht Debates and Beyond* (Boulder: Lynne Rienner, 1993), pp. 125–142; Wayne Sandholtz, "Choosing Union: Monetary Politics and Maastricht," *International Organization* 47 (Winter 1993):1–39.

4. *The Week in Germany,* June 15, 1990, p. 5; *Economist,* November 3, 1990, p. 97.

5. On the acceptance of German monetary norms and philosophy in Europe and their role in shaping the EMU agreement, see Sandholtz, "Monetary Bargains," pp. 125–142.

6. *Economist,* September 16, 1989, pp. 53–54; December 2, 1989, pp. 61–62.

7. W. R. Smyser, *The Economy of United Germany: Colossus at the Crossroads,* 2d ed. (New York: St. Martin's Press, 1993), pp. 273–274.

8. *Economist,* November 3, 1990, p. 97; November 17, 1990, p. 87; Committee of the Governors of the Central Banks of the Member States of the EC, "Draft Statute of the European System of Central Banks and the European Central Bank" (Brussels: EC, November 27, 1990).

9. *Economist,* November 3, 1990, p. 97; November 17, 1990, p. 87. On the structure and functions of the Bundesbank, see Deutsche Bundesbank, *The Deutsche Bundesbank: Its Monetary Policy Instruments and Functions* (Frankfurt: Deutsche Bundesbank, 1982); Ellen Kennedy, *The Bundesbank: Germany's Central Bank in the International Monetary System* (London: RIIA, 1991); and John B. Goodman, *Monetary Sovereignty: The Politics of Central Banking in Western Europe* (Ithaca: Cornell University Press, 1992), pp. 58–102.

10. *New York Times,* September 30, 1991, p. C2.

11. On Germany's unique "culture of stability" and its historical sources, see Wilhelm Nölling, *Monetary Policy in Europe After Maastricht* (New York: St. Martin's Press, 1993), pp. 15–24, 31–37.

12. *Economist,* April 7, 1990, p. 88.

13. *Economist,* November 16, 1991, pp. 100–101.

14. *Economist,* January 19, 1991, pp. 73–74. Also see George Ross, *Jacques Delors and European Integration* (New York: Oxford University Press, 1995), pp. 85–88.

15. Ibid.

16. *Economist,* March 9, 1991, p. 44.

17. Smyser, *The Economy of United Germany,* p. 280.

18. Ibid.

19. *Economist,* May 18, 1991, pp. 83–84.

20. *Economist,* September 14, 1991, p. 89.

21. *Economist,* September 28, 1991, p. 84.

22. *Financial Times,* November 6, 1991, p. 2; *Economist,* November 16, 1991, pp. 100–101.

23. *Financial Times,* December 4, 1991, p. 2.

24. See, for instance, Pöhl's statements at a June 11 meeting of EC finance ministers in Luxembourg, *The Week in Germany,* June 15, 1990, p. 5.

25. *Economist,* September 1, 1990, p. 48; September 15, 1990, pp. 61–62.

26. *Financial Times,* October 29, 1990 ("Survey on Germany"), p. 12; Deutsche Bundesbank, "Statement by the Deutsche Bundesbank on the Establishment of an Economic and Monetary Union in Europe," *Monthly Report of the Deutsche Bundesbank* 42, 10 (October 1990):40–44.

27. *Economist,* May 18, 1991, pp. 83–84; *Financial Times,* June 28, 1991, p. 6.

28. *Economist,* March 23, 1991, p. 15.

29. Smyser, *The Economy of United Germany,* p. 280.

30. *Financial Times,* August 1, 1991, p. 1.

31. Ibid.

32. *Economist,* September 14, 1991, p. 89.

33. *Economist,* September 28, 1991, p. 84.

34. *New York Times,* October 30, 1991, p. A3.

35. *Financial Times,* October 29, 1991, p. 2; *Economist,* November 2, 1991, p. 77.

36. *Financial Times,* December 3, 1991, p. 1.

37. *New York Times,* December 4, 1991, p. C2; December 7, 1991, p. A17.

38. *Economist,* January 19, 1991, pp. 73–74.

39. Ibid.; March 9, 1991, p. 44.

40. *Economist,* May 18, 1991, p. 83.

41. *Economist,* October 26, 1991, p. 106.

42. *Financial Times,* October 29, 1991, p. 2; *Economist,* November 2, 1991, p. 77.

43. *Financial Times,* November 26, 1991, p. 3.

44. *Financial Times,* December 4, 1991, p. 2.

45. *Economist,* September 15, 1990, pp. 61–62.

46. *Economist,* September 14, 1991, p. 89.

47. *Economist,* January 19, 1991, p. 74.

48. *Financial Times,* June 18, 1991, p. 16.

49. *Financial Times,* November 15, 1991, p. 18; *Economist,* November 16, 1991, p. 64.

50. *Financial Times,* November 18, 1991, p. 1.

51. *New York Times,* December 5, 1991, p. A4.

52. *Financial Times,* December 6, 1991, p. 20.

53. This was a view expressed by various EC and national leaders in interviews conducted by Sandholtz, "Monetary Bargains," p. 132.

54. *Financial Times,* November 28, 1991, p. 2.

55. *Financial Times,* November 17, 1991, p. 1.

56. For accounts of the Maastricht summit and the agreement on EMU, see *Financial Times,* December 10, 1991, pp. 1, 2; *New York Times,* December 10, 1991, p. A1; December 11, 1991, p. A1. For the final text of the EMU agreement, see "Treaty on European Union" (Luxembourg: Office for Official Publications of the European Communities, 1992). The provisions of the treaty pertaining to EMU are Articles 2, 3a, 4a, and 102a–109m inclusive; Protocol on the Statute of the European System of Central Banks and of the European Central Bank; Protocol on the Statute of the European Monetary Institute; Protocol on the Excessive Deficit Procedure; Protocol on the Convergence Criteria Referred to in Article 109j; Protocol on the Transition to the Third Stage of EMU; and Protocol on Certain Provisions Relating to the UK. Some of these articles and protocols are reprinted in Tommaso Padoa-Schioppa, *The Road to Monetary Union: The Emperor, the Kings, and the Genies* (Oxford: Clarendon Press, 1994), pp. 259–272.

57. Nölling, *Monetary Policy in Europe,* p. 148.

58. Sandholtz, "Monetary Bargains," pp. 136–137, n 66.

59. *Economist,* January 18, 1992, p. 49. The support of other EC countries for Bonn's position on the recognition of Slovenia and Croatia may also have been linked, although in a very informal and "offstage" way, to Germany's agreement to EMU at Maastricht. On this, and the role of the Yugoslavia crisis in the Maastricht negotiations, see John Newhouse, "The Diplomatic Round: Dodging the Problem," *New Yorker,* August 24, 1992, pp. 65–66. On the issue of EC diplomatic recognition for the ex-Yugoslav republics, see Chapter 5.

60. Cited in Nölling, *Monetary Policy in Europe,* p. 127.

4

Negotiating Maastricht: Political Union

In contrast to the EMU negotiations, the intergovernmental conference on European Political Union began without a clear agenda or plan. Also, whereas the EMU talks focused on a fairly narrow set of objectives, the EPU conference encompassed a wide array of topics and issues. These included the development of common foreign and defense policies, the reform of EC decisionmaking institutions, and the expansion of Community authority in such areas as social, environmental, industrial, and immigration policy. For this reason, the final outcome of the EPU conference was not nearly as clear-cut or decisive as that on EMU. It is somewhat ironic, therefore, that in the popular backlash against the Maastricht Treaty in 1992, the vague decisions on political union were an equally important target for criticism as the EMU agreement. In this chapter the negotiations on political union are examined more closely. After a brief survey of the positions of key national governments and the major areas of discussion, the actual course of the negotiations, leading up to the final agreements at Maastricht, is analyzed.

National Positions on Political Union

In the EPU conference, two main lines of division among EC countries were of significance. The first of these was based on size. Whereas smaller contries generally favored a stronger role for the commission, which they saw as an effective representative of their interests vis-à-vis large states,[1] the latter tended to prefer intergovernmental institutions such as the European Council and Council of Ministers, in which their greater relative size gave them more of a voice. Often cutting across this divide was the ideological cleavage between "federalists" and "intergovernmentalists," with the former wanting stronger European institutions and more common policies and the latter preferring cooperation among sovereign and independent states. With some qualifications, in the federalist camp were Germany, Italy, Spain, and the Benelux countries. Belonging to the second group were Britain, Denmark, Ireland, and Portugal. Somewhere in the middle was France, which, despite its basic intergovernmentalist leanings, was willing to consider more authority for EC institutions if this was in its interests. Beyond such general distinctions, however, the positions of key member countries on specific issues tended to reflect unique national interests and views.

The German government was a major proponent of political union.[2] In fact, it was Bonn's insistence on greater political union as a counterpart to EMU that was among the main reasons a parallel conference on EPU was launched in the first place. Moreover, from the very beginning the German government sought to link the results of the two conferences, declaring that an adequate agreement on political union had to accompany an EMU treaty. Chancellor Kohl stressed this theme repeatedly throughout the negotiations, implying that Germany would use the considerable leverage it derived from its central position in the EMU talks to force a satisfactory deal on political union. As Kohl stated in his first address to the all-German Bundestag on January 30, 1991, and again in many subsequent speeches, the German government wanted agreements on monetary and political union to be achieved together, and Bonn would not give its approval to a treaty in one area without a deal in the other.[3] In a speech in Washington, D.C., on May 20, Kohl declared that as far as he was concerned, the two sets of negotiations formed a single whole. "I consider it essential," he said, "that the scope and objectives of this treaty on political union should not come second to economic and monetary union."[4]

Even though some Europeans viewed this linkage strategy as simply a ploy to inhibit or slow down monetary union, the German support for political union was genuine, and Bonn desired this goal on its own merits. Since the founding of the FRG in 1949, it had been among the most consistent promoters of European union within the Community. After the opening of the Berlin Wall and unification, German leaders insisted on their continued support for European integration. They claimed that Germany had drawn the proper lessons from its disastrous past experiences with nationalism and unilateralism and now perceived its interests in terms of further integration into European institutions. Key government officials, such as Chancellor Kohl and Foreign Minister Genscher, held strong Europeanist convictions, and many Germans felt that their country had a unique role to play as a catalyst for peaceful European integration. In addition, as a federal system and a state that had developed with numerous external contraints on its sovereignty and independence, Germany was more easily reconciled to further political integration than were such centralized, unitary states as France and Britain.

Beyond such general convictions, there were also more specific benefits to Germany from EPU. Further integration in defense and foreign policy would help assuage the concerns of other Europeans about possible German independence and would provide Germany with an acceptable multilateral framework for exercising its increased power and influence. At the same time, a more integrated Community would give the German government a supranational context for resolving such controversial domestic problems as immigration and asylum and popular opposition to Germany's increased military and security role. Finally, an acceptable agreement on EPU and, in particular, the democratization of EC decisionmaking through a stronger European Parliament was necessary for domestic political reasons. Kohl believed that an agreement on EMU alone, featuring the establishment of a politically independent ECB, would appear much too elitist and technocratic. A strengthened European Parliament would therefore help offset democratic objections to EMU and help the Kohl government sell monetary union to a skeptical German public.[5] It would also help gain parliamentary ratification of an EMU treaty, for which the support of the opposition SPD and the federal states was required. In general terms, therefore, the German position at the conference favored a strengthening of the the EC's democratic and supranational elements.

In contrast to Germany, France was much less enthusiastic about political integration.[6] For much of the Community's history, France had resisted the growth of supranational power and its infringement on the sovereignty and independence of member states. France's position was best exemplified by President de Gaulle's empty chair policy of 1965 and the resulting Luxembourg compromise, which guaranteed the veto right of member governments and preserved the Community's basic intergovernmental character. The preferred French version of European union was a looser confederation of sovereign and independent nation-states—a "Europe of nation-states," in de Gaulle's formulation—under French leadership. This conception reflected France's proud history as a powerful actor in European and world politics and the French governmental tradition of statism.

Despite this basic orientation, France was willing to grant power to EC authorities whenever doing so served French interests, as in the cases of the ECSC and CAP. The former was necessary to gain access to German coal resources and integrate a rebuilding Germany into international institutions, and the latter protected the economic interests of French farmers. More recently, French support for European monetary union stemmed from the realization that France had already effectively lost monetary sovereignty within the EMS and that EMU would both reduce Germany's monetary dominance and help France regain control over economic policy. EMU was also a means for binding a united Germany more firmly to France and European institutions. Although Paris was willing to accept monetary union, it remained wary of deeper political integration and increased supranationalism and sought instead greater intergovernmental cooperation and the retention of as much sovereignty and independence of action as possible.[7] One particular area in which France favored further cooperation was foreign and defense policy. Cooperation in this realm was necessary not only to further constrain Germany but also to gain the long-standing French objective of greater European independence from Washington in defense and security affairs.[8]

With France promoting monetary union, and with Germany urging deeper political integration, Britain emerged as the primary defender of national sovereignty in Europe. Since its entry into the Community in 1973, Britain had been a problematic partner in the project of European integration.[9] In fact, London's decision to join the Community was mainly the product of economic necessity and did not represent an embrace of the political ideals of European union. A number of factors account for the British hostility toward European integration. To begin with, Britain's island location, and consequent geographical separateness, reinforces a sense of political and cultural distance from the Continent. In addition, an imperial legacy and special ties to the United States render Britain's attachment to the Continent only partial, with Europe representing, in the famous view of Winston Churchill, only one of three equally important spheres of external relations for Britain, the others being the Commonwealth and Anglo-American worlds. Also playing a role are divergent political-cultural and economic traditions, with liberal Britain opposed to the statism and protectionism that historically have been more characteristic of continental European countries.

British opposition to European integration, which had deep historical and cultural bases, intensified in the 1980s under the ideological leadership of Prime Minister Thatcher. Although Thatcher was a key supporter of the 1992 project, its liberalizing and deregulatory character being in accord with her own promarket views, she was strongly opposed to EMU, as well as any attempt to give a "social dimension" to the 1992 project through common EC social policies and standards. Thatcher viewed such moves as calculated steps in the direction of a federal Europe, something to which she was adamantly opposed, and argued that they required the surrender of too much national sovereignty and independence. She also believed that a Community social policy would reintroduce "socialism" into Britain through the back door of European regulations and legislation. Thatcher displayed her virulent opposition to European federalism in the late 1980s in verbal battles with Delors and his ideas on European union. Of particular note was Thatcher's September 1988 speech in Bruges (Belgium), in which she condemned federalist ideals and trumpeted the sovereignty and independence of the nation-state.[10]

Thatcher's intransigence on European integration was a key reason for her removal as Conservative Party leader in November 1990. Her successor as prime minister, John Major, was more positively disposed toward the Community and sought to increase Britain's role and influence in European affairs. Nevertheless, British skepticism about Europe remained, and Britain would serve throughout the Maastricht negotiations as the primary opponent of further integration. But Britain's position was not quite so isolated as has usually been portrayed. In this fairly consistent opposition to supranationalism, Britain has often acted on behalf of other member countries that may have harbored serious doubts about further integration, yet for various reasons were not able to publicly voice them. In this way, the British government served as a convenient lightning rod for the criticisms of federalists, a role that was not unappreciated by other EC governments.[11]

Foreign Policy and Defense

Among the key issues discussed in the EPU conference was a common foreign and defense policy. During the cold war, the need for such cooperation was minimal. The security of Western Europe was guaranteed by the United States, and European defense was organized within the framework of U.S.-dominated structures and institutions. At the same time, the cold war mandated foreign policy cohesion within the Western alliance, and European countries generally followed the lead of the United States.

The end of the cold war, however, dramatically altered the European security environment and generated new pressures for foreign and defense policy cooperation. To begin with, the collapse of communism transformed a stable bipolar order into a more uncertain security situation. Instead of military attack from the Soviet Union and its Warsaw Pact allies, Western Europe was now confronted by less direct and more diffuse security threats stemming from political and economic instability in the former Soviet bloc. These included ethnic and nationalist conflict, cross-border terrorism, massive immigration, destruction of the environment, and nuclear proliferation. Another challenge was posed by German reunification and the consequent need to firmly bind a united Germany to European political and security institutions. There was also the likely reduction of the U.S. security presence and role in Europe, posing the need for increased European self-reliance in defense and security affairs. Finally, the end of the cold war transformed not only the regional political and security environment but also that of the entire world. The so-called New World Order promised to be a much more complex and pluralistic system, with a greater role for new centers of economic and political power. As such, this order created new opportunities and challenges for the Community to fulfill its ambitions of becoming a unified external political actor.

Among EC countries, France was particularly interested in achieving more cooperation in the defense and security realm. For decades its key objective had been to diminish U.S. influence in Europe and gain more French and European autonomy in security affairs. In particular, France has wished to reduce the central role of NATO, which in the French view was a mechanism for U.S. dominance in Europe, and replace the organization with European-controlled structures. Beginning in 1989, Paris sought to bind Germany more firmly to French-influenced European institutions. The primary instrument for doing so was EMU, but increased defense and foreign policy cooperation was another means to this end. A key dilemma for France, however, was how to obtain these goals of increased international integration, yet not lose its basic autonomy and independence.

Germany, for its part, favored new initiatives on foreign and defense policy cooperation to assuage the fears of European neighbors about a more independent and assertive Germany and to guarantee German security in the post–cold war environment, especially given the prospects of U.S. disengagement from Europe. As the Community's easternmost member, Germany was the country most vulnerable to upheavals and instability in the former Soviet bloc and therefore most needful of effective international security arrangements. In addition, defense and security integration would provide Germany with an institutional framework for exerting its enhanced power and influence in post–cold war Europe, but in a way that would not frighten other countries. This integration would also help overcome domestic political resistance to a greater military and security role for Germany. Finally, a common foreign and defense policy would provide yet another means for cementing relations with France and preserving the Franco-German partnership as the primary basis of European integration. In pursuing these objectives, however, Bonn had to walk a tightrope between Paris and Washington, seeking to build European institutions and improve bilateral relations with France while at the same time not antagonizing the United States.

Britain was much more skeptical about European defense and security cooperation, particularly given the country's traditionally close ties to the United States. Unlike France, Britain strongly favored a continued central role for NATO and the United States in Europe after the cold war. London was therefore opposed to any European initiatives that might weaken NATO or undermine U.S. willingness to remain engaged in Europe.[12] These concerns about NATO were shared by other EC countries. Smaller countries such as Denmark and the Netherlands were concerned about German, or Franco-German, domination of post–cold war Europe and viewed NATO and U.S. influence as an effective counterbalance to such trends.[13]

Another potential hurdle to the development of a common foreign and security policy was posed by neutral member countries, such as Ireland, which believed that participation in such arrangements would violate that neutrality. This issue also affected the Community's future expansion, with such traditionally neutral countries as Austria, Finland, and Sweden being considered as possible new members.

There was some historical and institutional basis for a common foreign and defense policy.[14] The attempt to create an EDC in the early 1950s was largely a response to the need for German rearmament in the context of a hotter cold war. The failure of this ambitious plan underlined the centrality of NATO as the institutional framework for European defense and led to the integration of Germany into the Western European Union, a looser intergovernmental organization for defense cooperation. A second attempt at increased defense and security cooperation came in 1961, when France proposed the "Fouchet Plan," which called for the coordination of national defense and foreign policies outside of the EC institutional framework. Nevertheless, the Fouchet Plan also failed, leaving the WEU as the sole remnant of European efforts at defense cooperation. The WEU never did develop into a significant institution, however, and remained relatively moribund until the mid-1980s, when it was revived and subsequently became the focus of new efforts at European defense cooperation.[15] By this point the WEU had nine members—the original six members of the Community, plus Britain, Spain, and Portugal.

Also providing a basis for increased defense cooperation were previous Franco-German efforts in this area.[16] These began with the Franco-German Friendship Treaty (the Elysée Treaty) of 1963, which provided for regular bilateral consultations on defense and foreign policy matters. Bilateral defense cooperation was strengthened in the early 1980s, largely in response to growing French concerns about German neutralism in the midst of controversy over the deployment of new NATO missiles. Steps taken at this time included the establishment of a bilateral security and defense commission in 1982 and intensified cooperation between national defense and security officials. Also in the mid-1980s, French and German forces began to hold regular joint exercises and maneuvers, and in 1990 a joint Franco-German brigade was established.[17] In January 1988, Paris and Bonn signed an agreement to create a joint defense and security council, which involved France's commitment to a greater role in Germany's forward defense. This was a move that was greatly desired by Bonn after the 1987 U.S.-Soviet intermediate-range nuclear forces accords, which eliminated intermediate nuclear weapons from Europe but also generated unease about the future U.S. commitment to Germany's defense.[18]

The institutional basis also existed for a common foreign policy. After the failure of the EDC and Fouchet Plan, a new attempt at increased foreign policy cooperation came in the late 1960s. As a counterpart to policies toward Eastern Europe (*Ostpolitik*), the German government sought new initiatives on foreign policy cooperation with Western neighbors (*Westpolitik*) that were intended to offset concerns about growing German independence. These actions resulted in the establishment of European Political Cooperation in 1970, based on a joint proposal by Chancellor Willy Brandt and President Georges Pompidou. EPC was essentially a vehicle for promoting intergovernmental cooperation.[19] Decisions on joint foreign policy initiatives were made by unanimous vote in the European Council. Otherwise, EPC consisted of regular meetings of foreign ministers and lower-level Foreign Office functionaries. The national government that held the EC's rotating presidency also chaired EPC. Nevertheless, EPC was outside the Community's formal institutional structure, and its decisions were not subject to judgment by the European Court of Justice. A link to the Community did exist, however, through the participation of the commission at all levels of the EPC process. Official ties between EPC and the Community were eventually established by the 1986 SEA. As a result, a permanent but small EPC secretariat was created and located in Brussels.

Over two decades of existence, EPC has registered some minor successes, including a joint European policy toward the Middle East after 1973 and a common position in international negotiations and institutions such as the Conference on Security and Cooperation in Europe (CSCE) and the United Nations. Nevertheless, in the early 1990s the EC was still far short of being able to boast of a common foreign and security policy. This reality was underlined by European indecision and division during the Persian Gulf crisis of 1990–1991, which led to increased calls for a common EC foreign and security policy.[20]

The EP and Democratic Deficit

A second major issue in EPU negotiations was the reform of EC decisionmaking institutions, particularly the European Parliament.[21] The EP was originally created less to be the true representative legislative assembly of the Community than to provide it with a veneer of parliamentary accountability. Its seats are apportioned to member states according to population, although the size of national delegations are only roughly proportional. Since 1979 members of the European Parliament have been directly elected by the citizens of EC countries.

Despite the democratic legitimacy that direct election confers, the EP has remained largely powerless as a decisionmaking institution. In many respects, the EP differs greatly from most national parliaments. The Rome Treaty granted the EP only limited powers over Community budgetary expenditures and prohibited it from raising revenues. The Parliament's powers in the legislative process are also quite limited. It cannot initiate legislation and has generally served as a consultative body to the commission and Council of Ministers. The EP's role was somewhat enhanced under the new "cooperation procedures" established by the 1986 SEA, which gave it limited powers to delay or amend legislation proposed by the commission. This power is exercised in areas where qualified majority voting within the Council of Ministers is in effect, mainly on matters related to the Single Market project. The EP also was given little control over the Community's executive. It can demand the resignation of the entire commission with a two-thirds vote (something that has never been done), but it cannot remove individual commissioners. The EP also does not have the power to appoint or approve the commission president. Among the new authority given the Parliament by the SEA was the power of assent on external agreements, which means that the EP's approval is required for community enlargement and all EC treaties and trade agreements with nonmembers.

The Parliament figures greatly in discussion of the Community's "democratic deficit."[22] This term refers to the growing gap between the power and authority of EC institutions, as more and more aspects of national sovereignty are transferred to the European level, and the ability of the citizens of European countries to exercise supervision and control over Community decisionmaking through their elected representatives, whether national parliaments or the EP. The result is a loss of democratic accountability. One proposed solution to this problem has been to strengthen the role of national parliaments in the Community decisionmaking process. Another has been to increase the powers of the EP, the only Community body that is directly elected. Such an increase would include giving Parliament the authority to raise revenues, the right to initiate legislation, increased powers of codecision with the commission and Council of Ministers in all areas of legislation, and the right to confirm and remove the president and individual members of the commission. In other words, the EP would become an institution with similar powers to those of national parliaments. An additional suggestion for increasing the influence and role of the Parliament is to move it permanently from Strasbourg, where it is somewhat marginalized and out of the mainstream of Community events, to Brussels, where its effectiveness would be enhanced by a closer proximity to other EC institutions.

Support for a stronger Parliament has come not only from those seeking to reduce the Community's democratic deficit but also from European federalists. Many within this group regard a stronger EP as necessary for building a supranational European state since it would confer increased democratic legitimacy and authority to EC institutions. By increasing direct citizen involvement in EC decisionmaking, a stronger Parliament would also help generate public interest in, and support for, the Community and thereby contribute to a transnational sense of European identity and citizenship. A strong Parliament, therefore, is a key aspect of the federalist vision for Europe.

Going into the political union conference, national governments were quite divided in their views on the EP. Germany was perhaps the strongest supporter of increased powers for the Parliament; there was much support within the country for making the Community more democratic, and supporters felt that an agreement giving enhanced powers to the EP would help offset the expected domestic opposition to EMU. Furthermore, as the Community's largest country, a united Germany would have the EP's largest delegation and would thus exert considerable influence within this body. Also supporting additional powers for the EP were Italy, Spain, and the Benelux countries.

France was much less keen on the idea of a stronger Parliament. Such a move contradicted the constitutional principles of the Fifth Republic, which favored a strong executive, but also conflicted with the basic French goal of retaining as much national sovereignty and independence as possible within European institutions. Instead of more supranationalism, France favored a concentration of authority in the Community's intergovernmental organs—the European Council and Council of Ministers.[23] In November 1990, President Mitterrand declared that no democratic deficit existed in the EC since "true democracy" was represented by the role of independent democratic states in the European Council.[24] Siding with France on this issue was Britain, whose own tradition of "parliamentary sovereignty" and fundamental opposition to European federalism led it to oppose a stronger EP. Also opposed to enhanced powers for the EP were smaller Community countries, whose relatively small delegations would give them little voice within a stronger Parliament.

Extending the Community's Reach

A third key aspect of EPU negotiations concerned the expansion of EC authority in areas of policy that had largely remained the province of national governments. These areas included environmental protection, industrial and technology policy, social policy, internal police and security matters, and immigration and asylum policy. To some extent, these were areas in which greater cooperation between national governments had become necessary as a result of increased interdependence. Of particular importance in this regard was the 1992 Single Market project, which generated a variety of spillover pressures for increased cooperation in different policy areas.

Among the most controversial issues in the EPU talks was the issue of Community social policy. The Single Market project, with its emphasis on deregulation and market liberalization, had been strongly criticized by organized labor, the political left, and some national governments for its potentially negative social consequences. Specifically, these forces feared that liberalization of the Community's internal market would tip the social balance of power even more decisively in favor of employers against labor, mainly as a result of the mobility advantages of capital. Liberalization would also place considerable pressure on already-eroding social and labor laws at the national level. The end result, many felt, would be an acceleration of "social dumping," whereby companies shifted investment and jobs out of high-wage and heavily regulated countries and to less economically and socially protected ones. Such dumping, in turn, would spur increased "social competition," in which countries would be forced by intensified international competition to dismantle social and labor protections to make themselves more attractive to potential investors.

Although the claims of labor and its allies regarding the social impact of 1992 were not universally accepted, they did have the endorsement of President Delors. They were also supported by some national governments, for reasons of ideology, domestic politics, or national economic interest. Together with Delors, these groups began to push for Community guarantees of worker rights. The result, in December 1989, was the approval by EC leaders of a charter of fundamental social rights. Although essentially a statement of broad principles to which member states were expected to adhere, the charter was also intended to serve as the basis for more specific EC legislation.[25] The question of to what extent these principles should be transformed into binding Community social policies was a key focus of debate in the EPU conference.

In the case of social policy, as elsewhere, the effective development of EC policies necessitated the reform of Community decisionmaking procedures. Most important, it required the extension of majority voting procedures within the Council of Ministers. The SEA had extended qualified majority voting to areas of policy related to the single market, thus enabling the 1992 project to be implemented. The existence of diverse national interests necessitated further use of majority voting, however, if the Community was to play an effective role in such areas as social, environmental, and industrial policy. Working against the extension of majority voting was the desire of national governments to preserve their sovereignty and independence and to avoid the surrender of too much authority to EC institutions. More majority voting meant the increased possibility that national governments would be forced to submit to policies they did not support or agree with, thereby further diluting the national veto right enshrined in the Luxembourg compromise.

A further consideration in this regard was the power and role of the European Commission. Any extension of majority voting within the Council of Ministers would enhance the importance of the commission by increasing its ability to play a mediatory role and forge coalitions of interest among national governments. Extension would also create the possibility for alliances between the commission and Parliament. An increased role for the commission was favored by European federalists, as well as by most smaller EC countries, which wanted a stronger commission to offset the dominance of larger states within the Council of Ministers and Parliament. Large member states, including both Germany and France, generally opposed any strengthening of the Commission.

At the start of the EPU negotiations, the views of member governments on specific policy issues tended to vary greatly in accordance with national interests and traditions. Germany favored more common policies in the areas of environmental protection and social policy, reflecting domestic political pressures and institutions. It also wanted common immigration and asylum policies, a consequence of both the steady influx of asylum seekers into Germany after 1989 and the domestic and foreign policy difficulties of dealing with this problem unilaterally. Nevertheless, Bonn was opposed to stronger EC industrial policies, which conflicted with its more market-oriented approach to economic competitiveness. France, in contrast, wanted an expanded European industrial and technology policy, which would reinforce its own state-led efforts to promote economic competitiveness.[26] The French government also favored a Community social policy but was much less enthusiastic about EC intervention in environmental matters. Britain, under the Conservative leadership of Thatcher and Major, was vehemently opposed to any form of EC social policy and was against the expansion of Community authority more generally.[27]

The Luxembourg Draft

In the early months of the EPU conference, much of the debate centered on the role of the Community's supranational authorities—the commission and the Parliament—in new areas of common action. Although initially discussions on political union had assumed a unitary decisionmaking structure, it soon became apparent that most member countries were satisfied to deal with cooperation in some new areas, such as foreign policy and internal security matters (police, immigration) through separate arrangements outside of normal Community structures. France, in particular, with its commitment to intergovernmentalism and long-standing opposition to enhancement of the powers of the commission vis-à-vis national governments, agitated for a "pillarized" concept of European union. This would entail, alongside the established EC structures, which would continue to deal mainly with economic matters, the creation of new institutional frameworks for cooperation in the areas of defense and foreign policy and immigration and internal security matters. These frameworks would each be based on new treaties, leaving the Rome Treaty to govern only conventional EC business and thereby marginalize the role of the commission and the EP in the new areas of common action. This French design for a European union, it appeared, was broadly supported by other EC countries, the most vocal dissenter being the Netherlands. As might be expected, the commission also strongly disagreed with this design.[28]

By April 1991, the outline of a possible EPU agreement was beginning to take shape. Luxembourg, holder of the EC presidency in the first six months of the year, had submitted a proposal for a draft treaty on April 12, which attempted to both synthesize the discussions of the previous months and move the negotiation process forward. Leaning heavily on the French proposals, the draft treaty called for the formation of three distinct communities. The first of these, based on an amended Rome Treaty, would cover economic and monetary policy, as well as other normal EC business. Two additional communities, one to cover foreign and security policy and the other, interior ministry and police cooperation, would have separate arrangements for decisionmaking and would not be a part of normal EC structures. This concept of European union as a "temple with columns" was designed to reduce the power of the commission and Parliament and preserve the intergovernmental character of much Community decisionmaking. As such, this design clearly bore the imprint of British and French visions of European integration and aroused the opposition of those who favored a more federalist design for Europe.[29]

In a response to the Luxembourg draft, Delors argued against the pillarized design for European union. He declared that the EPU conference should negotiate a single treaty that consisted of amendments to the Treaty of Rome and that provided for a unitary institutional structure for European union. Of particular concern for Delors was the possibility that common defense and foreign policies might be organized outside of the Treaty of Rome framework. He also argued against the intergovernmentalist bias of the Luxembourg draft and urged instead that the supranational or federal option be retained for the future. At an EC foreign ministers meeting in Dresden (Germany) in early June, Delors won the support of eight countries, including Germany, for a single treaty structure and for the attachment of a preamble to the treaty that explicitly kept open the federal option.[30]

Responding to these criticisms, Luxembourg produced a revised draft treaty in June that dropped the temple with columns design and suggested instead a more unitary vision of European union—a "tree with branches." In this version, a single institutional framework would remain. Decisionmaking in the areas of foreign and security policy and Interior Ministry cooperation would initially be conducted through separate arrangements, with little or no involvement of the commission and Parliament, but would eventually be fused into normal EC structures. Under the new draft treaty, EC countries would be committed to review the decisionmaking procedures in the two new areas by 1996, with the possibility of then merging them into established EC institutions. The new draft treaty also committed member states, through a phrase in the preamble, to "a process leading gradually to a union with a federal goal." This wording was supported by Germany, along with most other EC countries. It was strongly opposed by Britain, however, which objected to use of the word "federal" in the treaty, claiming—in contrast to the understanding of the word shared by continental countries—that it connoted centralization and implied the creation of a European superstate. The British government emphatically preferred instead the original Rome Treaty formulation of "ever-closer union" as a long-term goal for the Community.[31]

The revised draft treaty was the basis for discussion on political union at the June 28–29 EC summit in Luxembourg. In the days leading up to the meeting, however, it had become apparent that there was little consensus on EPU. One subject for disagreement was the extension of majority voting in the Council of Ministers to new areas of policy. Most EC countries favored the Luxembourg draft's plan for the use of majority voting in areas such as social, environmental, technology, infrastructure, and development policy. Britain, however, was against the extension of majority voting. It was particularly opposed to EC involvement in social and labor policy, whereas most other Community members were willing to consider this.

Also controversial was the issue of increased powers for the European Parliament. The Luxembourg draft provided the EP with new powers to veto Community legislation in certain, limited areas of policy. These would be, for the most part, areas in which majority voting within the Council of Ministers was in effect. The granting of new powers of codecision to the Parliament was supported by Germany, Italy, Belgium, the Netherlands, and Spain. France, Britain, Denmark, and Portugal were strongly opposed.

A third key area of debate was the subject of a common foreign policy. The draft treaty provided for the European Council to decide by unanimous vote what foreign policy subjects should be dealt with in common. Among those areas in which the document called for common policies were arms control, U.N. peacekeeping operations and Security Council decisions, negotiations in the CSCE, and relations with the United States and Soviet Union. Within these areas of common policy, the European Council would determine the general guidelines of policy, which was to be implemented in detail by the Council of Ministers. The European Council could also decide to allow for majority voting within the Council of Ministers on some policy matters. This foreign policy design was acceptable to most countries—but was opposed by Britain, Denmark, and Ireland, all of which were against the use of any majority voting on foreign policy.

Yet another controversial part of the draft treaty concerned defense policy. The document called for the WEU to implement European Council decisions on defense. It also suggested that the links between the EC and WEU be reviewed in 1996, with the possibility that the two institutions could be formally merged once the terms of the 1948 Brussels Treaty that had originally created the WEU expired in 1998. France, Germany, Italy, Spain, and Belgium wanted a more definite commitment to an eventual common defense policy and a mandatory 1996 review of the WEU's links to the Community. Britain, however, together with the Netherlands, Denmark, Portugal, and Ireland, was opposed to any organic link between the WEU and EC, arguing that this would undermine the primary role of NATO and the U.S. commitment to European security.[32]

Given these major differences, EC leaders decided that the June summit should be merely a stock-taking exercise on EPU and that a final decision on political union would have to await the Maastricht summit in December.[33] Before that point, considerably more bargaining among national governments would have to take place.

The Dutch Draft

After the Luxembourg summit, little work was done on the EPU conference while everyone awaited a new draft treaty being prepared by the Netherlands, which had taken over the EC presidency in July. In September the Dutch government produced a document that differed significantly from the Luxembourg draft treaty and also managed to arouse widespread opposition among Community members. The Dutch version of the treaty was much more federalist in orientation. It dropped the proposal of the Luxembourg draft for three separate communities and instead suggested a more centralized European union with a single EC structure to incorporate Interior Ministry and police matters as well as foreign policy.[34] For those opposed to a federalist design for Europe, this design was not acceptable, and the resulting disagreement threatened to block progress on the treaty. According to one participant in the negotiations, "While the Luxembourg presidency [of the EC] sought the middle ground, the Dutch seem to be engaged in a moral crusade for a supranational Europe." This crusade, he indicated, marked a step backward for negotiations on political union.[35]

In addition to the federalist nature of the Dutch draft treaty, it managed to alienate some countries for other reasons. The French, beyond objecting to the involvement of the European Commission and Parliament in foreign policy decisions, were upset that the draft altogether neglected defense policy, this being something that the Netherlands—as a strongly pro-NATO country—preferred to exclude from EPU negotiations. In this objection, France was joined by Germany, which otherwise favored the document's emphasis on increased powers of codecision for the Parliament and its proposal to bring Interior Ministry and immigration matters within formal EC structures.[36]

The Dutch draft treaty did not survive for very long. At an EC foreign ministers meeting on September 30, it was heavily criticized and rejected by a ten-to-twelve vote. The ministers then decided to return to the earlier Luxembourg document as a basis for further discussion.[37] A new dispute soon erupted, however, over a joint British-Italian proposal on defense that was unveiled on October 5.[38] As a means of strengthening Europe's security posture, the two countries suggested that the WEU be enhanced through the creation of a rapid-deployment force, linked to the NATO command, to be used in conflicts outside of the NATO area. This proposal was heavily criticized by Germany, France, and Spain, which argued that security and defense questions should be handled within EC structures and that the WEU should be answerable only to the Community.[39]

By the middle of October, German authorities were becoming increasingly frustrated with the progress of the EPU talks, which was not matching that on monetary union, and warned that Bonn would adhere to its strict linkage of the two conferences at the Maastricht summit. According to one federal government official familiar with the negotiations, Germany would withhold its signature from any document on EPU that did not go far enough in meeting German demands for radical reform of the Community's political institutions. In particular, the official stressed the need for "substantial steps forward on strengthening the European Parliament and definition of a common foreign and security policy" as a precondition for Germany's agreement to the treaties. Among other things, Bonn was concerned that an inadequate agreement on political union would hurt the treaty's chances of being ratified by the Bundestag. Representatives of that body had begun to make clear that they would link ratification of an EMU treaty to an agreement on political reform that sufficiently strengthened the codecision powers of the Parliament and provided for more Community coordination of foreign and defense policies.[40]

In an effort to spur forward the lagging EPU talks, but also address growing criticisms at home that Bonn was losing interest in political union, Germany joined with France to release a letter on October 15 that made new proposals in the realm of defense and foreign policy. In countering the earlier British-Italian ideas on defense, the Franco-German initiative—the greater part of which was drafted by the Chancellor's Office[41]—suggested a strengthened WEU that would be more closely linked to the EC and perhaps even in the future merged with existing Community structures. The WEU would have as its core a multinational force based on an expansion of the existing Franco-German brigade, and it would be usable within the NATO area. With respect to foreign policy, the letter called for common EC policies in a number of different areas, including relations with the United States and Soviet Union, action within international organizations such as the United Nations and CSCE, and arms control and peacekeeping.[42]

Among the key critics of the new Franco-German proposals was Britain, which had otherwise proved itself to be the most skeptical EC country on EPU. As German concern about the possible failure of EPU talks mounted, the Bonn government—by now clearly the primary advocate of political union—targeted Britain for an intensive round of bilateral diplomacy. Over a period of several weeks in October and November, German and British officials at different levels and in various departments met frequently in an attempt to hammer out compromises on issues where there was a significant divergence of views. These were numerous and included enhanced powers for the Parliament, a stronger EC role in defense policy, the use of majority voting in foreign policy, the inclusion of immigration and internal security matters within normal Community structures, the development of Community social and labor policies, and the use of the term "federal" in an EPU treaty. On each of these issues, while the Germans were among the most ardent representatives of the federalist position, the British were the strongest defenders of national prerogative and sovereignty. Meetings between Chancellor Kohl and Prime Minister Major on November 1 and 10 did little to bridge these differences, although at a November 12–13 meeting of EC foreign ministers Britain and its partners did reach partial agreement on the subject of enhanced powers for the Parliament. Nevertheless, with the opening date for the Maastricht summit rapidly approaching, it was obvious that serious problems remained and would have to be overcome if an EPU treaty was to be signed in December.[43]

The British position on political union was criticized by Chancellor Kohl and President Mitterrand when they met in Bonn on November 15 and 16. In a personal postsummit plea to other EC leaders but directed primarily at Britain, Kohl claimed that failure to achieve success at Maastricht would be "catastrophic for the development of Europe." He argued that if the Community did not seize the "historic opportunity" presented to it at Maastricht, this would set back the project of European integration for years, and it would be "more than a generation before we are able to take up the threads of Europe again." In fact, he warned, failure at Maastricht could mark "the beginning of the collapse of our Community."[44]

To prevent such a failure, in the weeks immediately preceding the Maastricht summit the Kohl government, realizing that there was too much opposition to its views among other EC countries, greatly relaxed its position on political union. In a speech before the Bundestag on November 28, Kohl indicated a willingness to compromise, while at the same time he prepared the German public for a more modest agreement on EPU than he had originally desired. Instead of demanding final decisions on some contentious issues at Maastricht, Kohl announced that Bonn would now allow them to be put off until a future date. On issues such as increased powers for the EP, internal security cooperation, and foreign and defense policy, Germany was now hoping for first steps toward integration, perhaps involving the coordination of policies on an intergovernmental basis with an agreement on future dates for possible treaty revision. In return for such "interim solutions," however, Kohl demanded that the Maastricht conference set in motion an "irreversible process" toward European economic and political union.[45]

The revised German position created the basis for compromise with Britain. That compromise began to take shape in a flurry of bilateral meetings among national and EC leaders in late November and early December.[46] As a result, on the eve of the opening of the Maastricht summit, even though significant differences between national governments remained, sufficient agreement existed to allow treaties on monetary and political union to be signed. Nevertheless, some nervousness about the final outcome remained. In an article that appeared on the day before the summit began, Foreign Minister Genscher gave one last warning to those who would block an agreement: "The train to European Union is standing at the platform. It is about to leave. Anyone who does not climb on board will not stop it going. They will be left standing all alone. That is a fact which everyone must consider."[47]

The Maastricht Agreement on EPU

The Maastricht Treaty on European Union was in the end made possible by the willingness of other EC members to allow an intransigent Britain to opt out of certain key provisions. This was the case not only with EMU but also with the treaty chapter on social policy. In a last-minute compromise reached during the summit, the chapter on social policy was removed from the treaty, thereby allowing it to be signed as a separate protocol. This meant that the other eleven EC countries would proceed with the creation of common social and labor policies, but in a manner that would not make these a part of EC law, in effect creating a separate "European Social Community." Although this maneuver raised all sorts of complex legal and institutional questions, it allowed the Community to avoid the potential roadblock posed by a reluctant Britain.[48] Thus, according to Delors, "eleven countries have not slowed down their rhythm because a twelfth wanted to stop it."[49]

The agreement on social policy was indicative of the compromise-laden nature of the EPU treaty in general.[50] As a result, whereas the decisions on EMU were fairly clear and precise, the EPU agreement was convoluted and murky. On the issue of political reform, there was only a modest closure of the democratic deficit. The Parliament's powers were enhanced somewhat through the introduction of new "codecision" procedures, which gave the EP the right to veto and amend some legislation that was subject to qualified majority voting within the Council of Ministers. This change represented an enlargement of the EP's role but fell considerably short of what Germany and some other countries had originally wanted. The treaty also expanded Community authority in such policy areas as education, health, culture, environmental protection, research and technology, infrastructure, consumer protection, and development. Nevertheless, the use of qualified majority voting in these and other areas was extended only modestly.

The treaty also established separate intergovernmental arrangements for decisionmaking on a common foreign and security policy (CFSP). The CFSP would be outside the EC's normal institutional framework and would therefore not involve the commission and Parliament or be subject to judgment by the European

Court of Justice. Decisionmaking on foreign policy would be by unanimous vote in the European Council, although majority voting would be used for the implementation of agreed-on policies. Even so, individual countries could choose to opt out of common policies if their national interests compelled them to do so. In the area of defense, EC members decided to strengthen the WEU and increase its links to the Community but maintain coordination with NATO. Separate mechanisms for intergovernmental cooperation were also established for justice and internal security affairs (immigration, asylum, police). Finally, it was agreed that a constitutional review should be conducted in 1996. This review would assess the progress of intergovernmental cooperation in CFSP and justice and internal security matters and decide whether decisionmaking in these areas should be incorporated into normal EC structures.[51]

Once ratified by member states, the Maastricht Treaty established a new European Union. This was a three-pillared structure, or temple, that in addition to the previously existing EC structures consisted of the new intergovernmental arrangements for CFSP and justice and internal security affairs. The treaty also enshrined, in Article 3b, the principle of "subsidiarity," which states that the "Community shall take action . . . only if and insofar as the objectives of the proposed action cannot be sufficiently achieved by the Member States and can, therefore, by reason of the scale or effects of proposed action, be better achieved by the Community."[52] In addition, by providing opt-outs for Britain on EMU and social policy, the treaty set an important precedent for an "à la carte" or "variable geometry" pattern of integration in the future. Because of these features, it has been argued that the Maastricht Treaty—or its EPU provisions, at least—rather than paving the way for a supranational European union, has instead reinforced the sovereignty of the EC's constituent nation-states.[53]

According to this assessment, the commission and Delors were among the main "losers" at the Maastricht summit. In particular, Delors objected to the treaty's pillarized structure, which excluded the commission from any major role in CFSP.[54] The primary "winners" among EC institutions were clearly the intergovernmental bodies: the European Council and Council of Ministers. Somewhat more difficult to assess was the position of the Parliament. Although the EP did not gain full powers of codecision in EC legislation, or the power to appoint and remove individual commissioners, the Maastricht Treaty did confer on the EP the power of "assent" to EC treaties with third parties and the admission of new members and the right to approve the entire commission. Some members of the EP, in fact, admitted after the Maastricht summit that the Parliament had gained more from the treaty than they had originally expected.[55]

Among national governments, Britain was widely considered a big "winner" at Maastricht. Not only was that country able to gain opt-outs on EMU and social policy, but also—of considerable symbolic importance for the Major government—the final version of the treaty's preamble dropped any reference to a federal vocation for the Community and retained instead the Treaty of Rome formulation of an ever-closer union as the EU's long-term political goal. Also, Britain greeted with approval the limited progress on, and intergovernmental arrangements for, common foreign and defense policies, as well as the emphasis on subsidiarity. As a result, at the summit Major was able to proclaim the outcome as "game, set, and match for Britain."[56]

France could also claim to be among the victors at Maastricht. Of greatest importance, the treaty secured a firm German commitment to EMU. With respect to EPU, there was not as much progress on developing common foreign and defense policies as the French government had originally hoped for, but steps were taken in what Paris considered to be the right direction. At the same time, the arrangements created by the treaty for CFSP and justice and internal security affairs adhered to the intergovernmentalist pattern favored by France. The French government could also be pleased about the strengthening of the European Council and the containment of the role and influence of the commission. On the negative side, France had to accept more powers for the Parliament than it had wanted to concede.[57]

With respect to EPU, at least, Chancellor Kohl and the German government were considered among the major "losers" at Maastricht. Only one week prior to the summit, Kohl had declared that Germany would not agree to EMU if political union remained "only a castle in the air."[58] In the end, however, the German government not only agreed to an EMU process with firm deadlines and the possibility of politically modified convergence criteria, but also to an EPU treaty that fell considerably short of what Bonn had originally desired. Most notably, the EP did not gain the enhanced powers and role that Germany had sought. Also, the agreements providing for intergovernmental cooperation on CFSP and immigration policy were much weaker than Germany wanted. Finally, the chancellor had strongly favored a unitary treaty structure but in the end was forced to accept the pillarized temple with an agreement on a 1996 review conference instead. As a result, despite being able to claim that Germany had proved its European commitment and credentials at Maastricht, the Kohl government was severely criticized at home for not achieving enough on EPU to justify surrendering the D-mark and monetary sovereignty.[59]

Notes

1. On the support of small states for the commission, see Erik Jones, "Small Countries and the Franco-German Relationship," in Patrick McCarthy, ed., *France-Germany, 1983–1993: The Struggle to Cooperate* (New York: St. Martin's Press), 1993, p. 126.

2. On the German position and role in the EPU talks, see Christa van Wijnbergen, "Germany and European Political Union," in Finn Laursen and Sophie Vanhoonacker, eds., *The Intergovernmental Conference on Political Union: Institutional Reforms, New Policies, and International Identity of the European Community* (Dordrecht, The Netherlands: Martinus Nijhoff, 1992), pp. 49–61.

3. "Regierungserklärung von Bundeskanzler Helmut Kohl vor dem Deutschen Bundestag am 30. Januar 1991"; reprinted in *Europa-Archiv* 5, 46 (March 10, 1991):D135. See also "Die Rolle Deutschlands in Europa: Rede des Bundeskanzlers auf der Tagung 'Forum für Deutschland' in Berlin," *Bulletin* 33 (Bonn: Presse- und Informationsamt der Bundesregierung, March 22, 1991), p. 245.

4. "The Agenda of German Politics for the Nineties," Speech by Dr. Helmut Kohl in Washington, D.C., on May 20, 1991, *Statements and Speeches* 14, 5 (New York: German Information Center, June 6, 1991), p. 3.

5. On Kohl's view that an EMU agreement without a stronger European Parliament would appear too elitist, see George Ross, *Jacques Delors and European Integration* (New York: Oxford University Press, 1995), p. 187.

6. On French views on EPU, with emphasis on divergence from German views, see Roger Morgan, "France and Germany as Partners in the European Community," in McCarthy, ed., *France-Germany, 1983–1993*, pp. 93–112, esp. pp. 108–109.

7. On the French preference for intergovernmentalism, despite rhetorical appeals to the goal of federal union, see Françoise de la Serre and Christian Lequesne, "France and the European Union," in Alan W. Cafruny and Glenda G. Rosenthal, eds., *The State of the European Community,* vol. 2, *The Maastricht Debates and Beyond* (Boulder: Lynne Rienner, 1993), p. 146. See also Enrico Martial, "France and European Political Union," in Laursen and Vanhoonacker, eds., *The Intergovernmental Conference on Political Union,* pp. 121–125.

8. On French foreign policy objectives and their relation to the EC, see Patrick McCarthy, "France Looks at Germany, or How to Become German (and European) While Remaining French," in McCarthy, ed., *France-Germany, 1983–1993,* pp. 51–72.

9. Stephen George, *An Awkward Partner: Britain in the European Community* (New York: Oxford University Press, 1990).

10. Stephen George, "The British Government and the Maastricht Agreements," in Cafruny and Rosenthal, eds., *The State of the European Community,* pp. 177–180.

11. Ibid., p. 182.

12. On British defense and security interests in post–cold war Europe, see Robert Wester, "The United Kingdom and European Political Union," in Laursen and Vanhoonacker, eds., *The Intergovernmental Conference on Political Union,* pp. 197–199.

13. Jones, "Small Countries and the Franco-German Relationship," p. 126.

14. For a historical overview of past efforts, see Sophie Vanhoonacker, "A Critical Issue: From European Political Cooperation to a Common Foreign and Security Policy," in Laursen and Vanhoonacker, eds., *The Intergovernmental Conference on Political Union,* pp. 25–33.

15. The attempt to revive the WEU in the mid-1980s was led by France and Germany. See Philip H. Gordon, *France, Germany, and the Western Alliance* (Boulder: Westview Press, 1995), p. 19.

16. On Franco-German defense and security cooperation before 1989, see ibid., pp. 9–30.

17. Julius W. Friend, *The Linchpin: Franco-German Relations, 1950–1990* (New York: Praeger, 1991), pp. 67–70; Philip Gordon, "The Franco-German Security Partnership," in McCarthy, ed., *France-Germany, 1983–1993,* pp. 143–150.

18. *Economist,* February 13, 1988, p. 79. See also Werner J. Feld, "Franco-German Military Cooperation and European Unification," *Journal of European Integration* 12, 2–3

(1988):151–164; Werner J. Feld, *The Future of European Security and Defense Policy* (Boulder: Lynne Rienner, 1993), pp. 102–103.

19. On the structure and functioning of the EPC, see Alfred Pijpers, Elfriede Regelsberger, and Wolfgang Wessels, eds., *European Political Cooperation in the 1980's: A Common Foreign Policy for Western Europe?* (Dordrecht, The Netherlands: Martinus Nijhoff, 1989); Roy Ginsberg, *Foreign Policy Actions of the European Community: The Politics of Scale* (Boulder: Lynne Rienner, 1989); Martin Holland, ed., *The Future of European Political Cooperation* (New York: St. Martin's Press, 1991); Simon J. Nuttall, *European Political Cooperation* (New York: Oxford University Press, 1992).

20. Finn Laursen, Sophie Vanhoonacker, and Robert Wester, "Overview of the Negotiations," in Laursen and Vanhoonacker, eds., *The Intergovernmental Conference on Political Union,* p. 8. In a March 7, 1991, speech in London, Delors claimed that the "limitations of the European Community in the Gulf [were] yet another argument for moving towards a form of political union embracing a common foreign and security policy" (cited in Gordon, *France, Germany, and the Western Alliance,* p. 39).

21. On the structure and functions of the EP, see Francis Jacobs, Richard Corbett, and Michael Shackleton, *The European Parliament* (Boulder: Westview Press, 1993).

22. On the democratic deficit and suggestions for closing it, see Shirley Williams, "Sovereignty and Accountability in the European Community," in Robert O. Keohane and Stanley Hoffmann, eds., *The New European Community* (Boulder: Westview Press, 1991), pp. 155–176; Desmond Dinan, *Ever Closer Union? An Introduction to the European Community* (Boulder: Lynne Rienner, 1994), pp. 288–292; Juliet Lodge, "The European Parliament and the Authority-Democracy Crises," *Annals of the American Academy of Political and Social Science* 531 (January 1994):69–83.

23. Martial, "France and European Political Union," pp. 121–122.

24. *Economist,* November 3, 1990, p. 56.

25. On the Social Charter and the debate over EC social policy in the wake of the 1992 project, see Beverly Springer, *The Social Dimension of 1992: Europe Faces a New EC* (New York: Praeger, 1992). See also Dinan, *Ever Closer Union?* pp. 394–400.

26. On French EC industrial policy goals, see de la Serre and Lequesne, "France and the European Union," p. 148.

27. On Britain's position on EC social policy and on EPU more generally, see Wester, "The United Kingdom and European Political Union," pp. 195–201.

28. *Economist,* March 30, 1991, p. 48; May 4, 1991, p. 51. On the French idea of a pillarized or temple model, see Martial, "France and European Political Union," pp. 124–125. On the commission's opposition to this model, see Robert Wester, "The European Commission and European Political Union," in Laursen and Vanhoonacker, eds., *The Intergovernmental Conference on Political Union,* p. 211.

29. Laursen, Vanhoonacker, and Wester, "Overview of the Negotiations," pp. 14–15.

30. *Financial Times,* June 13, 1991, p. 2; Laursen, Vanhoonacker, and Wester, "Overview of the Negotiations," p. 16.

31. *Economist,* June 8, 1991, p. 54; June 22, 1991, p. 53; *Financial Times,* June 13, 1991, p. 2; June, 21, 1991, p. 2; June 24, 1991, p. 2. For documentation, see "Draft Treaty on the European Union from the Luxembourg Presidency"; reprinted in Laursen and Vanhoonacker, eds., *The Intergovernmental Conference on Political Union,* pp. 358–406.

32. On the British position on the WEU, see the article by Foreign Minister Douglas Hurd in *Financial Times,* April 15, 1991, p. 13.

33. *Financial Times,* June 24, 1991, p. 2; June 25, 1991, p. 1; June 26, 1991, p. 18; June 28, 1991, 16.

34. Laursen, Vanhoonacker, and Wester, "Overview of the Negotiations," p. 17.

35. *Economist,* September 21, 1991, p. 64.

36. Ibid.; *Economist,* September 28, 1991, p. 59; *Financial Times,* October 2, 1991, p. 14.

37. *Economist,* October 5, 1991, p. 58; Laursen, Vanhoonacker, and Wester, "Overview of the Negotiations," p. 18.

38. "An Anglo-Italian Declaration on European Security and Defense"; reprinted in Laursen and Vanhoonacker, eds., *The Intergovernmental Conference on Political Union,* pp. 413–414.

39. *New York Times,* October 13, 1991, p. A20; Laursen, Vanhoonacker, and Wester, "Overview of the Negotiations," p. 18.

40. *Financial Times,* October 18, 1991, p. 2.

41. *Financial Times,* October 30, 1991, p. 23; November 14, 1991, p. 18.

42. *New York Times,* October 17, 1991, p. A1; *Economist,* October 19, 1991, p. 54; Laursen, Vanhoonacker, and Wester, "Overview of the Negotiations," pp. 18–19. The text of the Franco-German letter is reprinted in Laursen and Vanhoonacker, eds., *The Intergovernmental Conference on Political Union,* pp. 415–418.

43. *Financial Times,* October 24, 1991, p. 1; November 1, 1991, p. 24; November 5, 1991, p. 1; November 6, 1991, p. 18; November 9–10, 1991, p. 2; November 11, 1991, p. 1; November 12, 1991, p. 1; November 13, 1991, p. 1; November 14, 1991, p. 1; November 15, 1991, p. 1; *New York Times,* October 30, 1991, p. A3; November 12, 1991, p. A6; November 14, 1991, p. A1; *Economist,* November 9, 1991, pp. 47–48; November 16, 1991, pp. 63–64.

44. *New York Times,* November 16, 1991, p. A5; *Financial Times,* November 17, 1991, p. 1.

45. *Financial Times,* November 28, 1991, pp. 1, 2; *New York Times,* December 2, 1991, p. A3.

46. *Financial Times,* November 29, 1991, p. 1; *New York Times,* December 2, 1991, p. A3; Laursen, Vanhoonacker, and Wester, "Overview of the Negotiations," p. 20.

47. *Financial Times,* December 7–8, 1991, p. 24.

48. Laursen, Vanhoonacker, and Wester, "Overview of the Negotiations," p. 21.

49. *Europe,* December 12, 1991, p. 7.

50. For analysis of the EPU provisions of the treaty, see William Nicoll, "Maastricht Revisited: A Critical Analysis of the Treaty on European Union," in Cafruny and Rosenthal, eds., *The State of the European Community,* pp. 19–27; Brigid Laffan, "The Treaty of Maastricht: Political Authority and Legitimacy," in Cafruny and Rosenthal, eds., *The State of the European Community,* pp. 35–51; Andrew Duff, "The Main Reforms," in Andrew Duff, John Pinder, and Roy Pryce, eds., *Maastricht and Beyond; Building the European Union* (London: Routledge, 1994), pp. 19–35.

51. *Financial Times,* December 11, 1991, pp. 1, 2; December 12, 1991, p. 14; *New York Times,* December 11, 1991, p. A1.

52. "Treaty on European Union" (Luxembourg: Office of Official Publications of the European Communities, 1992), p. 14.

53. Nicoll, "Maastricht Revisited," pp. 22–27.

54. Wester, "The European Commission and European Political Union," pp. 213–214.

55. Laffan, "The Treaty of Maastricht," pp. 45–47; Sophie Vanhoonacker, "The European Parliament and European Political Union," in Laursen and Vanhoonacker, eds., *The Intergovernmental Conference on Political Union,* pp. 222–224.

56. *Financial Times,* December 12, 1991, p. 3. On the British government's view of the Maastricht Treaty, see Wester, "The United Kingdom and European Political Union," pp. 199–200.

57. Martial, "France and European Political Union," pp. 125–126.

58. *Financial Times,* January 29, 1992, p. 12.

59. Van Wijnbergen, "Germany and European Political Union," p. 60.

5

The Ratification Crisis

Although the basic outlines of the Treaty on European Union were agreed to at Maastricht, it was not formally signed by national leaders until February 7, 1992. Now all that remained was for the treaty to be ratified by each of the Community's twelve member countries, according to their own national laws and procedures. Ratification was scheduled to take place over the course of the next ten months so that the treaty could take effect at the beginning of 1993. Initially, at least, there was little reason to doubt that ratification would occur as planned. Within only months, however, the Community was plunged into one of its most difficult crises. In June Danish voters narrowly rejected the treaty in a national referendum, thereby triggering a popular rebellion against Maastricht that threatened the ratification process in a number of countries. There were also successive exchange-rate crises in 1992 and 1993, which almost destroyed the ERM and with it the economic and institutional basis for EMU. EC leaders were, however, able to contain the situation, and the Maastricht Treaty was finally ratified in October 1993. Nevertheless, the ratification and currency crises put full implementation of the treaty into serious doubt and generated a new wave of pessimism about the future of the Community and European integration.

A Difficult Beginning

Because of the compromise-laden nature of the Maastricht Treaty, it was a disappointment to some, including European federalists, for whom the treaty failed to produce the decisive step toward political union that they desired. Also unhappy was commission president Delors, who criticized the EPU agreement as being too vague and halfhearted, claiming that its pillarized structure amounted to an "organized schizophrenia."[1] In particular, Delors was critical of the treaty's provisions for a common foreign and security policy, which omitted the Commission from any important role.[2] Also dissatisfied with the Maastricht outcome were some members of the European Parliament, who felt that the EP's powers should have been even more substantially enhanced.[3] Sharing this disappointment was the German government, which had been forced to accept much less on

EPU than it had originally wanted. This much was admitted by Chancellor Kohl himself in an address to the Bundestag just three days after the Maastricht summit. Nevertheless, Kohl insisted that the overall results of the intergovernmental conferences were a tremendous success, and he declared that now "the way to European unity is irreversible."[4]

Despite the optimism of Kohl and others, the post-Maastricht atmosphere in Europe soon became one of disunion, one reason for which were actions taken by German political and monetary authorities in the immediate aftermath of the Maastricht summit. Less than two weeks after the summit, the Bundesbank decided to raise interest rates. Bank authorities defended this rate hike as necessary to keep in check domestic inflationary pressures, which had been generated by government spending to rebuild eastern Germany and by a growing budget deficit. The Bundesbank also claimed that higher interest rates sent a needed message to unions and employers to keep wage settlements limited in upcoming collective bargaining rounds. Nevertheless, the Bundesbank's actions were interpreted by some within the Community as an expression of the basic hostility of German monetary authorities toward EMU and as an attempt to perhaps even sabotage it. At the very least, higher rates were a way of sending a signal to other EC countries that EMU, if it occurred, would not undermine German monetary stability and would take place on German terms of strict adherence to the tough convergence criteria established at Maastricht. Others viewed the Bundesbank's actions as an attempt to force a two-speed EMU by driving a wedge between strong and weak EC economies.[5]

Equally upsetting for other European countries were German actions on Yugoslavia. After the eruption there of full-scale civil war in summer 1991, Bonn had begun to push for early EC recognition of the independence of Slovenia and Croatia. The German position was motivated by the presence of a large Croatian minority in Germany and by widespread public sympathy for the independence demands of the breakaway republics. Most other EC countries, however, including France and Britain, were strongly opposed to early recognition, fearing that this would only exacerbate the conflict while setting an unfortunate precedent by sanctioning the dissolution of a European state.[6]

Seeking to preserve European unity before the Maastricht summit, Bonn initially bowed to the wishes of its EC partners and agreed to not recognize Croatia and Slovenia until the rest of the Community was prepared to do so. In early December, however, the German government broke ranks and informed the two republics that it would recognize their independence by Christmas. Nevertheless, under intense pressure from other governments, Bonn appeared to compromise. At an EC foreign ministers meeting on December 16, Germany agreed to postpone any diplomatic action until the middle of January, when the Community as a whole would extend formal recognition provided the two republics were found to meet a list of tough human rights criteria. Despite this agreement, the Kohl government pressed ahead and announced on December 23 that it would automatically grant recognition to Slovenia and Croatia in January, regardless of the findings of the commission established to review their adherence to the criteria. Seeking to avoid public disunity immediately after the Maastricht conference, other EC countries were left with little choice other than to go along. As a result, formal Community recognition of Slovenia and Croatia was extended on January 15, despite strong reservations expressed in the Badinter Commission report about the latter's treatment of the Serbian minority within its border.[7]

The German unilateralism on Yugoslavia marked, according to a Dutch government official, "a very unhappy beginning" for the Community's attempt to forge a common foreign and security policy.[8] Together with the actions of the Bundesbank, it also provoked renewed fears of German power and dominance and raised additional questions about Bonn's commitment to the goal of European union. In remarks made in early January, President Mitterrand complained that German assertiveness on monetary and foreign policy had contradicted the spirit of unity established at Maastricht.[9] Such criticism was dismissed by Bonn officials as the inevitable result of enhanced German size and influence.[10] Neverthless, other Europeans could not help but be disconcerted by the obvious satisfaction Chancellor Kohl took in the "great victory for German foreign policy" on Yugoslavia,[11] or the public celebration in Germany of Bonn's first "unilateral action in foreign policy" since the founding of the Federal Republic in 1949.[12]

In addition to concerns about German power and assertiveness, a number of other developments were souring the political mood within the Community in early 1992 and casting a cloud over the optimism created at Maastricht. As might be expected, Germany's display of monetary and political power had created problems in relations with France. Bilateral tensions were further exacerbated, however, by conflicts over other issues. This included a dispute over global trade negotiations, with Bonn pressing for a General Agreement on Tariffs and Trade (GATT) deal that would liberalize international trade and France obstructing such a deal with fierce resistance to reductions in CAP subsidies to farmers. There was also disagreement over Community industrial policy, with France pushing for more EC intervention to promote the competitiveness of European firms and a more market-oriented Germany strongly opposing such a move.

Further problems within the Community were posed by a sharp dispute over the EC budget. At Maastricht national leaders had agreed to expand Community activities in a number of policy areas. They had also consented to set up a cohesion fund to transfer greater amounts of money from wealthy to poor EC countries. On February 12, just four days after the Maastricht Treaty was formally signed, Delors presented the bill for these decisions in the form of his five-year (1993–1997) plan for the EC budget. This called for the establishment of a $3 billion Cohesion Fund by 1997 and an overall increase in the Community budget from $81.9 billion to $107.6 billion.[13]

The Delors budget proposals met with strong opposition from Germany, which as the EC's largest net contributor would see its payments to the Community increase considerably. Faced with the mounting costs of unification, the German government could not accept a budget increase. Moreover, with public discontent over EMU already growing, Bonn believed that increased German contributions would provide further ammunition to domestic anti-Maastricht forces. Also voicing objections to the budget proposals were Italy and Britain. Poor EC states, in contrast, viewed the resistance to budget increases as a retreat by rich states from their pledge at Maastricht to provide poor states with more economic assistance. Supporting the demands of the poor countries was Delors, who argued that the Cohesion Fund was necessary to promote the convergence required for EMU. With the budgetary package due to be voted on at a June EC summit in Lisbon, conflicts over this issue threatened to complicate the ratification process in several countries.[14]

There was also growing unease about EC bureaucratization and the centralization of political power in Brussels. Much of this stemmed from public statements made by Delors in spring 1992. In response to growing pressures for the Community to "widen" through the admission of new members, Delors claimed that the supranational powers of EC institutions would have to be strengthened considerably. Only in this way, he argued, could a Community of possibly up to thirty-five states function effectively. For this reason, he favored making the commission into a more powerful political executive whose head would be elected by the Parliament and which would be accountable to the EP and European Council. Delors also called for a modification of majority voting to make it more difficult for intransigent countries to block EC legislation and for doing away with the right of all EC countries to appoint a member of the commission.[15]

The Delors proposals on institutional reform, which were scheduled to be debated at Lisbon, provoked considerable protest from those opposed to the idea of a federal Europe. In a speech at The Hague (Netherlands) on May 15, former Prime Minister Thatcher condemned commission plans to create "a tightly regulated, centralized bureaucratic federal state, imposing uniform standards throughout the continent."[16] Although not apparent at the time, Delors's statements were also having an impact on the ratification debate in many EC countries, particularly in Denmark, where it fed already substantial fears about the centralization of political power in Brussels and the submergence of national identity in a European superstate.[17]

Despite these problems, the ratification process appeared on schedule. In April the European Parliament, whose support was not required for ratification, voted its approval of the treaty and urged all member states to ratify it as soon as possible; this despite serious misgivings about the treaty's failure to grant more power to the EP. In May France took the first step toward ratification when the National Assembly approved constitutional revisions required by the treaty.[18] Later that month, formal debate on the Maastricht Treaty began in the British Parliament.

Although Britain had been the most critical and hesitant country at Maastricht, the concessions gained on EMU and the social chapter were expected to make ratification of the treaty relatively easy.[19]

The Danish Veto

The rejection of the Maastricht Treaty by Danish voters on June 2 came as an unexpected shock. Despite long-standing skepticism about European integration in Denmark, political experts felt that most Danes had accepted the inevitability of further integration. As one observer had commented following the 1986 referendum to approve the SEA, "When the chips were down and the voters' choice was real rather than hypothetical, a majority would stick with the EC."[20] Indeed, the Maastricht Treaty had been supported by the government and most of Denmark's political and economic establishment, as well as by the country's major newspapers. And in opinion polls taken just days before the referendum, the "yes" vote appeared to be headed for victory. Nevertheless, in the actual vote the treaty was rejected by an extremely narrow 50.7 to 49.3 percent margin.[21]

Playing a major role in the Danish vote against Maastricht were specific economic and political considerations, such as the impact of further integration on the important fisheries industry, the negative consequences for Denmark's advanced social welfare and environmental policies, and the possibility of being forced to go along with common European defense policies. For the most part, however, opposition centered on broader fears about the loss of national sovereignty and identity. There was also concern about the erosion of democratic legitimacy and control through the increased power of bureaucratic and nonaccountable European institutions. In addition, many worried that in a more integrated Europe a small state such as Denmark would be easily dominated by larger countries, especially France and Germany. Although the "no" vote did not signify that most Danes wanted to leave the EC, it did constitute a rejection of further deepening and, in particular, of political integration.[22]

The Danish veto represented a huge setback for the Community and presented it with a number of political and legal problems. Technically, the Danish vote meant that the Maastricht Treaty could not go into effect as planned since EC law required that amendments to the Rome Treaty be approved by all member states. For the treaty to survive, therefore, a second Danish referendum—this time with a more positive outcome—would probably be necessary. A second referendum, in turn, might require a renegotiation of the treaty's contents to satisfy popular objections. But most EC leaders believed that reopening the complex treaty to negotiation would be tantamount to opening a Pandora's box. For exactly this reason, the EC had already rejected Ireland's request to revise a treaty clause that protected that country's constitutional ban on abortion. Another possibility was for the other eleven countries to somehow proceed outside of the Treaty of Rome framework, thereby bypassing Denmark and establishing a two-tiered Community. This possibility, however, raised a multitude of difficult legal questions.[23]

By far the most serious challenge posed by Denmark's rejection of the treaty was its possible negative impact on the ratification process in other countries. Perhaps the most immediate effect was felt in Britain, where the Danish vote was hailed as a great victory by opponents of European integration. It also significantly bolstered the position and spirits of the so-called Euroskeptics within Major's own Conservative Party.[24] As a result, while continuing to proclaim his confidence that Britain would ratify the treaty, Major decided one day after the Danish referendum to temporarily suspend parliamentary debate on the Maastricht Treaty.[25]

Of greatest concern, however, was the situation in Germany, where the treaty was facing mounting criticism. Strong popular resistance to surrendering the D-mark had emerged at the time of the Maastricht summit and had grown since. On the day after the summit, the mass-circulation newspaper *Bild-Zeitung* ran an enormous headline proclaiming "The End of the D-mark." In the accompanying article the paper claimed that at Maastricht a funeral bell "tolled for the symbol of German prosperity, of the economic miracle."[26] In a public opinion poll taken just before the summit, some 71 percent of Germans surveyed indicated they wanted a decision on creating a single currency postponed, while only 3 percent thought that monetary union would benefit Germany. In the same poll, 75 percent of the respondents expressed their doubts that a new European currency would be as good as the D-mark, and 79 percent said they would favor a national referendum before the D-mark was abolished.[27] After the signing of the treaty, these concerns did not diminish, and opinion polls taken over the following months consistently showed that a solid majority of Germans opposed giving up their "wonderful money."[28]

The widespread popular opposition to EMU revealed the considerable emotional attachment of Germans to the D-mark, demonstrating the extent to which it had become "a part of [the] national subconscious."[29] Equally disconcerting for the government, however, was the opposition to EMU coming from the business and financial establishment, including the German Federation of Industry, whose president had expressed the fear that EMU could lead to a loss of economic stability.[30] Also critical of the EMU agreement was the conservative, business-oriented newspaper *Frankfurter Allgemeine,* which in an editorial on December 9 argued that EMU would alter the "quality" of German monetary policy, making it more difficult to meet the traditional objectives of price and monetary stability.[31] As with popular opinion in general, concern about EMU among the business class grew in the months that followed the Maastricht summit. According to a survey of international business leaders published in April, only 35 percent of German companies thought EMU was a good idea, compared with a majority of their counterparts in other EC countries.[32] Then, as if to underscore the uncertainty created by the Danish referendum, on June 11 a group of sixty leading German economists issued a statement opposing the EMU agreement, claiming that it was premature and that, if carried out, would not only create higher inflation but also divide Europe even further into weak and strong currency zones.[33]

The Bundesbank continued to have strong reservations about EMU, which it made public in a document released in early February[34] and in numerous public statements over the following months, all clearly timed to influence the looming parliamentary debate on the treaty. Among other things, Bundesbank officials were critical of the firm timetable for EMU agreed to at Maastricht, which they believed could result in a premature move to stage three or lead to political pressures for a relaxation of the convergence criteria in the interest of European union.[35] Officials also argued that the Maastricht Treaty did not provide for sufficient political union, which was necessary for stricter controls on the budgetary and fiscal policies of member states. According to Bundesbank vice president Hans Tietmeyer, further progress toward political union was "indispensable for the lasting success of monetary union"; without it EMU was "doomed to failure."[36] Bundesbank criticism of the EMU agreement was reinforced by comments made in May by former bank president Pöhl, who argued that the agreement did not allow time for sufficient economic convergence between member countries and that there had not been enough progress on political union.[37]

Responding to such criticisms, the Kohl government mounted a spirited defense of the EMU agreement. It repeatedly stressed that the D-mark and German monetary stability were not being sacrificed for Europe but rather that Europe was accepting the D-mark system.[38] In a speech in early March in Karlsruhe (Germany), Kohl's chief negotiator in the EMU talks, Horst Köhler, claimed that the German government "managed to achieve far more, in my view, in the economic and monetary union than could have been expected at the beginning of negotiations." He countered the Bundesbank's criticisms by pointing out that bank officials had agreed "word for word" with the negotiating brief. He also assured his listeners that Germany would make certain that the convergence criteria were strictly interpreted and adhered to and that there would be no relaxation of these standards. Köhler went on to say that there should be no fears about the stability of a common European currency since monetary policy under EMU would be guided by even more stringent stability requirements than currently existed in Germany.[39] This remark echoed Chancellor Kohl's earlier claim, made in his December 13, 1991, address to the Bundestag, that "important elements of the [Maastricht] Treaty are more clearly and unambiguously formulated than the Bundesbank Law."[40] In addition to such statements, the Kohl government sought to assuage fears about EMU by stepping up its campaign to have the new EMI and future European central bank located in Frankfurt.[41]

Also threatening the Maastricht Treaty were demands made by the opposition Social Democrats. Since a two-thirds majority was required in the Bundestag to ratify the treaty, the SPD's support was necessary. With its own strong pro-EC tradition, the SPD had already announced that it would not block ratification.[42] Nevertheless, the party did want to attach some conditions to its support for the treaty. In particular, the SPD demanded a full parliamentary debate and vote before the final decision to begin stage three of EMU. Among other things, this debate would consider whether the established convergence criteria had been adequately adhered to, thus guaranteeing that a future German government would not abandon the commitment to price and monetary stability in the face of political pressure from other EC states. The debate would also determine whether there had been sufficient progress toward the goal of political union. Following the Maastricht conference, the SPD had been highly critical of the Kohl government for not securing greater powers for the European Parliament, thereby ensuring that a future European Union would be democratic enough.[43] For this reason, the SPD now demanded that the Parliament be "substantially strengthened" before full EMU could begin. Rather than the already planned automatic transition to stage three in 1997 or 1999, the SPD wanted to preserve the right to assess and "take stock" of affairs before making the final leap. Critics of this provision argued that it amounted to an opt-out right similar to that secured by Britain in the Maastricht negotiations.[44]

Another potential roadblock was posed by the sixteen federal states, or *Länder*. Since ratification also required a two-thirds majority in the Bundesrat—the parliamentary body that represents the interests of the states—the *Länder* were in a position to block approval of the treaty. They were determined to use this leverage to ensure that transfers of governmental authority to the EC not be made without their consent and that their own considerable powers in various areas of policy not be diminished as a result of European integration. The states therefore demanded, as the price for their assent to the Maastricht Treaty, a constitutional amendment that would guarantee them a role in any future decisions concerning the transfer of sovereignty to supranational institutions.[45] By early June, bargaining between the states and federal government on such an amendment was still ongoing.

Parliamentary debate on the Maastricht Treaty in Germany had begun in April, and the Kohl government was originally optimistic that final voting on the treaty could take place sometime in the fall or early winter. After the Danish veto, however, the government feared that domestic opposition to the treaty might enjoy an upsurge of support. As a result, in early June the prognosis for ratification in Germany remained uncertain. This prompted Chancellor Kohl to warn, "If we don't link German unification with European unity, if what we undertook in Maastricht fails and we don't achieve European Union in the last decade of this terrible century, then we will revert to nationalist disputes in Europe next century."[46]

The French Referendum

In the aftermath of the Danish vote, the Community vowed to press forward with ratification of the treaty. The strongest statement in this regard came from Chancellor Kohl and President Mitterrand, who in a joint announcement on June

3 declared their determination to "proceed unswervingly and firmly with the achievement of European union."[47] On the following day, EC foreign ministers meeting in Oslo (Norway) proclaimed that the other eleven countries would continue with plans to ratify the existing treaty by the end of the year, with the hope that Denmark would reconsider its decision and join the EU. They also ruled out any renegotiation of the treaty.[48] Perhaps the most notable gesture was made by France's Mitterrand, who the day after the Danish vote announced that he would take the constitutionally unnecessary step of submitting the Maastricht Treaty to a national referendum in September. Among other reasons for this move, Mitterrand felt that a decisive yes vote in France, where there was traditionally strong support for European integration, would help counter the negative effects of the Danish veto and provide the treaty with a much-needed boost.[49]

Before the French vote, the Maastricht Treaty had to clear the hurdle of a popular referendum on June 18 in Ireland. Besides Denmark, Ireland was the only EC country required by its constitution to ratify the treaty in this manner. In its campaign for the treaty, the Irish government stressed the considerable economic benefits of Community membership for Ireland. In the end, a substantial majority of 67 percent voted in favor of the treaty, with 31 percent voting against. With a rather low voter turnout of only 57 percent, and given the traditionally strong support for European integration in Ireland, this vote represented something less than a ringing endorsement for the treaty.[50] Nevertheless, following close on the heels of the Danish disaster, the positive outcome of the Irish referendum was greeted with considerable relief by the Community.[51]

Attention now focused on France. The decision by Mitterrand to submit the Maastricht Treaty to a popular referendum had been something of a gamble. In addition to Mitterrand's wish to give the treaty a critical boost, there were important domestic political considerations behind this move. With the right-wing opposition parties severely divided on European integration, Mitterrand hoped that the debate over Maastricht would split them even further. In this manner, a referendum would be a convenient means for the governing Socialists to regain domestic political advantage. There was, of course, the possibility that the president's considerable unpopularity among the French people could damage the treaty's chances. Nevertheless, at the time of the decision public support for Maastricht was high, with opinion polls showing that two-thirds of French voters favored the treaty, and an easy victory appeared certain.[52]

Throughout the summer, however, opposition to the Maastricht Treaty mounted in France. Promoting the no position was an unlikely coalition, including a majority of the main conservative opposition party—the Gaullist Rally for the Republic—the far right National Front, the Communists, and Socialist Party dissidents. A key argument of the opposition was that further integration would only limit French autonomy and independence rather than enhancing it, as claimed by the government. This was the case not only in economic policy, where France would become subject to the dictates of the Bundesbank or nonaccountable European institutions, but also in foreign and security policy. The opposition also claimed that the Maastricht Treaty, by further centralizing political power in the hands of faceless bureaucrats in Brussels, represented a massive threat to French democracy and national identity. Opposition also grew out of the economic interests of particular groups, including industrial workers, who were critical of the treaty's weak provisions for industrial and social policy, and farmers, who feared further reductions of CAP subsidies. Late in the ratification debate, the question of German power and hegemony became a central issue, with the opposition claiming that Maastricht and EMU would mean domination of France by its stronger neighbor. Just the opposite was argued by treaty supporters, who asserted that further integration was the only way to exert control over Germany in post–cold war Europe.[53]

Opposition claims about German dominance were bolstered by the Bundesbank's decision in July to raise interest rates yet again, thus placing further pressure on a French economy that was already burdened with extremely high levels of unemployment.[54] One week prior to the referendum, however, the Bundesbank relented and agreed to lower rates, a move that was widely perceived as calculated to bolster the chances of the yes vote on September 20.[55]

As a result of the skillful campaign waged by the treaty's opponents, and a rather complacent attitude on the part of the government, by late August opinion polls showed that the no vote had drawn even and was possibly inching ahead. Shocked by the possibility of defeat, the government mobilized a major effort in the final weeks before the referendum, claiming that failure of the Maastricht Treaty would be a catastrophe for France and Europe and could possibly mean the end of the EC. Such an outcome, the government argued, would nullify the work of four decades of French diplomacy, strengthen the global dominance of the United States and Japan, and pave the way for German hegemony in Europe. Providing a boost for the yes vote was the appearance of Chancellor Kohl with Mitterrand during a televised debate on September 3, in which Kohl argued against the claims that Maastricht would lead to German hegemony. Also intervening in the debate were other national and EC leaders, including Delors, who threatened to resign as commission president should the treaty be defeated.[56]

In the end, the Maastricht Treaty was saved, and on September 20 the yes vote won a razor-thin victory, with 51.05 percent opting for the treaty and 48.95 percent voting against.[57] Nevertheless, the outcome of the vote was something of double-edged sword. On the one hand, Community leaders could now breathe a sigh of relief and push forward with the ratification process. On the other, the narrowness of the win in one of the Community's most important countries underscored the considerable reservations many Europeans had about the treaty and further integration. Even though EC leaders could correctly attribute much of the no vote to anti-Mitterrand sentiment, and therefore interpret the vote as being as much a referendum on the president as on Maastricht,[58] it was also the case that such factors as concern about the loss of national sovereignty and identity, questions about the democratic legitimacy of the Community, and fear of German domination played a key role, as did concerns about the economic consequences of further integration.

Despite the narrow win for the Maastricht Treaty in France, Kohl and Mitterrand remained undaunted. Just days after the referendum, the two leaders met in Paris and reaffirmed their determination to forge ahead with European union. Spurring their efforts were the strong commitment of both men to this goal and their mutual belief that Europe had to act now to exploit the window of opportunity for further integration that existed. As the chancellor was reported to have said prior to his meeting with Mitterrand, "While both alive, François and I have to make Europe's unification irreversible. . . . Our successors will never manage it."[59]

The First Currency Crisis

Reinforcing the gloom created by the narrow approval of the Maastricht Treaty in France was the currency crisis that erupted simultaneously with the referendum. For months the Bundesbank had refused to lower interest rates, thereby releasing its tight-money stranglehold on the European economy, arguing the need to combat inflation in Germany and maintain the Bundesbank's domestic and international credibility. On September 14, however, the Bundesbank finally relented and agreed to slightly lower rates in return for devaluation of the weaker Italian lira and Spanish peseta. The Bundesbank also suggested that Britain devalue the pound, which London refused to do. Instead, the British government attempted to support the value of its currency by raising interest rates even further. Two days later, following remarks by Bundesbank chief Helmut Schlesinger that indicated Germany would not act to defend the sliding pound, Britain decided to remove its currency from the ERM, thereby allowing it to float dramatically downward. On September 17, Italy followed suit.[60]

The currency crisis provoked an extraordinarily bitter exchange of accusations between Britain and Germany. British officials and commentators blamed the crisis on public suggestions by German authorities that the pound was overvalued against the D-mark. They also chastised the Bundesbank for promoting economic tensions in Europe through its stubborn refusal to lower interest rates. In response, German officials denied any responsibility for the run on the pound, arguing that the real problem was Britain's weak economy and London's attempt to maintain the pound's value at an unrealistically high level.[61]

After the French referendum, currency speculators increasingly targeted the franc, raising the possibility that the French currency might be forced out of the ERM as well. The Bundesbank and German government acted to strongly support the French currency, however.[62] On September 23, the governments and central banks of Germany and France released a joint statement declaring their determination to defend the value of the franc.[63] The Bundesbank therefore essentially staked its reputation on defense of the franc and proclaimed there would be no realignment of currencies within the EMS. After several days, it became apparent that Franco-German efforts to defend the franc had been successful, and the currency crisis subsided.[64]

The dramatic bilateral action to save the franc had major political repercussions. In Britain angry comparisons were drawn between German defense of the franc and the earlier lack of support for the pound. German officials argued, however, that this defense had less to do with politics than economics. German actions, they claimed, were not motivated by a preference for relations with Paris over London but by the basic solidity of the French economy and the belief that the franc was not unstable or overvalued.[65] Nevertheless, it was clear that politics did play an important role in German defense of the franc. The Franco-German relationship was the central axis of the Community and primary force behind European integration. If the franc had been forced to devalue or depart the ERM, this would have been a potentially fatal blow to hopes for EMU and European union. By coming to the aid of the French currency, the German government had sent a clear signal of its commitment to these goals. The successful bilateral effort to preserve the franc, therefore, was both a reaffirmation of Franco-German partnership and a symbolic political victory for the idea of European union.[66]

The currency crisis and defense of the franc spurred renewed talk of a two-speed EMU, with Germany and France proceeding ahead together with the Benelux countries. There were also rumors of a secret plan for immediate Franco-German monetary union, with a common central bank located in Frankfurt but headed by a French citizen.[67] Such speculations were further fueled by Pöhl's statement, made while on a trip to Washington, that a quick monetary union between the two countries was possible and that indeed a two-speed EMU with a Franco-German core was desirable.[68] Nevertheless, Bonn continued to officially deny any plans for a two-speed EMU.[69] And at a meeting in London on September 28, EC finance ministers stated their opposition to this approach as well.[70]

Despite such official proclamations, it was clear that European economies were diverging rather than coming closer together. As a result of the exchange-rate crisis, the currencies of two of Europe's largest economies had been forced to abandon the ERM altogether, and those of several other countries—Spain, Portugal, and Ireland—were able to remain within the system only through major devaluations and a reversion to national capital controls. At the same time, economic stagnation and rising unemployment continued throughout Europe. According to most experts, unless something changed drastically—such as a decision by the Bundesbank to substantially lower interest rates—further economic and currency crises could be expected.[71]

Along with economic problems, the Community was also experiencing a severe political crisis. Since the Danish referendum, and now reinforced by the narrow endorsement of the Maastricht Treaty by France, a growing popular backlash had emerged against the perceived accumulation of power by Brussels and the commission. Linked to this backlash were concerns about the loss of national sovereignty and identity within a more integrated Europe. To counter such fears, EC and national leaders had been forced to abandon ambitious rhetoric about European union and instead stress the principle of subsidiarity and the decentralization of political power. The ratification crisis also made apparent the existence of a huge gap between the views of most political and business elites and those of most citizens; unless the gap could be closed, it threatened further progress in Community integration. In addition, the Community was now threatened by conflict between member governments. In particular, significant tensions had emerged between Britain and other EC countries, especially Germany and France, since the currency crisis in September.[72]

In Britain itself, the government of Prime Minister Major was in deep political trouble. Following the decision to devalue the pound in September, Major had narrowly survived a parliamentary vote of confidence and was now under increasing attack by opponents of European integration within his own party. Nevertheless, he continued to insist that Britain would ratify Maastricht, but only after popular concerns about EC bureaucracy and intrusiveness had been adequately dealt with, the ERM reformed, and the Danish problem resolved.[73]

In an effort to repair damaged intra-Community relations and assuage popular fears about integration, EC leaders held a special summit on October 16 in Birmingham (England). At this meeting, they declared their intention to go forward with the Maastricht ratification process but also pledged that further integration would not take place at the expense of the interests or identity of national states. "Greater unity," the leaders claimed, "can be achieved without excessive centralization." To ensure this outcome, they promised to examine ways for making the Community more democratic and respectful of national concerns and to discuss these at the December European Council in Edinburgh (Scotland). They also agreed to take up the issue of Danish objections to the treaty at that time and announced that Denmark would have until December to decide how to ratify the treaty.[74]

The Edinburgh Summit

By fall 1992, the issue of subsidiarity had risen to the top of the Community agenda. In broad terms, this is the principle that policy decisions should be made as close to the people as possible and that the EC should act only when measures cannot be more effectively taken at the national or local levels.[75] The subsidiarity principle was anchored in the Maastricht Treaty in Article 3b, yet was formulated in a vague and imprecise manner. With the onset of the ratification crisis, this formerly obscure principle became the focal point of both opponents and proponents of the treaty. Among the former, especially in Britain, it was the key to efforts at limiting the erosion of national powers to the EC. For the latter, it became a means for assuaging the fears of nervous Europeans about the loss of national identity and the emergence of an overweening superstate, while at the same time preserving the possibility for expanding Community powers in the future.[76]

Following the Danish referendum, Delors backtracked furiously from his ambitious proposals to make the commission into a more powerful political executive. Instead, he began to give much greater emphasis to the principle of subsidiarity. He also recognized popular concerns about excessive bureaucratization, admitting that the Community had in the past been "too elitist and technocratic."[77] Delors's proposals on political reform had originally been scheduled for discussion at the June 26–27 Lisbon summit. At that meeting, EC leaders instead stressed subsidiarity and promised to limit the power of the commission and Brussels. They also claimed that the goal of European union was not to create a "superstate."[78]

The narrow approval of the Maastricht Treaty in France further spurred efforts to clarify and strengthen the principle of subsidiarity. In October the commission produced a lengthy statement on subsidiarity.[79] The issue was also discussed by EC leaders at Birmingham, but they decided that any firm action on this matter should await the regular European Council planned for December 11–12 in Edinburgh. At the Edinburgh summit, after much discussion EC leaders adopted a lengthy statement on subsidiarity, in which they attempted to define the concept more precisely, offer guidelines for its application, and give concrete examples with respect to existing and pending legislation. In general, EC leaders concluded that EC legislation should be judged according to two key criteria: the "need for action" and "proportionality." Also at Edinburgh, leaders approved measures aimed at making the EC decisionmaking process more open and transparent, once again seeking to counter criticism that the Community was too elitist and nondemocratic.[80]

In addition to subsidiarity, the Edinburgh summit tackled a number of other difficult issues. Foremost among these was the question of Denmark. By the fall, the Danish government had decided to submit the Maastricht Treaty to a second referendum in spring 1993. For this referendum to be successful, however, many of the objections expressed by voters in the initial vote would have to be overcome. In early October, the Danish government had produced a paper suggesting various ways in which Denmark might be able to ratify the treaty, including special concessions that would allow it to avoid certain treaty obligations.[81] This paper was followed several weeks later by a Danish proposal for special treaty supplements. These would provide Denmark with opt-outs from key Maastricht agreements that were of special concern to voters, including EMU, European citizenship, a common defense policy, and cooperation in police and internal security affairs.[82]

The Danish proposal for legally binding opt-outs was greeted with considerable uncertainty by other governments and EC authorities. In addition to the question of making exceptions, it was also not clear whether exemptions could be granted without renegotiating the treaty, which other EC governments had stead-fastly refused to do.[83] In the end, but not until after furious negotiations before and during the summit, an agreement was reached at Edinburgh. Among other things, this agreement gave Denmark the right to not participate in stage three of EMU, as well as aspects of CFSP that had defense implications. In concluding the agreement, EC leaders were careful to state that the Danish opt-outs did not con-stitute an alteration of the treaty, nor did they apply to any other member coun-try.[84] Nonetheless, it was clear to many observers that the Danish opt-outs, on top of those already granted to Britain at Maastricht, only reinforced the Community's movement in the direction of an à la carte or variable geometry de-sign.

In addition to the Danish question, the Edinburgh summit dealt with the prob-lem of the EC budget. After being made in February, the Delors budget proposals for 1993–1997 were to be discussed at the June summit in Lisbon. Sharp criticism of the budget package by key governments, however, resulted in the decision to postpone action until December. Nevertheless, as the date for the Edinburgh summit approached, widespread disagreement remained. In particular, wealthy EC countries continued to resist increases in the budget, most of which would come from them and go to poor countries in the form of regional and economic development aid. As a result, the Spanish government, acting on behalf of other poor countries, pushed the wealthy governments to honor the agreements they had made at Maastricht and threatened to hold up a budget deal if they did not.[85] Among the issues affected by the budget dispute were plans for EC enlargement. The Community had decided to begin negotiations on EC membership with sev-eral European Free Trade Association (EFTA) applicants, but only once there was an agreement on the budget. Entry talks with Sweden, Finland, Austria, and Norway were scheduled to begin in January, but these would have to be post-poned if a budget deal could not be reached. On this matter as well, however, the Edinburgh summit forged a last-minute compromise, and a budget deal that in-cluded a doubling of EC Cohesion Funds was approved.[86]

With agreements having been reached on the Danish opt-outs, subsidiarity, and the budget, the Edinburgh summit helped put the Community and the ratifi-cation process back on track. Nevertheless, major hurdles remained. One of these was posed by ratification difficulties in Britain. After suspending parliamentary debate on Maastricht in the wake of the Danish veto, Prime Minister Major had reinitiated the ratification process in the fall. The government's political position at this time was not a strong one, however. Following the September currency cri-sis, the government had narrowly survived a vote of no confidence in the House of Commons. In addition, a series of policy blunders in the fall had led to plum-meting popularity ratings for the prime minister, who also faced a mounting re-bellion by treaty opponents within his own Conservative Party. As a result, after the treaty only barely won a preliminary vote in the House of Commons on November 4, Major decided to put off a final parliamentary vote on the treaty until after the second Danish referendum.[87] This decision provoked dismay and out-rage among other Community leaders, who saw it as further delaying and endangering the Maastricht ratification process.[88]

Besides Britain and Denmark, however, by the end of 1992 all other EC countries had ratified the Maastricht Treaty. Of considerable importance was Germany's ratification of the treaty, which took place in December by large majorities in both houses of parliament. To secure ratification, however, the Kohl government had to concede significant new powers over EC affairs to the federal states and Bundestag. As a result, Article 23 of the constitution (Grundgesetz), which declared European union an official state goal, was amended to specify that approval by both the Bundestag and Bundesrat would be required for future transfers of sovereignty to European institutions.[89] The Bundestag also attached a resolution to its approval of the treaty, which the federal government accepted, that called for a positive vote of assent by the Bundestag before Germany could begin stage three of EMU.[90] The SPD, in justifying its vote for the treaty, claimed that it did not want to provide further opportunities for the gathering forces of nationalism in Germany. Nevertheless, the SPD remained critical of the insufficient social and environmental provisions of the Maastricht Treaty and of the fact that progress on political integration and EC democratization had not matched the pace of EMU.[91]

The Second Danish Referendum

After the Edinburgh summit, the Community awaited the second Danish referendum, which was scheduled for May 18. The intervening months, however, were not without interesting or important developments. On January 1, 1993, the Single European Market formally became a reality. Although by this point much of the legislation to permit the barrier-free movement of goods, services, labor, and capital had not yet been implemented, sufficient progress toward this goal had been achieved to allow the Community to celebrate. Nevertheless, after the bruising struggles over the Maastricht Treaty in the previous year, the official opening of the Single Market was something of an anticlimax.

Another important development for the Community was the initiation of formal entry negotiations with Sweden, Austria, and Finland on February 1, with Norway expected to soon join the talks as well.[92] In the previous year, these four members of the EFTA had signed an agreement with the EC making them a part of the European Economic Area (EEA). This arrangement allowed them to participate in the Single Market, yet meant that they would have to play by the economic rules established by the Community without having any voice in making them. As a result, even before signing the EEA agreement, several of the EFTA countries had applied for full membership in the Community.[93]

The application of the EFTA countries frustrated the original intent of the EEA arrangement for Delors. He had viewed the EEA as a means for deferring Community enlargement, thereby allowing the EC to focus on deepening integration among current members. Widening the Community before deepening it, Delors believed, would make further integration more difficult to achieve. For exactly this reason, the EEA was also favored by France, which believed that early enlargement would hinder its effort to bind Germany into a more integrated Community. Precisely because widening the Community would likely inhibit deepening, Britain favored doing so as quickly as possible. The German government was also pushing harder for enlargement. Not only would the membership of EFTA countries benefit Germany economically and politically, but it would also clear the path for the next round of enlargement, this time into Eastern Europe. Among other things, as the EC's easternmost member, Germany had a strong security interest in the Community's eastward expansion.[94]

By fall 1992, the French perspective on EC enlargement had shifted somewhat. With the Maastricht Treaty under fire and the ratification process stalled, France and other opponents of early enlargement now saw it as a means of sustaining the Community's momentum. Nevertheless, even though France was now willing to concede an EC of fifteen or sixteen members, it continued to reject an early enlargement into Eastern Europe. In June 1991, Mitterrand had remarked that it would be "decades and decades" before Eastern European countries would be ready to join the EC.[95] As an alternative to enlargement, Mitterrand promoted his idea of a "European confederation," which would relegate Eastern European countries to a looser relationship with a deepening EC.[96] This proposal was roundly rejected, however, by the Eastern European countries and Germany, who favored instead full membership for the postcommunist states. Britain, for its part, also welcomed the beginning of enlargement talks and the prospect for further widening into Eastern Europe. As a result, by spring 1993 the British government could take increasing satisfaction in EC trends and claim that the Community was now moving in a direction (widening) Britain had long favored.[97]

On May 18, the EC overcame an important hurdle when Danish voters approved the Maastricht Treaty, with 56.8 percent voting for the agreement and 43.2 percent voting against. A key reason for the treaty's success in the second referendum was the opt-outs secured by Denmark at the Edinburgh summit. The treaty also benefited from a change of government in January, with a majority Social Democratic coalition taking over from the minority center-right government. The Social Democrats were therefore able to apply more pressure on reluctant supporters to vote for the treaty. For the most part, however, it was the fear of being left behind by the rest of Europe and isolated, and the possibility of being forced out of the Community altogether, that played the largest role in motivating Danish voters to support the treaty.[98]

Despite Denmark's approval, the Maastricht Treaty was not yet home free. It still awaited ratification by the British Parliament, where a final vote was being delayed by a series of parliamentary maneuvers. The government also had to hold off growing calls for the treaty to be submitted to a popular referendum before ratification.[99] In addition, final ratification had not yet been achieved in Germany, where after parliamentary approval in December the treaty was challenged in several suits to the Federal Constitutional Court. Among other things, these claimed that the treaty illegally undermined national sovereignty and constitutional guarantees of individual rights and democratic procedure. The Court was scheduled to hear these challenges in June. Only if it ruled against them could the federal president sign the Maastricht Treaty and formalize its ratification.[100]

The Second Currency Crisis

Before these developments could take place, the Maastricht Treaty sustained yet another severe blow. In late July and early August, a second major currency crisis erupted, this time almost destroying the exchange-rate mechanism of the EMS and with it the institutional basis for EMU.

Since the first currency crisis in September 1992, the EC had experienced a succession of lesser upheavals. In November heavy speculative pressure had forced devaluations of the Spanish peseta and Portugese escudo. Also coming under pressure at this time were the French franc, Danish krone, and Irish pound, although all three countries had managed to preserve established rates in the ERM.[101] Renewed currency turbulence occurred in early 1993, forcing devaluations of the escudo and Irish pound. There was also increased pressure on the French franc. Once again, this upheaval was met with coordinated intervention by the Bundesbank and Bank of France, following a joint Franco-German statement in support of the franc on January 5. A slight reduction of interest rates by the Bundesbank in early February was also construed as a move to aid the franc.[102]

The currency troubles of early 1993 and the concerted Franco-German response provoked renewed talk about a two-speed EMU led by Germany and France. As before, this option was explicitly ruled out by Bonn and Paris, although at a joint press conference on January 21 Kohl and Mitterrand held out the possibility of shortening stage two of EMU. Doing so would permit a more rapid leap into full monetary union for France and Germany, as well as other countries that were prepared for it. Afterward, however, this statement was quickly downplayed by officials of both governments.[103]

Nevertheless, developments in spring and early summer gave further support to speculation that if EMU was to occur, it would be on a two-speed basis. In mid-May during the run-up to the second Danish referendum, a new round of currency turmoil forced devaluations of the peseta and escudo.[104] At the same time, however, the French franc appeared to be strengthening. After coming to power in March, the new conservative government of Prime Minister Edouard Balladur announced its determination to continue with the established "franc fort" (strong franc) policy, which centered on maintaining the French currency's parity with the D-mark. The Balladur government also outlined its plans to make the French central bank independent of government control, thus not only allowing improved ties to the Bundesbank and fulfilling a key prerequisite for EMU, but also bolstering the credibility of the franc and French monetary policy.[105] In June France was able to reduce key interest rates to below German ones for the first time in twenty-six years, a source of considerable national pride. Together with the D-mark's decline against the U.S. dollar and Japanese yen, the reduction prompted talk of the franc becoming the new anchor currency of the ERM.[106]

Such talk was drastically premature, for despite an inflation rate (2 percent) that was less than half of Germany's, the French economy remained weak, with nearly 12 percent unemployment and record high budget deficits. For months domestic critics had called for the government to abandon its franc fort policy and to substantially lower interest rates in a national "dash for growth," even if this meant devualuing the franc and leaving the ERM altogether. In pressing for such a change in policy, critics held up Britain as an example. Since leaving the ERM in September, the British government had been free to slash interest rates, and the pound had dropped nearly 20 percent against the D-mark, thus helping spur renewed economic growth and trade competitiveness. Demands for a devaluation were firmly rejected by the French government, however, which asserted that preserving the franc's parity with the D-mark was, as Balladur put it, "a national objective."[107] Although simple national pride was a factor in this determination, it was also motivated by the desire to maintain close Franco-German ties as the basis for EMU and future European integration.[108]

In mid-July, however, the French position began to crumble as currency speculators bet that a reduction of French interest rates was both necessary and imminent. The Bundesbank responded with massive intervention, and Finance Minister Waigel declared Germany's intention to defend the franc. On July 23 the governments of France and Germany issued a joint statement in support of the franc's parity with the D-mark. Despite such actions, pressure on the franc grew when the Bundesbank refused to cut interest rates at meetings of its executive council on July 15 and 29. Also coming under increased pressure at this time were the krone, peseta, escudo, and Belgian franc. The final act of the crisis came on the weekend of July 31–August 1 with an emergency meeting of EC finance ministers and central bankers in Brussels. After prolonged, and at times acrimonious, negotiations, they decided in the early hours of August 2 to widen the band of permissible fluctuation within the ERM to 15 percent around the established central rate, rather than the previous 2.25 percent band. The exception to this would be the Dutch guilder, which would keep its narrow band vis-à-vis the D-mark.[109]

The decision to widen fluctuation bands gave European governments much greater room for maneuver in their economic policies while preventing the ERM from falling apart altogether. At the same time, this move helped France save face by allowing it to avoid formally devaluing the franc. Nevertheless, the crisis led to increased tensions between France and Germany. In particular, the French were furious with the Bundesbank for not lowering interest rates at the height of the currency turmoil. A major reason for the crisis, the French government charged, was that the Bundesbank refused to put European needs ahead of narrower domestic concerns. In fact, a key motivation for the Bundesbank's decision was its determination not to be perceived as bowing to political pressure for lower rates, thereby preserving its autonomy and credibility. France and its EC allies moved quickly to deflect criticism from the Bundesbank and repair relations with Germany, however, by focusing blame on "Anglo-Saxon" speculators, who, Delors and others claimed, sought to sabotage European monetary union.[110]

Also damaged by the currency crisis were the Maastricht plans for EMU. With economic convergence a precondition for this goal, the turmoil in exchange rates only reemphasized the continuing divergence among European economies. At the same time, the Maastricht guidelines specified that currencies had to remain within the narrow (2.25 percent) fluctuation bands for two years prior to the beginning of stage three. With a reintroduction of the narrow bands nowhere in sight, the initial Maastricht EMU goal of 1996 now appeared highly unlikely. Nevertheless, the commission reaffirmed the Maastricht timetable at a meeting on August 6.[111] At a meeting on August 26, Chancellor Kohl and Prime Minister Balladur also claimed that the original EMU schedule was still valid.[112] Much more realistic, however, was Kohl's admission more than two weeks previously that EMU might have to be delayed "by a year or two."[113]

Final Ratification

It is ironic, or perhaps appropriate, that Britain's formal ratification of the Maastricht Treaty would come in the midst of the second currency crisis, which effectively buried any hopes for early EMU and struck a further blow at pretensions to European unity. Nonetheless, after enduring a tortuous route through Parliament, fending off demands for a popular referendum, and surviving in July another vote of confidence and a last-minute court challenge, the British government finally secured ratification of the Maastricht Treaty in early August.[114]

Now all that remained was final German ratification, which was awaiting a decision by the Federal Constitutional Court. This came on October 12. In the ruling, the Court rejected claims that the Maastricht Treaty involved the loss of national sovereignty and might force Germany into monetary union under terms to which it objected. The Court also rejected calls for a popular referendum on Maastricht, yet argued that the Community should strive to become more democratic.[115] The Court's verdict was pleasing to the Kohl government, which was nevertheless somewhat embarrassed that Germany, among the chief promoters of the treaty, was the last country to ratify it.[116]

On October 29, EC leaders held a special summit in Brussels to celebrate ratification of the Maastricht Treaty, which was to come into force on November 1. From this date, the Community officially became known as the European Union. At the Brussels meeting, Community leaders reaffirmed the Maastricht timetable for EMU, although after the currency adventures of the previous fourteen months few now believed that the timetable could actually be followed. As if to reinforce the claim that it would, EC leaders announced that stage two would begin on January 1, 1994, as planned and that the new EMI, which was to begin operation on this date, would be based in Frankurt.[117]

Notes

1. *Financial Times,* December 12, 1991, p. 14.

2. On the commission's reaction to the EPU treaty, see Robert Wester, "The European Commission and European Political Union," in Finn Laursen and Sophie Vanhoonacker, eds., *The Intergovernmental Conference on Political Union: Institutional Reforms, New Policies, and International Identity of the European Community* (Dordrecht, The Netherlands: Martinus Nijhoff, 1992), pp. 213–214.

3. On the other hand, some members of the EP felt the treaty gave more to the EP than had been originally expected. On the Parliament's reaction to the Maastricht Treaty, see Sophie Vanhoonacker, "The European Parliament and European Political Union," in Laursen and Vanhoonacker, eds., *The Intergovernmental Conference on Political Union,* pp. 222–224. See also Andrew Duff, "Ratification," in Andrew Duff, John Pinder, and Roy Pryce, eds., *Maastricht and Beyond: Building the European Union* (London: Routledge, 1994), pp. 65–66.

4. *New York Times,* December 14, 1991, p. A5.

5. *Financial Times,* December 20, 1991, pp. 1, 2; January 13, 1992, p. 12.

6. *New York Times,* July 2, 1991, p. A6; July 3, 1991, p. A5; July 7, 1991, p. A4. On EC policy toward Yugoslavia, see Pia Christina Wood, "European Political Cooperation: Lessons from the Gulf War and Yugoslavia," in Alan W. Cafruny and Glenda G. Rosenthal, eds., *The State of the European Community,* vol. 2, *The Maastricht Debates and Beyond* (Boulder: Lynne Rienner, 1993), pp. 233–244.

7. *New York Times,* December 8, 1991, p. A7; December 24, 1991, p. A3; January 16, 1992, p. A6. *Financial Times,* December 17, 1991, p. 1; *Economist,* December 21, 1991, p. 57; Wood, "European Political Cooperation," pp. 235–236.

8. *Financial Times,* January 16, 1992, p. 16.

9. *New York Times,* January 11, 1992, p. A4.

10. Ibid.; *Financial Times,* January 11–12, 1992, p. 2; January 18–19, 1992, p. 6. On the dispute between France and Germany over Yugoslavia and its impact on Franco-German relations, see Philip H. Gordon, *France, Germany, and the Western Alliance* (Boulder: Westview Press, 1995), pp. 53–66.

11. *New York Times,* January 24, 1991, p. A3.

12. Quote from *Der Spiegel;* cited in *New York Times,* January 7, 1992, p. A2.

13. *Financial Times,* February 10, 1992, p. 10. On the "Delors II" budget package, see Michael Shackleton, "The Community Budget After Maastricht," in Cafruny and Rosenthal, eds., *The State of the European Community,* pp. 373–389. See also Andrew Scott, "Financing the Community: The Delors II Package," in Juliet Lodge, ed., *The European Community and the Challenge of the Future,* 2d ed. (New York: St. Martin's Press, 1993), pp. 69–88.

14. *Financial Times,* February 22–23, 1992, p. 2; March 17, 1992, p. 2; March 24, 1992, p. 1.

15. *Financial Times,* April 8, 1992, p. 2; May 5, 1992, p. 18.

16. *Financial Times,* May 16–17, 1992, p. 4.

17. *Economist,* December 19, 1992, p. 19. See also Justin Morris and Juliet Lodge, "Appendix: The Referendums," in Lodge, ed., *The European Community and the Challenge of the Future,* p. 386.

18. *Financial Times,* May 14, 1992, p. 3.

19. *New York Times,* May 17, 1992, p. A8; May 22, 1992, p. A6.

20. Kenneth E. Miller, *Denmark: A Troubled Welfare State* (Boulder: Westview Press, 1991), p. 181.

21. *New York Times,* June 3, 1992, p. A1. On Danish views on European integration, see Morton Kelstrup, ed., *European Integration and Denmark's Participation* (Copenhagen: Copenhagen Political Studies, 1992); Hanne Norup Carlsen, Ross Jackson, and Neils I. Meyer, eds., *When No Means Yes: Danish Visions of a Different Europe* (London: Adamantine Press, 1993).

22. Ibid.; *Financial Times,* June 4, 1992, p. 6.

23. *Financial Times,* June 4, 1992, p. 1.

24. On the impact of the Danish veto on the Maastricht debate in Britain, see Stephen George, "The British Government and the Maastricht Agreements," in Cafruny and Rosenthal, eds., *The State of the European Community,* pp. 185–189.

25. *New York Times,* June 4, 1992, p. A1; June 12, 1992, p. A3.

26. Cited in *Financial Times,* December 12, 1991, p. 3. See also the various articles under the cover headline "Angst um die Mark," *Der Spiegel,* December 9, 1992, pp. 124–131.

27. *Financial Times,* December 7–8, 1991, p. 3; December 12, 1991, p. 3.

28. The phrase "our wonderful money" (*unser schönes Geld*) is taken from a front-page headline of *Bild-Zeitung,* December 5, 1991. In a poll conducted in February, 57 percent of responding Germans were opposed to EMU; see *Der Spiegel,* February 17, 1992, p. 47. After the Danish veto, 52 per cent of Germans polled claimed they would vote against the Maastricht Treaty in a referendum; see *Der Spiegel,* June 29, 1992, p. 44.

29. "Survey of Germany" (Special Supplement), *Economist,* May 23, 1992, p. 15.

30. *Financial Times,* December 6, 1991, p. 2; *Financial Times,* December 12, 1991, p. 16.

31. Cited in *Financial Times,* December 11, 1991, p. 2. The conservative press was not alone in arguing that EMU would subvert German monetary stability. For criticism of EMU from the liberal or left-of-center press, see *Der Spiegel,* February 17, 1992, p. 20.

32. *Financial Times,* April 29, 1992, p. 2.

33. *New York Times,* June 12, 1992, p. A3.

34. Deutsche Bundesbank, "The Maastricht Decisions on the European Economic and Monetary Union," *Monthly Report of the Deutsche Bundesbank* 44, 2 (February 1992): 51–52. For articles on this document, see *Financial Times,* January 29, 1992, p. 1; February 8–9, 1992, p. 2.

35. See comments by Wilhelm Nölling, president of the state (*Land*) central bank of Hamburg; cited in *Financial Times,* February 26, 1992, p. 2. See also comments by Otmar Issing, a member of the Bundesbank's executive board; cited in *Financial Times,* March 7–8, 1992, p. 2. For a more detailed critical analysis of the Maastricht EMU agreement by a member of the Bundesbank's governing Central Bank Council, see Wilhelm Nölling, *Monetary Policy in Europe After Maastricht* (New York: St. Martin's Press, 1993), pp. 167–195.

36. *Financial Times,* March 24, 1992, p. 4. See also earlier comments by the Bundesbank's Issing that imply that the final stage of EMU should await further agreement on political union; cited in *Financial Times,* March 7–8, 1992, p. 2. The Bundesbank's emphasis on political union as a precondition for EMU was not necessarily new. In a September 27, 1990, speech in London, Bundesbank vice president Schlesinger had argued that EMU required the creation of "relevant political structures"; reprinted in *Auszüge,* October 1, 1990, pp. 1–5. The need for political union as a basis for EMU was also stressed

by Tietmeyer in a speech delivered in Venice on November 22, 1991; cited in *Financial Times,* November 23–24, 1991, p. 2.

37. Pöhl's comments were made in a book published in May and were cited in *Financial Times,* May 15, 1992, p. 2.

38. See, for instance, the comments made by Finance Minister Waigel; reported in *Financial Times,* December 23, 1991, p. 2.

39. *Financial Times,* March 6, 1992, p. 16.

40. Cited in Nölling, *Monetary Policy in Europe,* p. 146.

41. *Financial Times,* March 30, 1992, p. 1; May 5, 1992, p. 3; *Economist,* May 23, 1992 ("Survey on Germany"), p. 16.

42. This announcement was contradicted, however, by the call for outright rejection of the Maastricht Treaty made in March by Oskar Lafontaine, the SPD's candidate for chancellor in the 1990 elections. Lafontaine's statement embarrassed others in the SPD and was repudiated by the party leadership. See *Financial Times,* March 7–8, 1992, p. 2; March 10, 1992, p. 1.

43. See comments by SPD chairman Björn Engholm; cited in *Financial Times,* December 12, 1991, p. 3.

44. *Financial Times,* March 7–8, 1992, p. 2; March 10, 1992, p. 1.

45. *Financial Times,* March 13, 1992, p. 14.

46. *International Herald Tribune,* June 8, 1992; quote cited in Hugh Miall, *Shaping a New European Order* (London: RIIA, 1994), p. 85.

47. *New York Times,* June 4, 1992, p. A1.

48. *Financial Times,* June 5, 1992, p. 1; *New York Times,* June 5, 1992, p. A4.

49. *Financial Times,* June 4, 1992, p. 4.

50. Desmond Dinan, *Ever Closer Union? An Introduction to the European Community* (Boulder: Lynne Rienner, 1994), pp. 185–186. See also Morris and Lodge, "Appendix," pp. 392–393.

51. *New York Times,* June 21, 1992, p. A7.

52. *Financial Times,* June 4, 1992, p. 4; June 5, 1992, p. 2.

53. On the ratification debate in France, see Patrick McCarthy, "France Looks at Germany," in Patrick McCarthy, ed., *France-Germany, 1983–1993: The Struggle to Cooperate* (New York: St. Martin's Press, 1993), pp. 67–68; Françoise de la Serre and Christian Lequesne, "France and the European Union," in Cafruny and Rosenthal, eds., *The State of the European Community,* pp. 153–155; Morris and Lodge, "Appendix," pp. 393–395.

54. *New York Times,* July 22, 1992, p. C1.

55. *New York Times,* September 14, 1992, p. A1; September 15, 1992, p. A1.

56. *Financial Times,* September 1, 1992, p. 1; September 4, 1992, p. 1; September 5–6, 1992, p. 6; *New York Times,* September 13, 1992, p. E5.

57. Dinan, *Ever Closer Union?* p. 187.

58. However, exit polls showed that only 10 percent of French voters cast their vote for or against the president, or for domestic political reasons; results cited in de la Serre and Lequesne, "France and the European Union," pp. 153–154.

59. *Der Spiegel,* September 28, 1992, p. 18.

60. *New York Times,* September 17, 1992, p. A1; September 18, 1992, p. A1; October 8, 1992, p. C1. For an account of the September 1992 EMS crisis, see Jörg Bosche, "Franco-German Economic Relations," in McCarthy, ed., *France-Germany, 1983–1993,* p. 88. See

also David M. Andrews, "The Global Origins of the Maastricht Treaty on EMU: Closing the Window of Opportunity," in Cafruny and Rosenthal, eds., *The State of the European Community,* pp. 115–117. For a description of Bundesbank actions during the ERM crisis, see Nölling, *Monetary Policy in Europe,* pp. 205–207.

61. *New York Times,* September 18, 1992, pp. A1, C5; September 19, 1992, p. A1.

62. For a description of Bundesbank efforts to aid the franc in September 1992, see Nölling, *Monetary Policy in Europe,* pp. 205–207.

63. The text of the Franco-German statement is quoted in ibid., p. 206.

64. *New York Times,* September 24, 1992, pp. A1, C6; September 25, 1992, p. C1; September 26, 1992, pp. A3, A17; *Economist,* October 3, 1992, p. 81.

65. Boche, "Franco-German Economic Relations," pp. 88–89. See also Roger Morgan, "France and Germany as Partners in the European Community," in McCarthy, ed., *France-Germany, 1983–1993,* pp. 94–95.

66. *New York Times,* September 24, 1992, p. C6.

67. *Der Spiegel,* September 28, 1992, pp. 18–19.

68. "Pöhl: Währungsunion zwischen Deutschland und Frankreich möglich," *Frankfurter Allgemeine Zeitung,* September 22, 1992; cited in Dana Allin, "Germany Looks at France," in McCarthy, ed., *France-Germany, 1983–1993,* p. 44. See also *Der Spiegel,* September 28, 1992, pp. 23–28.

69. "Gegen EG der zwei Geschwindigkeiten," *Frankfurter Allgemeine Zeitung,* September 30, 1992; cited in Allin, "Germany Looks at France," p. 44.

70. *New York Times,* September 29, 1992, p. C1.

71. *New York Times,* October 7, 1992, p. C2.

72. *New York Times,* October 1, 1992, p. A4; October 7, 1992, p. C2.

73. *Financial Times,* October 2, 1992, p. 1; October 3–4, 1992; October 10–11, 1992, p. 1; *New York Times,* October 6, 1992, p. A5; October 11, 1992, p. A11.

74. *Financial Times,* October 17–18, 1992, pp. 1, 2; *New York Times,* October 17, 1992, p. A1; October 18, 1992, p. A5.

75. For discussion of the principle of subsidiarity, see Andrew Duff, ed., *Subsidiarity Within the European Community* (London: Federal Trust, 1993). See also Brigid Laffan, "The Treaty of Maastricht: Political Authority and Legitimacy," in Cafruny and Rosenthal, eds., *The State of the European Community,* pp. 43–44; "Twelve Men in Search of a Common Meaning," *Financial Times,* December 7, 1992.

76. The principle of subsidiarity is also important for subnational governments, such as the German *Länder,* in their efforts to prevent constitutionally delegated powers from being usurped by Brussels. On the various interpretations of the principle of subsidiarity, see Kees Van Kersbergen and Bertjan Verbeek, "The Politics of Subsidiarity in the European Union," *Journal of Common Market Studies* 32, 2 (June 1994):215–236. See also Anthony Teasedale, "Subsidiarity in Post-Maastricht Europe," *Political Quarterly* 64 (April–June 1993):187–209.

77. *New York Times,* June 21, 1992, p. A7.

78. *New York Times,* June 27, 1993, p. A3.

79. *Financial Times,* October 13, 1992, p. 1.

80. *Economist,* December 19, 1992, p. 49; Dinan, *Ever Closer Union?* pp. 189–190.

81. *Financial Times,* October 10–11, 1992, pp. 1, 3.

82. *Financial Times,* October 29, 1992, p. 1.

83. *Financial Times,* October 30, 1992, p. 1; October 31–November 1, 1992; November 10, 1992, p. 1; *New York Times,* November 14, 1992, p. A3.

84. *Economist,* December 19, 1992, p. 48; Dinan, *Ever Closer Union?* p. 191. See also Morris and Lodge, "Appendix," pp. 386–391, which includes documentation of the Edinburgh agreement on the Danish opt-outs.

85. *Financial Times,* November 30, 1992; *Economist,* December 5, 1992, p. 56.

86. *Economist,* December 19, 1992, pp. 48–49.

87. *Financial Times,* November 6, 1992, p. 1.

88. *Financial Times,* November 10, 1992, p. 1; November 7–8, 1992.

89. *Frankfurter Rundschau,* December 3, 1992, p. 1. On the new powers for the federal states, see *Der Spiegel,* November 23, 1992, pp. 37–38; *Frankfurter Rundschau,* December 2, 1992, p. 7.

90. Duff, "Ratification," p. 61. For a text of the Bundestag resolution, see Nölling, *Monetary Policy in Europe,* p. 141.

91. *Frankfurter Rundschau,* December 3, 1992, p. 1.

92. *Economist,* February 6, 1993, p. 56.

93. *Financial Times,* February 4, 1992, p. 2; May 2–3, 1992, p. 2.

94. Barabara Lippert et al., *German Unification and EC Integration: German and British Perspectives* (London: RIIA, 1993), pp. 120–122.

95. Michael Sutton, "France and the European Union's Enlargement Eastward," *The World Today* 50, 8–9 (August–September):153–154.

96. Mitterrand originally made his proposal for a European confederation on December 31, 1989. On this concept, see Ernst Weidenfeld, "Mitterrands Europäische Konföderation: Eine Idee im Spannungsfeld der Realitäten," *Europa-Archiv* 46, 17 (1991):513–518. On the conflicts between France and Germany over Eastern Europe and EC enlargement, see Gordon, *France, Germany, and the Western Alliance,* pp. 46–53.

97. *New York Times,* April 25, 1993, p. A9; *Economist,* June 26, 1993, p. 64.

98. *Economist,* May 22, 1992, pp. 55–56.

99. *Economist,* February 13, 1993, p. 62; March 13, 1993, p. 64; July 17, 1993, pp. 56–57; *New York Times,* April 25, 1993, p. A9.

100. *Economist,* May 22, 1993, pp. 57–58.

101. *Financial Times,* November 23, 1992, p. 1.

102. *Economist,* January 9, 1993, pp. 67–68; February 6, 1993, pp. 76–77; March 6, 1993, p. 19; *New York Times,* February 1, 1993, pp. C1, C3; February 5, 1993, p. C1.

103. *Economist,* February 13, 1993, pp. 73–74.

104. *Economist,* May 15, 1993, pp. 16–17.

105. *New York Times,* April 9, 1993, p. C2; *Economist,* April 24, 1993, p. 76.

106. *Economist,* June 26, 1993, pp. 7, 82–83.

107. *New York Times,* April 9, 1993, p. C2. Similarly, during Bastille Day celebrations (July 14) President Mitterrand had declared that defense of the franc was "a priority" and that preserving its parity with the D-mark was "a necessity"; quoted in *Economist,* July 17, 1993, p. 41.

108. *New York Times,* April 9, 1993, p. C2; *Economist,* July 17, 1993, p. 41.

109. *Economist,* July 17, 1993, p. 69; July 31, 1993, pp. 65–66; August 7, 1993, pp. 21–22; *Financial Times,* December 23, 1993, p. 4.

110. *Financial Times,* December 23, 1993, p. 4; *Economist,* August 7, 1993, pp. 21–23; *New York Times,* September 23, 1993, p. C2.

111. *Economist,* August 14, 1993, p. 43.

112. *Economist,* August 28, 1993, p. 12.

113. *Economist,* August 14, 1993, p. 43.

114. *Economist,* August 7, 1993, p. 54.

115. *Economist,* October 16, 1993, p. 52.

116. For German reactions to the Court's decision, see *Der Spiegel,* October 18, 1993, pp. 28–32.

117. *Economist,* November 6, 1993, pp. 56–61.

6

Consolidating the Union

With the final ratification and enactment of the Maastricht Treaty in November 1993, the Community left behind its "period of waiting and gloom,"[1] and the new European Union was born. The new name for the Community was more than just symbolic, however, for it was abundantly clear to many that a new era of European integration had begun. In this chapter, the prospects for European integration in the post-Maastricht era are examined. After a brief analysis of the sources of the post-Maastricht crisis, developments within the EU since November 1993 are discussed. Since ratification of the treaty, the EU has entered a new phase of pragmatism and consolidation. At the same time, the EU has begun preparations for its next major intergovernmental conference, to be opened in 1996. The purpose of this conference, called for by the Maastricht Treaty, is both to review the intergovernment arrangements established by the treaty and prepare the future of European integration. After a brief survey of some of the key items on the agenda of the 1996 conference, the chapter concludes with a discussion of some important future challenges for the Community.

Evaluating the Post-Maastricht Crisis

After the Maastricht Treaty was agreed on in December 1991, the Community fell victim to two separate, though interrelated and overlapping, developments. The first of these was the popular backlash against the Maastricht Treaty and further European integration; this backlash led to a prolonged ratification crisis and delayed final ratification of the treaty by ten months. The second was the currency upheavals of 1992–1993; these nearly destroyed the ERM, a key institutional basis for monetary union, and called the Maastricht timetable for EMU into serious doubt.

The Anti-Maastricht Backlash

The widespread popular backlash against the Maastricht Treaty and further integration took European and national leaders by surprise. There is no simple explanation for this phenomenon. Certainly domestic politics and nationally specific factors played a key role in individual countries, especially those in which referendums on the treaty were held.[2] In addition, however, a number of more general concerns were important. One of these was fear of Germany. Although supporters of the treaty argued that further integration was needed precisely to limit German power and independence, many Europeans apparently felt that integration would only enable Germany to extend its dominance. In this regard, the visible linkage among German monetary policy, the Maastricht plans for EMU, and economic recession and unemployment throughout Europe only bolstered the claims of treaty opponents. Ironically, even though the citizens of some EC countries opposed Maastricht because of fears of German hegemony, many Germans were opposed to the treaty because they felt it would lead to a loss of national power and sovereignty.

Popular concern about the loss of national identity and sovereignty was an important reason for the backlash against Maastricht in other countries as well. This concern revealed the continued strength of national feelings and identities in Europe, indicating that these had not been diminished by growing interdependence and integration; in fact, they may even have been strengthened. It is also clear that many Europeans opposed the Maastricht Treaty because they feared the centralization of political power in the hands of distant and nonaccountable bureaucrats in Brussels. For this reason, the issue of subsidiarity became an important one during the ratification crisis. Despite the increased emphasis given to subsidiarity by both the commission and national leaders after June 1992, however, many Europeans remained unconvinced that the Maastricht Treaty did not represent a profound threat to national sovereignty and independence.

Opposition to the Maastricht Treaty also stemmed from the Community's democratic deficit—that is, to the limited democratic legitimacy and accountability of EC institutions. Through additional integration, political power would be further concentrated in institutions beyond the control of popularly elected representative assemblies, either the EP or national parliaments. For this reason, many Europeans feared that Maastricht would result in a loss of democratic control over government. Closing this democratic deficit remains a key task for the Community in the future.

Yet another dimension of the democratic deficit was the elitist manner in which the treaty was negotiated and then presented to the public for ratification. On several occasions during the intergovernmental conferences, Delors had made the seemingly perverse statement that only in reluctant Britain had the potential consequences of the treaty been openly discussed and debated.[3] The implication of his remark was that countries in which the treaty had not been properly debated could experience significant popular opposition once the Maastricht Treaty was presented to an unprepared public as more or less a fait accompli. Delors's fears proved to be well founded.

In the wake of the anti-Maastricht backlash, therefore, the general consensus was that the intergovernmental negotiations had been conducted in a manner that was much too secretive and did not sufficiently engage the public. Future intergovernmental conferences, all parties agreed, will have to be both more open and transparent and make greater efforts to involve and educate the public. That this lesson may have been learned is evidenced by preparations for the 1996 conference, with the commission emphasizing that it wants to "make Europe the business of its citizens." The commission's new head, Jacques Santer, has urged national governments to initiate public debate on integration before the end of the 1996 conference and has suggested the wider use of popular referenda to validate the conference's outcomes.[4]

Opposition to the Maastricht Treaty also reflected the general crisis of political institutions in Europe in the early 1990s.[5] In almost every European country at this time, there was a growing mistrust of established politicians and political parties. This feeling was manifested in such phenomena as the proliferation of far right and extremist parties, declining voter turnouts, and the diminished vote shares of mainstream parties of both the left and the right. Mistrust was also revealed in the abysmal popularity ratings of current leaders such as Mitterrand, Kohl, Major, and González, many of whom had been in office for more than a decade and whose leadership had begun to grow stale. Making things more difficult for the Maastricht Treaty was the fact that many of these now-unpopular leaders had been important actors in the negotiation process and were therefore closely identified with the treaty.

Among the main reasons for this general crisis of political institutions were Europe's severe economic and unemployment problems and the apparent inability of government to do much about them. There were also corruption scandals and abuses of political power in nearly every major country, nowhere more severe than in France and Italy, which only fanned the flames of popular mistrust of politicians and government. In this context, opposition to the further centralization of political power in the hands of nonaccountable EC bureaucrats is understandable. At the same time, voting against the Maastricht Treaty was a convenient means of punishing unpopular leaders, or entire political classes, that were closely associated with the treaty. The Maastricht Treaty, therefore, was in some ways a victim of this previously existing political crisis, the roots of which extend back at least a decade. Nevertheless, the treaty itself, given the elitist manner in which it was negotiated and its somewhat nondemocratic contents, contributed to and exacerbated this crisis.

In the final analysis, the popular rebellion against Maastricht revealed the existence of a sizable gap between the views of political elites and those of average citizens about European integration. For elites, integration was a means for dealing with large-scale economic and geopolitical problems, such as the management of growing interdependence and the control of a united and more powerful Germany. These were not the primary concerns of most citizens, however, who generally focused on more immediate problems of economic security and survival and did not see the link between international institutions/agreements and their own everyday economic situation. For this gap to be closed, European elites will have to do a much better job of convincing their publics that integration is necessary and that it can improve their lives. In the words of one top adviser to Chancellor Kohl, "The argument for the next steps of integration will have to be much more political than for Maastricht."[6]

The ERM Crisis

Also undermining the Maastricht Treaty and plans for further integration were the currency crises of 1992 and 1993. The functioning of the ERM and plans for EMU contributed to these crises, as did general economic stagnation and high unemployment throughout Europe. A major problem of the narrow-band ERM was its intermediate status, representing something in between a flexible floating-rate system and a permanently fixed exchange-rate regime. Instead, currency rates in the ERM were semifixed, meaning they could be adjusted by explicit government decision. As many experts have noted, such a system works well if governments are willing to occasionally adjust or realign rates according to economic needs and circumstances.[7] The ERM, however, became too rigid. After 1987, in fact, there were no currency realignments within the system until the September 1992 crisis. A primary reason for the absence of currency alignments was the EC's plans for monetary union, which began to take shape in 1988 with the work of the Delors Commission and which required substantial economic convergence as a precondition for membership. With governments throughout Europe staking their prestige on EMU, there was considerable resistance to currency devaluations and realignments.

The problem was that such realignments became increasingly necessary in the early 1990s, as Europe was plunged into recession and unemployment grew to record levels. To keep national currencies within the ERM at their established parities, and to meet the strict convergence criteria set at Maastricht, national governments and central banks had to push interest rates ever higher to match or exceed those of Germany's Bundesbank. By summer 1992, it was becoming increasingly clear that most EC countries could no longer afford to do this. The solution was either to significantly reduce interest rates and devalue currencies or to substantially lower German rates. With a primary focus on the domestic inflation picture, and a determination to preserve autonomy from government and political control, the Bundesbank adamantly refused the latter course of action. Nevertheless, other EC governments stubbornly resisted lower interest rates and devaluations, despite growing internal political pressure to do so. In an international currency market of more than $1 trillion per day, speculators were soon able to force EC governments to accept reality. When the pent-up pressure for realignment finally blew, it was almost enough to destroy the system altogether.

Thus, given the context of the unrestrained international movement of capital, the ERM provided an inadequate basis for achieving the Maastricht goals of convergence among sovereign countries with widely divergent economic conditions and needs. Not only was there no central political authority to enforce uniform economic and budgetary policies, thus prohibiting currency speculators from pressuring individual governments within the system, but also at the heart of the ERM was a national central bank (the Bundesbank) with no mandate, or inclination, to look beyond the domestic realm and make its policies with Europe-wide conditions in mind. After a lengthy study of the ERM, EC finance ministers in May 1993 concluded that there was nothing fundamentally wrong with the ERM mechanism. Instead, they argued that the problems of the previous months were largely the fault of bad policy decisions made by individual governments.[8] This may in large part be true, but in association with the political pressures created by plans for EMU, the ERM proved ineffective. Only two months after the finance ministers' report, the ERM almost collapsed.

The Maastricht EMU agreement only compounded the existing problems of the ERM. Motivated largely by the desire to integrate Germany, the Maastricht Treaty set the deadline of 1999 for achieving full EMU. Only in this manner, European political leaders felt, could an irrevocable German commitment to monetary union be gained and a united Germany be firmly bound to European institutions. The result of such politically motivated haste, however, was that, in the words of one unnamed Western official, "politicians got out ahead of the economies."[9] Because of considerable political determination to see EMU succeed, the Maastricht Treaty and European integration soon became synonymous in the minds of many Europeans with economic austerity, stagnation, and growing unemployment. Rising popular discontent with the economy not only fed the political rebellion against Maastricht but also made the economic policies of some national governments increasingly untenable in the minds of international currency speculators.

Clearly, a key factor in the breakdown of the ERM was German unification and its economic consequences. Although the initial economic impact of unification was largely positive, with an upsurge in German demand pulling in exports from other European countries, this effect was soon reversed.[10] After unification the federal government chose to finance the rebuilding of eastern Germany through borrowing rather than higher taxes. By 1991 massive government subsidies to the eastern states, growing public-sector deficits, and overly generous wage settlements for eastern workers were generating substantial inflationary pressures, thus forcing the Bundesbank to throw on the monetary brakes with higher interest rates. The consequences of this policy for the economies of other EC countries that were linked to Germany through the ERM, and for the Maastricht EMU plans, have already been discussed. In more normal economic times, it could be argued, without the historically unique complications of German unification, the Maastricht timetable for EMU might have been feasible, although the foregoing discussion of the ERM casts some doubt on this assumption as well. However, it is also possible that without the spur of German unification, the Maastricht agreement on EMU, at least in the form it eventually took, might never have been negotiated in the first place.

The New Pragmatism

As a result of the ratification and currency crises, the Community was plunged into a new period of pessimism. Also contributing to this new pessimism were a number of other events and problems. Among these were the bloody and intractable conflict in Yugoslavia and the Community's hesitant and ineffective response to it. At the beginning of the Yugoslav civil war in summer 1991, the foreign minister of Luxembourg—the current holder of the EC presidency—had bravely declared that this was now "the hour of Europe."[11] The Community's subsequent failure to resolve the turmoil in its own backyard, however, made a mockery of the Maastricht pretensions to a common foreign and security policy while revealing just how far the EC was from being a unified external political actor. What was instead displayed was the continued lack of European institutional capacity in foreign and security policy, as well as the absence of truly common interests and will.[12] The Yugoslavia debacle only increased skepticism about the Community among many Europeans, while it was profoundly embarrassing and demoralizing for EC leaders and proponents.

Another problem affecting the mood of the Community was the prolonged conflict over GATT trade negotiations. This conflict mainly pitted the United States against the EC over the issue of agricultural trade. It also, however, led to considerable friction within the Community, especially between France and Germany.[13] An agreement to conclude the multilateral Uruguay Round was originally slated to be signed in December 1990 but was scuttled by developments in Europe and the EC's focus on internal matters. Over the next three years, a GATT agreement was held up mainly by the French government's opposition to reduced CAP subsidies for farmers and French concerns about the effects of liberalized trade more generally. Export-oriented Germany, however, was more favorably disposed toward trade liberalization and pushed hard for a GATT deal. By the time a Uruguay Round agreement was finally concluded in December 1993, the tensions between France and Germany over this issue had become significant.[14]

The new pessimism within the Community led to renewed questions about the future of European integration. After the currency crisis of July–August 1993, if not before, there was no longer much doubt that EMU in 1997—the first possible date set for the beginning of stage three—was impossible; this despite the official rhetoric of EU officials and some national governments to the contrary. Equally questionable were plans for further political union. Although few believed that the EU would not hold together and remain an important trade and economic organization, there was now increased doubt about the political goal of achieving an ever-closer union of European nation-states. As the prestigious *Economist* magazine declared in August 1993, what the second ERM crisis and accompanying political turmoil signified, above all else, was "the death of Europe's federal illusions."[15] Similarly, after the Maastricht Treaty's final ratification in November 1993, a prominent member of Chancellor Kohl's own party alliance, Bavarian premier Edmund Stoiber, declared, "We [Germany] are no longer striving for a European federal state." Preferable to this, he claimed, was a "simple confederation" in which "nation states maintain a dominant role."[16] Even among the most ardent supporters of European Union, the Maastricht ratification crisis and related difficulties had generated considerable doubts about the EU's future identity and purpose.

One important consequence of this new pessimism was a new pragmatism in Brussels and national capitals. After the first Danish referendum, EC leaders became much more modest about political union goals. They also took pains to emphasize the principle of subsidiarity and stressed their opposition to further cessions of national sovereignty to Brussels. By spring 1993, at the latest, the focus had shifted even further from discussion of grandiose plans for institution building—or European "theology," as British prime minister Major liked to term it[17]—to more immediate and practical concerns, such as economic growth and jobs. A key lesson drawn by EC leaders from the anti-Maastricht rebellion was that average Europeans felt the Community had little relevance to their basic needs and concerns. Unless EC leaders could prove otherwise, and demonstrate what the EC could do to help improve Europe's dismal economic situation, Community leaders realized that plans for further integration had little chance of being accepted by an increasingly skeptical and disgruntled public.

As a result, the economy and unemployment were dominant themes at a June 21–22 EC summit in Copenhagen. At this meeting, Delors sketched his preliminary thoughts on promoting more economic growth and employment in the Community, as well as Europe's international competitiveness. His plan took the form mainly of coordinated spending by national governments on research and development and infrastructure projects. National leaders asked the commission to further develop these ideas and to present them at a December European Council meeting in Brussels.[18]

Despite the new emphasis on pragmatism, Delors could not resist the temptation to cast his ideas in grandiloquent terms and by fall was talking of Europe's need for "a New Deal so that it can be both powerful and more united."[19] The white paper on "Growth, Competitiveness, Employment" that he eventually presented to the EC summit in Brussels on December 10–11, however, was actually rather modest in scope. Instead of centralized Community policies, it proposed a list of nonbinding options for member governments within the context of coordinated measures for labor market deregulation, macroeconomic stability, and infrastructure spending. As such, the paper reaffirmed the movement away from centralized federalism and toward decentralization within the Community. It also, some believed, signaled a growing acceptance within Europe of the British or Anglo-Saxon view of economic policy, which emphasized market forces and labor-market deregulation as the best prescription for growth and employment, as opposed to the more statist and corporatist continental tradition.[20]

The new pragmatism within the EU was also manifested in the Community's increased focus on Eastern Europe. A key criticism of the Maastricht Treaty was that it did not give sufficient attention to the needs and interests of postcommunist countries, nor did it sufficiently recognize that "Europe" was more than just the member states of the EU (i.e., Western Europe). Germany, which had strong economic and security interests in the stability and prosperity of the countries to its east, particularly insisted that more attention be paid to Eastern Europe. Since 1989 the EU had negotiated a series of trade and economic association agreements with individual Eastern European countries, the most recent being the "Europe Agreements," the first of which were signed with Hungary, Poland, and Czechoslovakia in December 1991. Nevertheless, these agreements were riddled with exceptions and safeguard clauses aimed at protecting politically sensitive industries such as agriculture, textiles, and steel and fell far short of providing the access to Community markets that Eastern European countries required.[21] The EC had also given considerable multilateral economic assistance to Eastern Europe, much of it in the form of loans through the European Bank for Reconstruction and Development. And the Phare program provided technical aid and advice.[22] As with the trade agreements, however, Eastern European governments complained that these measures were not enough.

The subject of Eastern Europe was on the agenda of the June 1993 Copenhagen summit. At Copenhagen EC leaders agreed to accelerate the pace of trade liberalization measures and decided to increase formal political ties with Eastern European governments. They also promised eventual membership for postcommunist countries that met certain conditions. To qualify for membership in the Community, Eastern European countries would have to be stable democracies and market economies and be governed by the rule of law. They would also have to ensure adequate rights for ethnic and cultural minorities. A further condition was "the Union's capacity to absorb new members, while maintaining the momentum of European integration."[23] This condition, of course, hinged on the EU's internal politics and struggle for self-definition and in the end could prove more of an obstacle to Eastern European countries than the other conditions.

By early 1994, the issue of Eastern Europe had been given new urgency by the success of the ultranationalist Vladimir Zhirinovsky in Russian elections in December and by President Bill Clinton's demand, made at a January NATO summit, that the EU play a greater role in assisting the Eastern European countries. In response, Delors announced a wide-ranging study of EU relations with Eastern Europe, including the possibility of foreign policy cooperation and new security links through associate membership in the WEU. It was now time, Delors declared, to think in terms of a "Greater Europe."[24]

The integration of Eastern Europe received a further boost from Germany's EU presidency in the second half of 1994. On assuming the presidency, the German government declared the integration of Eastern Europe to be a central priority.[25]

This goal was reaffirmed by EU foreign ministers at a September meeting in Bansin (Germany).[26] Further movement in the direction of eastern enlargement was achieved at the December European Council in Essen (Germany). At this meeting, EU leaders promised to provide prospective Eastern European members with a firmer road map for accession by spring 1995. They also held out the prospect of membership for some Eastern European countries around the year 2000.[27] In May 1995, the commission produced the promised road map for accession; this consisted of a detailed listing of legal and administrative reforms Eastern European countries would have to make before they could be admitted to the Community. It also offered some technical assistance in support.[28] The hopes of Eastern European countries for early EU membership were further bolstered in early July 1995 when Chancellor Kohl, during an official visit to Warsaw, suggested that Poland could join the EU by 2000.[29]

Another key issue occupying the EU after ratification of the Maastricht Treaty was the EFTA enlargement. Formal negotiations with Austria, Sweden, and Finland had begun in February 1993 and were later joined by Norway. Much discussion in these negotiations focused on narrow economic issues that were of particular interest to individual countries, such as oil and fisheries for Norway and property ownership and transportation for Austria. Common to all the applicants were concerns about agriculture and regional aid. Also problematic was the subject of budgetary contributions for the new members. Nevertheless, these and other issues were successfully negotiated, and by mid-March 1994 the entry agreements were ready to be signed.[30]

The signing of the entry agreements was delayed, however, by a late-breaking dispute over the issue of voting procedures in the Council of Ministers. In question was the number of votes required for a "blocking minority" in qualified majority voting in the council. To this point, a blocking minority had required twenty-three votes out of a total of seventy-six, meaning that an alliance of two large countries and one small country was sufficient to block the approval of legislation.[31] With the increase of total votes in the council to ninety after enlargement, it was proposed to increase the size of the blocking minority proportionately to twenty-seven. This move was strongly opposed by Britain and Spain, which feared being more easily outvoted on issues of national importance in an enlarged EU. Instead, they favored retaining a blocking minority of only twenty-three votes. These demands angered other EU governments and put the enlargement talks at risk. In the end, a compromise was reached that changed the blocking minority to twenty-seven votes, yet allowed outvoted states to delay legislation for an undefined "reasonable period" to enable a consensus to be forged.[32]

With the dispute over voting procedures resolved, the entry agreements with Austria, Sweden, Finland, and Norway were signed on March 30,[33] and were then approved by the European Parliament in May. All that now remained before these countries could formally join the EU was for the citizens of each to ratify the entry agreements in popular referendums. Ratification was accomplished by Austria in a June referendum and by Finland and Sweden in votes held in the fall. A minor setback for the Community occurred, however, when the citizens of Norway failed to approve EU membership in a referendum on November 29.[34] Nevertheless, on January 1, 1995, Austria, Sweden, and Finland entered the EU, bringing the total number of Community member states to fifteen.

Another key turning point for the EU came in January 1995 with the departure from office of Jacques Delors. As it turned out, the December 1993 white paper on "Growth, Competitiveness, and Employment" was Delors's final major contribution to the Community and his last important act as commission president. In January Delors stepped down after ten years in office and handed over the reins of the EU executive to Jacques Santer, a former prime minister of Luxembourg. With Delors's departure, an extraordinary period in the history of European integration came to an end. This had been an era of considerable activity and ambition, although it had ended amid disappointment and frustration with the course of events since 1991. In an important sense, the change in commission leadership in January 1995 also signified the EU's shift to a more pragmatic and modest phase of development.[35] On assuming office, Santer made it amply clear that he did not favor bold new steps toward integration but rather sought to consolidate the gains made by the Community in recent years.[36]

The transition in commission leadership was not accomplished without difficulty, however. At a June 1994 European Council meeting on the Greek island of Corfu, the British government had vetoed the first choice of Germany and France—and all other EU member states—for commission president, Jean-Luc Dehaene of Belgium. Among other things, the Major government considered Dehaene too much of a federalist. Perhaps even more important, however, was Britain's objection to the high-handed manner in which the French and German governments had simply decided on and then announced their choice for commission president without fully consulting other EU countries. This action smacked too much of the traditional Franco-German axis and a way of doing things within the Community that Britain was committed to changing. What Britain's action at Corfu mainly accomplished, however, was to infuriate other EU member states—already upset by London's actions to delay the EFTA accession agreements—and further isolate Britain within the Community. Following the British veto of Dehaene, a compromise agreement on Santer as the new commission head was quickly reached and was announced on July 15.[37]

In the spirit of consolidating existing gains, in 1995 the Community moved to finally implement the Schengen Agreement to eliminate intra-EU border controls. This agreement had been originally signed in 1985 and was then renegotiated in 1990. The signatories to the agreement—France, Germany, the Benelux countries, Spain, Portugal, Italy, and Greece—had agreed to eliminate all physical border controls (i.e., passport and customs checks) by January 1993 so that the free movement of goods and people would coincide with the formal opening of the Single Market. A series of political disputes and technical problems repeatedly delayed implementation of the accord, however. Nevertheless, on March 26, 1995, all of the Schengen countries other than Italy and Greece removed border controls with each other.[38] Although the implementation of the Schengen Agreement represented a partial victory for European integration, the continued refusal of some EU countries to join the accord indicated a significant divergence of national views and interests within the Community. These differences were highlighted by France's announcement in June 1995 that it wished to further delay full implementation of the Schengen Agreement and retain its border control for another six months, a move that infuriated other agreement signatories.[39] Following a wave of terrorist bombings in Paris, the French government announced in September 1995 that the dismantling of border controls could be delayed even further.[40]

Toward 1996

The intergovernmental conference scheduled to begin in 1996 is the next major milestone for the EU. At this conference, called for in Article N of the Maastricht Treaty, national representatives will review the new intergovernmental arrangements for CFSP and judicial and home affairs created by the treaty and consider possible changes to the EU's institutional structure.

Although not officially on the conference agenda, one key issue in 1996 will be the question of how to proceed with EMU. By spring 1995, only tiny Luxembourg fully met the economic convergence criteria set at Maastricht, and it was apparent to most observers that a majority of the EU's fifteen member states would not meet these criteria by 1997, as required by the Maastricht Treaty if EMU is to occur at this date. This reality was underscored by the EMI's first annual report, issued in April 1995, which noted the considerable distance most EU countries had yet to travel before meeting the Maastricht convergence goals, especially in the area of allowable levels of public debt.[41] Even so, the commission and some member states, particularly France, had persisted in their optimism that EMU could occur in 1997.[42] Nevertheless, at the June 26–27 European Council in Cannes (France), national leaders formally abandoned the goal of EMU in 1997 and accepted 1999 as a much more realistic date.[43] The prospects for EMU occurring at this date remain uncertain as well, however, given Europe's continued economic dificulties and widespread popular opposition to further integration, not to mention the continued reluctance of the Bundesbank to surrender monetary sovereignty. Other problems still to be resolved include disputes about the actual implementation of stage three and the name for a common currency. At the Cannes summit, national leaders agreed that final decisions on these matters should await the December European Council in Madrid.[44]

In fall 1995, however, uncertainty about EMU grew after comments made by German Finance Minister Waigel; these appeared to suggest that Germany favored a further strenghtening of the Maastricht convergence criteria for EMU membership. Waigel also cast doubt on Italy's ability to qualify for stage three by 1999. These comments were taken as further indications of German reluctance to give up the D-Mark for a single currency and generated renewed turbulence in international currency markets.[45] To counter doubts about EMU and to calm currency markets, EU leaders meeting in Majorca (Spain) on September 23 reaffirmed both the Maastricht convergence criteria and the 1999 target date.[46] Nevertheless, comments made two days after the meeting by Waigel and Bundesbank President Tietmeyer made it clear that Germany was hardening its stance on which countries would qualify for stage three and that it would pursue a strict interpretation of the convergence criteria.[47] As a consequence, by late September there was growing speculation that the implementation of stage three could be delayed beyond 1999 to allow more countries to qualify, a prospect that EU and national governments continued to officially deny.[48]

A central purpose of the 1996 conference will be to assess the functioning of the intergovernmental arrangements, or pillars, for CFSP and judicial and home affairs (immigration, police) that were established by the Maastricht Treaty. A key question will be whether these arrangements should be incorporated into the EU's supranational decisionmaking structures, thus allowing a greater role for the commission, European Parliament, and Court of Justice. At this time (October 1995), such an incorporation appears highly unlikely because of the pronounced intergovernmentalist trend within the EU since the Maastricht ratification crisis.

Otherwise, a number of suggestions have been made for improving the effectiveness of these arrangements. Concerning the CFSP, for instance, a January 1995 commission report suggested the increased use of qualified majority voting and the appointment of an executive head of CFSP to give it more leadership and focus. The report also proposed the formation of an EU intervention force under common command.[49] Support within the Community for greater defense cooperation also appears to be growing, with most proposals centering on strengthening the role and effectiveness of the WEU. Considerable disagreement remains, however, over whether the WEU should be incorporated as the EU's defense arm or remain organizationally separate. In particular, Britain has opposed formally linking the two institutions.[50]

Also at the 1996 conference, national representatives will discuss the reform of EU decisionmaking institutions and procedures. It is generally recognized that such reforms are necessary to enable a much larger Community to function effectively and to enhance the EU's democratic legitimacy and accountability. The basic decisionmaking structures of the EU were established in 1957 by the Treaty of Rome, at a time when the Community had only six members. By 1995 the EU had expanded to fifteen member states, although with only minimal alterations of its decisionmaking institutions and procedures. A decisionmaking system that had already become highly complicated, and was often ineffective, now threatens to become totally paralyzed as a result of further enlargement.

Much attention at the conference will be given to the question of majority voting in the Council of Ministers. Many within the Community argue that an expanded use of qualified majority voting—and the consequent diminution of unanimity voting—is necessary for greater efficiency in the development of common policies, particularly in view of the Community's impending enlargement. Nevertheless, the question of majority voting is a highly sensitive one since the increased use of this procedure would dilute the assumed right of national veto over EU policy in cases of vital national interest, a right that has been honored within the Community since the 1966 Luxembourg compromise. The move to more majority voting, therefore, poses a direct challenge to national sovereignty and is for this reason strongly opposed by Britain and some other EU countries. Instead of more supranationality, the British government favors protecting national sovereignty through clearer development and stronger application of the principle of subsidiarity.

The issue of institutional reform will clearly be a central one at the 1996 conference, and decisions on reform will be necessary before further enlargement can be considered. Various ideas have already been put forward. Among these are proposals made in August 1993 by parliamentary leaders of Germany's governing CDU/CSU. These proposed the concept of a "double majority" for the Council of Ministers, whereby measures subject to majority voting would require support from a majority of member states representing a majority of the EU's population. Unanimity voting, according to this proposal, would be replaced by a "superqualified" majority of four-fifths or three-quarters of the member states representing an equal proportion of the EU population. Also proposed were a reduction in the size of the commission from seventeen to ten members and a rotation of the EU presidency between large and small states rather than alphabetically.[51] Another suggestion for institutional reform involves the creation of a longer, two- or three-year EU presidency. This would give the Community a more visible and stable political leadership and allow larger member states to exercise greater influence over EU policy. With many of these proposals, however, a key issue will be protection of the rights and interests of smaller member states and their position and role in the Community relative to larger countries.

Another institutional question to be considered at the conference concerns the powers and role of the European Parliament. Germany, in particular, has long favored increased powers for the EP, because of domestic politics and Germany's own federalist governmental structures and traditions. Also, as the EU's most populous member state, Germany has the EP's largest national delegation.[52] Beyond this, however, the German government views a stronger EP as a necessary democratic counterweight to the technocratic and politically autonomous European Central Bank called for in the Maastricht Treaty. Nevertheless, a stronger EP is opposed by other EU countries, especially France and Britain. France favors a dominant role for the EU's major intergovernmental institutions—the European Council and Council of Ministers—arguing that only through decisions made by the democratically elected governments of sovereign states will the EU achieve legitimacy and accountability. Otherwise, France has suggested a stronger role for national parliaments in EU affairs as a means of addressing the Community's democratic deficit.

At the 1996 conference, as in the Maastricht negotiations, a key conflict will pit those member states favoring a more deeply integrated federal Europe against proponents of a looser intergovernmental confederation. Among the federalists is Germany, which desires not only a greater role for the EU in foreign policy and defense, as well as in judicial and internal security affairs, but also more majority voting in the EU's Council of Ministers (i.e., the dilution or reduction of national veto rights) in these and other policy areas. At the same time, Germany has demanded expanded powers for the EP as a means of making the EU more democratic. Joining Germany in the federalist camp are Spain, Italy, and the Benelux countries, although many smaller states have concerns that their interests would find little voice in a more powerful, proportionally constituted EP. These states therefore differ from Germany in favoring a stronger commission as their primary representative.

In opposition to the federalists, those favoring an intergovernmental EU want to preserve national veto rights as far as possible. Although not necessarily opposed to greater cooperation in the realms of foreign policy and defense, countries such as France and Britain want decisionmaking in these sensitive areas to remain based on consensus while otherwise retaining a predominant role for large states in qualified majority voting. They also oppose stronger powers for either the EP or commission, instead favoring the leading role of the Council of Ministers and European Council. Beyond this, however, substantial differences exist between key states in the intergovernmentalist camp concerning the extent of EU involvement in different policy realms. Whereas France prefers more common efforts in such areas as industrial, technology, and social policy, Britain would like to keep EU involvement in national policies and affairs to a minimum. As this example indicates, beyond a simplistic differentiation between federalists and intergovernmentalists, it is difficult to generalize about the diverse positions and views of the EU's fifteen member states, each with their own histories, traditions, institutions, and patterns of domestic politics. As a result, the structure of national interests regarding European integration is exceedingly complex, meaning that interstate differences of interest will be a major factor inhibiting agreement on the EU's future institutional development.

A second key division between member states that will affect the outcome of the 1996 conference, and the future of European integration more generally, is that between rich and poor member countries. Since the 1970s, integration has been facilitated by the transfer of economic resources from wealthy northern European countries to poor southern ones, mostly in the form of regional development aid and cohesion funds. Such transfers helped mitigate the gap between rich and poor countries while also buying the votes of poor countries for further integration—a move necessitated by the unanimity required to approve treaty amendments to the Community's constitution. Economic hardship and the growing resentment of taxpayers in rich countries, however, have led to a declining willingness to fund north-south transfers of wealth. In particular, Germany, which is the largest net contributor to the EU budget and which since 1990 has been faced with the tremendous economic costs of rebuilding its eastern states, has balked at continuing in its role as "paymaster for Europe." Conflict between rich and poor states, therefore, will have a major impact on the direction, pace, and uniformity of future EU integration. It will also affect EU enlargement into Eastern Europe since this will lead to even more competition for available regional assistance.

A final item on the 1996 conference agenda is the fundamental question of the future shape and purpose of the EU. This question is even more vital in view of the EU's impending enlargement, which will only further diversify the Community and enhance the potential for interstate conflicts of interest. One possibility for reviving the momentum of integration may involve rethinking the basic design of the EU and deciding to proceed according to a multispeed approach. In this manner, those countries that are both economically able and politically willing to proceed with futher integration may do so and not be held back by those that are either unable or unwilling. The idea of a multispeed EU is a highly controversial one, however, since it implies the creation of a "core-periphery" Europe or a Europe of different classes of states. Nevertheless, the increased discussion of this concept since fall 1994 indicates that a multispeed approach to further integration could be used in the future.[53]

Future Challenges

Beyond the 1996 conference, several key issues will play an important role in the future of European integration. These issues include enlargement, the democratic deficit, and the continued German problem.

Enlargement

Among the most pressing issues confronting the EU in the future will be the matter of enlargement. Queued up behind the three EFTA countries that joined the EU in January 1995 are a host of other prospective members, most of them in Eastern Europe. First in line are the postcommunist states that have made the most progress toward economic and political reform and are the closest geographically to the EU: Poland, Hungary, and the Czech Republic. Each of these countries has already formally applied for EU membership; entry negotiations will probably begin sometime after the conclusion of the 1996 conference. Behind these three countries are a number of other Eastern European states, including Slovakia, Romania, Bulgaria, the Baltic states, and the former Yugoslav republics of Slovenia and Croatia. These countries are relative laggards in economic and political reform and are also geographically more distant from the EU. For these reasons, membership for them is a possibility only in the long-term future.

Finally, there are also the Mediterranean applicants Malta and Cyprus, as well as the reluctant EFTAns: Switzerland, Iceland, and Liechtenstein.

The issue of enlargement raises a number of serious problems for the EU and its member states.[54] There is, quite obviously, the question of institutional reform, necessary for a larger Community of up to two dozen members to function effectively. Even with such reform, however, the prospect of a larger and more diverse EU calls into serious question the ability of a Community of more than two dozen members to achieve its ultimate goals of full economic and political union.

Another problem raised by enlargement is the economic threat to heavily protected EU farmers and basic industries posed by lower-cost producers in Eastern Europe. Such threats could prompt resistance to enlargement by EU member states in which these economic sectors are important. Attempts to protect such interests have already limited the access of Eastern European producers to the Community market under the economic association agreements negotiated since 1989. There is also the question of the CAP, which will have to be drastically reformed or eliminated before Eastern European countries can be admitted since to include these highly inefficient agricultural economies in the current system would simply be too costly. However, given the highly political and symbolic nature of the CAP, and the problems experienced with past efforts at agricultural reform, CAP reform promises to be extremely difficult.[55]

A further problem posed by enlargement concerns labor markets. Full membership in the EU would mean that the citizens of Eastern European countries would be free to move throughout the Community in search of employment. For EU countries that are already experiencing an average unemployment rate of over 10 percent, however, the prospect of labor markets suddenly flooded with thousands of skilled Polish, Czech, and Hungarian job seekers is not a pleasant one. There is also the issue of EU development and regional assistance since new Eastern European entrants would compete with current member states for an already limited amount of funds. The poorer EU countries that currently receive the lion's share of regional assistance, therefore, are likely to oppose enlargement without a consequent increase of such funds. Any attempt to enlarge this segment of the EU budget, however, is certain to encounter stiff resistance from wealthier, yet financially strapped, member states such as Germany.

Also affected by enlargement, and therefore another key factor determining its pace, will be the EU's internal political balance, especially among the largest member states. Within a larger EU Germany's influence would most likely be enhanced, while that of France would decrease because an EU that widens to the east will have Germany at its geographical center, with France pushed to the periphery. Because of this geographical centrality and close cultural and economic ties with Central and Eastern European countries, Germany would undoubtedly be the political center of a wider EU. At the same time, within a wider EU control of Germany through integration would become even more difficult since a larger and more diverse Community would presumably be much harder to integrate.[56]

Nevertheless, because of Germany's vital interests in Eastern Europe—Chancellor Kohl has termed it "unthinkable" that Germany's border with Poland "shall remain the eastern border of the European Union"[57]—enlargement may be necessary to resolve the German problem. As Delors has emphasized, "If the rest of the Community wants Germany to remain firmly anchored inside the EC, Eastern Europe cannot be left outside it."[58] France also appears to increasingly realize that its support for EU enlargement is necessary to preserve close Franco-German relations.[59] It is not only Germany, however, that favors a rapid enlargement of the Community. Enlargement is also desired by Britain, precisely because this would presumably inhibit deeper integration. In Britain's view, a larger EU would be more likely to become the looser association of independent nation-states—a sort of glorified free trade area—that it prefers.

The internal political implications of enlargement were evident in conflicts that emerged over the entry of Austria and the Nordic countries. While Germany and Britain pushed for the early admission of these countries, France resisted, wanting greater consolidation among existing EC members before any discussion of Community widening. Only with the onset of the Maastricht ratification crisis did the French government change its mind, becoming convinced that enlargement was necessary to maintain the momentum of European integration. Nevertheless, France and other countries were upset by the ardor that Germany displayed in pushing the pace of entry negotiations; in particular, they objected to the use of heavy-handed tactics by German officials to bring the negotiations to a successful conclusion.[60] Although these tensions reflected concern about increased German assertiveness, they also stemmed from fears about the German agenda for EU enlargement into Eastern Europe.[61] Partly to counter the growing eastward tilt of the Community promoted by Germany, although also motivated by the real perception of growing security threats from Islamic fundamentalism and immigration, France stressed greater attention to the Mediterranean and Northern Africa during its EU presidency in the first half of 1995.[62]

The Democratic Deficit

A second key issue affecting the future of European integration is the problem of the democratic deficit, meaning the limited accountability of EU decisionmaking institutions to democratically elected representative assemblies and the lack of transparency and openness in EU decisionmaking. Both of these factors, in turn, contribute to the most crucial element of the democratic deficit: the EU's lack of democratic legitimacy. As the popular backlash against Maastricht demonstrated, the nation-state continues to be widely regarded as the proper locus of legitimate political authority, and there is little public support for the further transfer of government power to the EU level. Whether this is due mainly to concerns about the lack of accountability, the opacity of technocratic-bureaucratic decisionmaking, or fears about the loss of national identity and sovereignty is not quite clear, although undoubtedly each of these factors is involved to some extent.

One thing that the Maastricht debate did make clear is the extent of the gap between elite and popular views on European integration. With some notable exceptions, European governments and political elites regard further integration as a necessity to allow national governments to better meet the challenges of interdependence and to contain the power of a united Germany. The popular reaction to Maastricht, however, indicates that these views are not widely shared by average Europeans or at least that they have quite different concerns. In fact, among many Europeans the perception is not that EU integration represents the solution to pressing economic and political problems but that it is instead a key cause of these problems. In many cases, the Maastricht ratification process provided European citizens with their first opportunity to directly voice an opinion about the acceleration of EU integration since the late 1980s, and the critical response indicates that many are not too happy with the results thus far.

Undoubtedly, a major reason for the negative popular response to Maastricht was the elitist manner in which decisionmaking and the treaty negotiation process had taken place, allowing for little public discussion and debate. This process, however, was nothing particularly new since European integration had always been pretty much an elite affair. Although this elitism was largely by design,[63] it was also the case that European publics had consistently displayed a high degree of disinterest in matters concerning Europe, as evidenced by the poor turnouts for EP elections since these were begun in 1979. The anti-Maastricht backlash, however, indicates that this "permissive consensus" no longer exists.[64] It also indicates that the elitist-technocratic model of European integration—or "integration from above"—may finally have reached its limits and that future integration efforts must consciously inform and involve average Europeans.[65] Doing so, of course, will only make the integration process slower and more politicized and therefore more problematic. As such, the democratic legitimacy problem of the EU and the necessary steps to correct it will pose a major barrier to further integration.

This barrier is even more significant in view of the new directions that European integration has taken since the late 1980s. Prior to the Maastricht Treaty, the Community focused primarily on negative integration through the removal of barriers to trade and economic activity between member states.[66] Such integration may limit the capacity of states to make independent policies in certain areas, but it does not require them to formally surrender or cede sovereignty. Instead, as some have argued, by enabling governments to more effectively confront the challenges of interdependence, negative integration can actually enhance national sovereignty.[67] With the Maastricht Treaty's plans for EMU and greater political union, however, EU member states have begun to engage in positive integration, or the joint provision of public goods through the construction of common institutions and policies. In contrast to negative integration, positive integration involves the potential transfer of significant aspects of national authority to supranational institutions.

The movement toward positive integration is perhaps a major reason for the erosion of the permissive consensus among European publics and the heightened political salience of the democratic deficit.[68] Because of the essentially negative nature of EC integration, European publics were easily indifferent to the Community and the integration process in previous decades. It is unrealistic to expect that they will remain so, however, now that the EU's institutional development has moved onto a qualitatively new and different plane. What is more, these new integration efforts are taking place in policy areas (money, foreign policy, security, and defense) that are generally regarded as core aspects of national sovereignty and identity. As such, efforts to integrate in these areas can be expected to provoke strong feelings and reactions among the citizens of European countries.

At the same time, it is doubtful that European citizens will assent to the transfer of key elements of national sovereignty and substantial decisionmaking authority to EU institutions without the accompanying extension of mechanisms for democratic accountability and control. Until now democratic accountability and legitimacy have been the exclusive properties of nation-states. While the absence of democratic accountability in EC institutions may have been acceptable for intergovernmental cooperation and negative integration, it is plainly inadequate for the sort of supranational "high politics" union that is envisioned for the future and toward which the Maastricht Treaty points. Wanting to retain ultimate sovereignty and political authority, however, while at the same time ceding ever-more-important parts of national power to European institutions, national governments are bound to resist such an enhancement of the EU's democratic legitimacy, thus setting up what could be an epic struggle for governmental power and rights in the future.

In the final analysis, European integration is no longer simply an elite project. Instead, the changing nature of integration efforts, from sovereignty-enhancing negative integration to sovereignty-undermining positive integration, has served to mobilize popular interest and participation in EU affairs. Initially, at least, this mobilization is likely to be essentially a defensive engagement as European publics react to the possible loss of national sovereignty and identity and increased bureaucratic centralization. Such defensiveness, in fact, appears to describe much of the popular opposition to the Maastricht Treaty. In the longer term, however, one can expect that popular engagement will turn more positive, seeking to extend links of democratic accountability and control from the national to European level, parallel to the actual transfer of government powers and authority to EU institutions. Finding ways to do this, while at the same time preserving national autonomy and distinctiveness, will be a major challenge for the EU and its member states in the future.

The Continued German Problem

A third key issue for the future of European integration is the German problem. After 1989 Germany sought to answer questions about its commitment to

European integration by agreeing to EMU and by acting as a primary advocate of further political union. Nevertheless, questions about Germany's future orientation and role in Europe remain, as does the basic problem of how to accommodate within European institutions a Germany that is too large to be treated as just another country, yet not dominant enough to be truly hegemonic.[69]

For the forseeable future, much of EU politics will continue to revolve around the German problem, and the path of European integration will be greatly shaped by the interplay of its two complementary sides: on the one hand, actions taken by other countries out of fear of German power and dominance and, on the other, the actual use by Germany of its enhanced leverage and influence. This situation poses a potential dilemma: Given substantial economic and political interests in the EU, and a desire to assuage the fears of neighbors through further self-containment, Germany can be expected to continue to push for more European integration. Such pressure, however, is likely to be viewed with suspicion by other EU countries, which might resist or seek to delay what they perceive as a German attempt to extend dominance through regional institutions. In a similar fashion, Germany's desire for rapid enlargement into Eastern Europe could be resisted by its EU partners, for which stability in the former communist bloc is not of the same pressing economic and political importance. The result could be increased German frustration with the EU and a declining tendency for Germany to regard its own national interests and those of the Community as identical. In this manner, fears of German independence and unilateralism could, in the end, become a self-fulfilling prophecy.[70]

One factor promoting more German assertiveness and independence in the future will be domestic politics. From the opening of the Berlin Wall until the signing of the Maastricht Treaty, Germany's European policy was conducted in a fairly autonomous fashion by Chancellor Kohl and other top government officials. Since December 1991, however, there has been an upsurge of public interest in European integration, motivated primarily by concern about loss of the D-mark and monetary sovereignty. At the same time, with the initial shock and euphoria of unification over, many Germans have begun to question whether they want to surrender further sovereignty to the EU at precisely the moment that Germany has fully regained or newly acquired it and is now once again in a position to exercise power and influence in the world.

In the future, therefore, Germany's European policy will likely be increasingly driven and constrained by domestic politics, leaving the federal government less able to act in an autonomous fashion in the EU arena. Among other things, this constraint is ensured by new constitutional provisions that require approval by both houses of parliament for future integration agreements. It is also ensured by the growing centrality of European issues in domestic politics and elections, as indicated by the formation in January 1994 of a new political party (the Free Citizens' Alliance) dedicated mainly to opposing further integration.[71] Within Chancellor Kohl's own CDU/CSU as well, there is a growing skepticism about European integration.[72] In addition to opposing EMU, many Germans have become increasingly resentful of Bonn's traditional role as the financial paymaster for Europe and feel that Germany should give more attention to its interests in Eastern Europe.

That such an upsurge in German national consciousness is occurring should not be surprising. After unification many prominent Germans sought to assure other countries that Germany had adequately absorbed the lessons of the past and as a result of its unique postwar experiences of limited sovereignty and integration into international institutions represented a new type of "postnational" state. For this reason, according to Foreign Minister Genscher, a united Germany rejected the "power politics of the past" in favor of a new "politics of responsibility."[73] He also claimed that "we want to commit Germany to Europe, not to the nation-state ideal."[74] As some have argued, however, this postnational *Sonderweg* (special path) was largely a product of the unique circumstances of the cold war, making it inevitable that a united Germany would return to more hardheaded calculations of national interest.[75] It has also been suggested that Community enlargement could affect Germany's behavior since within a larger and more diverse EU, Germany's focus on specific national interests will become both more necessary and likely.[76] Unification and the end of the cold war, in other words, have accelerated the process of Germany becoming a normal nation-state.

A key aspect of the German problem is the Franco-German relationship. Traditionally the foundation of European integration, this crucial bilateral partnership has come under considerable stress as a result of unification and the end of the cold war. It has thus far survived, however, mainly through cooperation to achieve and promote the Maastricht Treaty. Nevertheless, disagreements on a number of issues since 1991, including Yugoslavia, monetary policy, GATT trade negotiations, and EU enlargement, have further strained the relationship. At the same time, the enhancement of German power at the expense of France after 1989 has significantly altered the essential balance between these two countries and created a structural basis for future conflict and rivalry. How Germany and France resolve the problems created by this new imbalance of power will be a major factor affecting the future development of the EU and European integration.

Notes

1. These were the words of Delors; cited in *Economist*, October 16, 1993, p. 51.

2. For the argument that domestic politics was the key factor promoting opposition to the Maastricht Treaty in countries holding referenda, see Mark Franklin, Michael Marsh, and Lauren McLaren, "Uncorking the Bottle: Popular Opposition to European Unification in the Wake of Maastricht," *Journal of Common Market Studies* 32, 4 (December 1994): 455–472.

3. *Financial Times*, April 23, 1992, p. 16.

4. *Financial Times*, May 11, 1995, pp. 2, 14.

5. On the crisis of political institutions in Europe, see Martin Jacques, "The End of Politics," *Sunday Times*; reprinted in *World Press Review* (November 1993):23–25. See also *New York Times*, August 11, 1993, p. A1.

6. Quoted in *Economist,* July 3, 1993 ("Survey of the European Community"), p. 7.

7. For analysis of the ERM's flaws, see *Economist,* October 23, 1993, pp. 25–27. For a critical assessment of the ERM that is nevertheless more positive about the future of EMU, see Peter G. Rogge, "Monetary Union in Europe: End of a Dream or Beginning of a Nightmare?" in Paul Michael Lützeler, ed., *Europe After Maastricht: American and European Perspectives* (Providence: Berghahn Books, 1994), pp. 113–124.

8. *Economist,* May 29, 1993, pp. 74–89.

9. Quoted in *New York Times,* September 27, 1992, p. E6.

10. For an analysis of German economic policy afer unification and its impact on the rest of Europe, see Paul J.J. Welfens, "The New Germany in the EC," in Alan W. Cafruny and Glenda G. Rosenthal, eds., *The State of the European Community,* vol. 2, *The Maastricht Debates and Beyond* (Boulder: Lynne Rienner, 1993), pp. 159–176. See also David M. Andrews, "The Global Origins of the Maastricht Treaty on EMU: Closing the Window of Opportunity," in Cafruny and Rosenthal, eds., *The State of the European Community,* pp. 114–115.

11. *Financial Times,* July 1, 1991, p. 1.

12. On EC policy toward Yugoslavia, see Pia Christina Wood, "European Political Cooperation: Lessons from the Gulf War and Yugoslavia," in Cafruny and Rosenthal, eds., *The State of the European Community,* pp. 233–242.

13. On the GATT negotiations, with an emphasis on the conflict between the United States and EC, see Finn Laursen, "The EC, the United States, and the Uruguay Round," in Cafruny and Rosenthal, eds., *The State of the European Community,* pp. 245–263.

14. *Economist,* October 2, 1993, pp. 49–50; *New York Times,* November 30, 1993, p. C1; December 14, 1993, p. C7.

15. *Economist,* August 7, 1993, p. 15.

16. *Economist,* November 6, 1993, p. 61; *Financial Times,* November 3, 1993, p. 1.

17. *Economist,* June 26, 1993, p. 53.

18. Ibid., pp. 53–54.

19. *Economist,* November 6, 1993, p. 56.

20. *Financial Times,* December 13, 1993, p. 21; *Economist,* December 11, 1993, pp. 53–54.

21. On the Europe Agreements, see Jackie Gower, "EC Relations with Central and Eastern Europe," in Juliet Lodge, ed., *The European Community and the Challenge of the Future,* 2d ed. (New York: St. Martin's Press, 1993), pp. 290–293.

22. On EC economic assistance to Eastern Europe, see ibid., pp. 294–297.

23. *Economist,* June 26, 1993, pp. 53–54.

24. *Financial Times,* January 29–30, 1994, p. 2; March 7, 1994, p. 1.

25. Klaus Kinkel, "Germany in Europe" (The Aims of the German Presidency of the European Union), *Statements and Speeches* 17, 7 (New York: German Information Center, 1994), pp. 3–4.

26. *Deutschland Nachrichten,* September 16, 1994, p. 2.

27. *Financial Times,* December 12, 1994, pp. 1, 2.

28. *Financial Times,* May 4, 1995, p. 2.

29. *Financial Times,* July 8–9, 1995, p. 22.

30. On the entry negotiations, see *Economist,* December 4, 1993, p. 58; February 12, 1994, pp. 49–50; February 19, 1994, p. 59; March 5, 1994, pp. 52–57; March 19, 1994, p. 64.

31. For majority voting in the Council of Ministers, the voting weight of EU member states is apportioned roughly according to size: Germany, France, Britain, and Italy have

ten votes each; Spain, eight; the Netherlands, Greece, Belgium, and Portugal, five; Denmark and Ireland, three; and Luxembourg, two. Under the terms of the March entry agreements, Sweden and Austria would have five votes each; Finland and Norway, three.

32. On the dispute over voting procedures, see *Economist,* February 26, 1994, p. 51; March 13, 1994, pp. 53–54; March 19, 1994, p. 64; April 2, 1994, p. 55; *Financial Times,* March 14, 1994, 13; March 17, 1994, p. 3; March 18, 1994, p. 1; March 23, 1994, p. 1.

33. *Economist,* April 2, 1994, pp. 49–50.

34. *Economist,* June 18, 1994, pp. 55–57; *New York Times,* November 30, 1994, p. A1.

35. For an analysis of the EU during the Delors years, with a particular emphasis on the period after 1990, see George Ross, *Jacques Delors and European Integration* (New York: Oxford University Press, 1995).

36. In a May 1995 speech in London, for instance, Santer insisted that "together we must now consolidate the EU. Perhaps now we need a little less ideology and more management and more concrete achievements"; quoted in *Financial Times,* May 5, 1995, p. 1. See also *Financial Times,* February 16, 1995, p. 1; April 21, 1995, p. 3.

37. *New York Times,* July 16, 1994, p. A3.

38. *Financial Times,* March 25–26, 1995, p. 2; March 27, 1995, p. 1; *New York Times,* March 27, 1995, p. A4. Austria, an observer member of the Schengen group since July 1994, was to fully implement the accord in April 1995. On the Schengen Agreement more generally, see Alan Butt Philip, "European Immigration Policy: Phantom, Fantasy, or Fact? *West European Politics* 17 (April 1994): 168–191. See also Juliet Lodge, "Internal Security and Judicial Cooperation," in Lodge, ed., *The European Community and the Challenge of the Future,* pp. 321–323.

39. The French move was possible since the original implementation of the accord was only for a three-month trial period. *Financial Times,* June 30, 1995, pp. 1, 3.

40. *Financial Times,* September 6, 1995, p.1.

41. *Financial Times,* April 5, 1995, p. 2.

42. The French government remained officially optimistic about a 1997 date for EMU at least until April 1995. See *Financial Times,* April 8–9, 1995, p. 1.

43. *Financial Times,* June 27, 1995, p. 1.

44. *Financial Times,* June 28, 1995, p. 2.

45. *Financial Times,* September 12, 1995, p. 2; September 23/24, 1995, p. 1.

46. *New York Times,* September 24, 1995, p. A8; *Financial Times,* September 25, p. 1.

47. *Financial Times,* September 26, 1995, p. 1.

48. *Financial Times,* September 27, 1995, p. 1; September 28, 1995, p. 4; *New York Times,* October 2, 1995, p. C2.

49. *Financial Times,* January 28–29, 1995, p. 2.

50. *Financial Times,* March 2, 1995, p. 12; March 16, 1995, p. 2.

51. *Financial Times,* August 25, 1993, p. 12; *Economist,* October 16, 1993, pp. 51–52.

52. As a result of unification, at the December 1992 Edinburgh European Council it was decided to increase the size of the German delegation from eighty-one to ninety-nine. The delegations of the other large member states (Britain, France, and Italy) were also increased from eighty-one to eighty-seven members each.

53. Increased discussion of a multispeed approach began with publication by the German CDU/CSU in September 1994 of a paper in which the creation of a "core Europe" centered on France and Germany was advocated. The CDU/CSU paper and the multispeed model are considered in more detail in the Conclusion.

54. On the issue of enlargement and the problems it poses for the EU, see John Redmond, "The Wider Europe: Extending the Membership of the EC," in Cafruny and Rosenthal, eds, *The State of the European Community*, pp. 209–225. See also Anna Michalski and Helen Wallace, *The European Community: The Challenge of Enlargement*, 2d ed. (London: RIIA, 1992).

55. On the problem of the CAP and its relationship to the EU's eastern enlargement, see *Economist*, August 20, 1994, p. 42. See also *Financial Times*, October 3, 1994, p. 19.

56. On the French position on EU widening, see Ronald Tiersky, "France in the New Europe," *Foreign Affairs* 71, 2 (Spring 1992):131–146. For a discussion of the conflicts between France and Germany over EU enlargement, see Philip H. Gordon, *France, Germany, and the Western Alliance* (Boulder: Westview Press, 1995), pp. 46–53.

57. *Financial Times*, March 24, 1994; cited in ibid., p. 52.

58. G. Merritt, *Eastern Europe and the USSR: The Challenge of Freedom* (London: Office for Official Publications of the EC, 1991); quote cited in Gower, "EC Relations with Central and Eastern Europe," p. 289.

59. Michael Sutton, "France and the European Union's Enlargement Eastwards," *The World Today* 50, 8–9 (August–September 1994):156.

60. *Financial Times*, March 17, 1994, p. 14; March 18, 1994, pp. 2, 16.

61. *Economist*, March 26, 1994, pp. 57–58.

62. *Financial Times*, December 12, 1995, p. 2; *Economist*, January 14, 1995, pp. 45–46.

63. For the argument that the European Community was originally designed in an elitist-technocratic manner, see Kevin Featherstone, "Jean Monnet and the 'Democratic Deficit' in the European Union," *Journal of Common Market Studies* 32, 2 (June 1994):149–170.

64. The concept of permissive consensus is developed in Leon N. Lindberg and Stuart A. Scheingold, *Europe's Would-Be Polity* (Englewood Cliffs, N.J.: Prentice-Hall, 1970), pp. 45–63. The authors also suggested that this consensus was relatively superficial and might not withstand a major increase in the scope or capacity of the Community (p. 277).

65. The limits to the technocratic-elitist model of integration were also recognized in Brussels. According to Delors's chief of staff, Pascal Lamy, in July 1992: "Europe has been built in a St. Simonian way from the beginning, this was Monnet's approach. The people weren't ready to agree to integration, so you had to get on without really telling them too much about what was happening. Now St. Simonianism is finished. It can't work when you have to face democratic opinion"; quoted in Ross, *Jacques Delors and European Integration*, p. 194.

66. On the distinction between negative and positive integration, see John Pinder, "Positive Integration and Negative Integration—Some Problems of Economic Union in the EEC," *The World Today* 24 (1968):88–110. See also Andrew Moravcsik, Book Review in *American Political Science Review* 88 (June 1994):510.

67. The argument that European integration has actually enhanced, rather than undermined, national sovereignty has been made most strongly by Alan Milward, *The European Rescue of the Nation State* (Berkeley and Los Angeles: University of California Press, 1992). See also David Calleo, "Rebalancing the U.S.-European-Soviet Triangle," in Gregory Treverton, ed., *Europe and America Beyond 2000* (London: RIIA, 1989), p. 49; Stanley Hoffmann, "Reflections on the Nation-State in Western Europe Today," *Journal of Common Market Studies* 21, 1–2 (September–December 1982):21–37.

68. For a similar argument, see Franklin, Marsh, and McLaren, "Uncorking the Bottle," p. 460.

69. This problem was recognized as early as 1967 by Chancellor Kiesinger, who stated that a united Germany would have a "critical size . . . too big to play no part in the balance of forces and too small to keep the forces around it in balance by itself"; cited in Timothy Garton Ash, "Germany's Choice," *Foreign Affairs* 73 (July–August 1994):67.

70. A similar scenario is painted by Steven Muller, "Democracy in Germany," *Daedalus* 123 (Winter 1994):53–55.

71. *Financial Times,* January 24, 1994, p. 12. In EP elections in June 1994, the Free Citizens Alliance and other anti-Europe parties did not perform very well.

72. *Financial Times,* September 4–5, 1993, p. 3; November 3, 1993, p. 1; November 5, 1993, p. 1; November 12, 1993, p. 1; *New York Times,* November 12, 1993, p. A5. See also Lothar Gutjahr, "Zwischen Politischer Union und nationaler Normalität: Die Europakonzepte der Regierungsparteien," *Die Neue Gesellschaft/Frankfurter Hefte* 6 (June 1994):533–542.

73. From a May 1990 speech at Georgetown University; quoted in *New York Times,* May 27, 1990, p. A25.

74. Comments made in a mid-1991 television interview; quoted in Peter H. Merkl, *German Unification in the European Context* (State College: Penn State University Press, 1993), p. 380.

75. See, for instance, Heinrich August Winkler, "Abschied von einem deutschen Sonderweg," *Die Neue Gesellschaft/Frankfurter Hefte* 7 (July 1993):633–636.

76. Hans-Peter Schwarz, "Germany's National and European Interests," *Daedalus* 123 (Spring 1994):86.

Conclusion: The End of the Cold War and the Future of European Integration

A key question posed at the beginning of this book was how the EC would adapt to the new geopolitical situation created by the end of the cold war and German unification. The initial impact of these developments was to push the Community toward further deepening of integration, as exemplified by the Maastricht Treaty, with its provisions for monetary and political union. Such deepening was deemed necessary to bind a united and more powerful Germany to the Community and put it in a better position to serve as the architectural cornerstone for a New Europe. At the same time, the Maastricht Treaty was a means for rebalancing the new internal political relations of the Community and for preserving the crucial Franco-German relationship. As this book has shown, the Maastricht Treaty was only partially successful in attaining these goals, and the problems posed by German power and the challenge of organizing the New Europe remain largely unresolved.

As this book has also discussed, this initial impulse toward deepening has faltered in the face of popular opposition to further integration and economic difficulty and uncertainty. The anti-Maastricht backlash led to a prolonged ratification crisis, which delayed the final ratification and enactment of the treaty by ten months while delivering a severe psychological blow to the Community. At the same time, instability in international currency markets, especially the successive currency crises of fall 1992 and summer 1993, nearly wrecked the ERM and raised serious questions about the Maastricht timetable for EMU.

Not all of these developments within the Community can be attributed to the geopolitical changes in Europe since 1989, of course. Even before the opening of the Berlin Wall, the EC had been moving toward EMU, with the Delors Plan for monetary union having already been prepared and approved by national leaders. What the events of 1989 did was to accelerate action on EMU, making it a matter of much greater geopolitical urgency, while at the same time generating pressures for adding political union to the EC agenda.

155

By the same token, the end of the cold war and German unification did not directly cause the Maastricht ratification crisis. These events did, however, contribute to this crisis in less direct ways. The geopolitical earthquake of 1989 was simply the latest in a series of profound changes affecting Western Europe since the early 1970s, including both accelerated economic globalization and intensification of EC integration. Among the consequences of globalization and integration have been levels of unemployment not seen since the 1930s and growing pressures on European welfare states, thus leading to a heightened sense of economic uncertainty and insecurity for many Europeans. To the extent that globalization and integration have promoted a shift of state functions to the EC and international institutions or to the market, they have also generated mounting confusion about the proper role of the state and national government authority in European societies.

The geopolitical changes in Europe since 1989 have been every bit as disorienting as the political-economic changes of the past two decades. The demise of the iron curtain and accompanying developments led to a tremendous influx of immigrants and asylum seekers into economically beleaguered Western Europe and further fueled already-mounting antiforeigner and nationalist sentiments. At the same time, the reunification of Germany regenerated primordial fears of German power and hegemony among many Europeans, however irrational these might appear to more detached political observers. Also, the prospect of U.S. disengagement from Europe threatened the protected niche within which prosperous Western European civilian powers had existed for more than four decades and raised troubling new questions about the future of European security in a potentially more unstable regional and global political environment.

In the face of such unsettling changes, European publics in the early 1990s were not in the mood to endorse bold new steps toward European integration. In fact, rather than representing a necessary step for dealing with new challenges and problems, as most European governments claimed, integration, in the view of many Europeans, was a major source of present economic and social difficulties. The transfer of even more power from the national level to Brussels could only exacerbate the problems created by two decades of change. It may, therefore, take some years before a disoriented and suspicious European public can accept greater economic and political integration.

At the same time, the geopolitical urgency of integrating Germany may have contributed to an overly ambitious schedule for EMU, one that got too far ahead of both public opinion and economic conditions. Yet another outgrowth of the end of the cold war with consequences for the Community was the costly unification process in Germany. Government spending to rebuild the east generated inflationary pressures in Germany, leading to increased interest rates by the Bundesbank in response. These increases placed considerable pressure on other EC countries, which could ill-afford to match high German rates. Economic strangulation by the ERM also led to increased resentment of Germany in other countries and thereby undermined public support for a German-centered EMU. German interest rate policy also placed the ERM under considerable strain, making it an irresistible target for international currency speculators.

Three Key Consequences

Beyond such immediate effects, what are the longer-term consequences of the end of the cold war and German unification for the EU and European integration? This book has argued that there are three. The first of these stems from the disappearance of the old iron curtain, which divided democratic and capitalist Western Europe from communist Eastern Europe. Among other things, this disappearance means that the EU cannot remain a fairly small and exclusive club and must confront its historical task of becoming an organization for all of Europe. The question of enlargement, or widening, therefore, is now on the Community's agenda.

As we have seen, the EC's initial response after 1989 was to deflect the question of enlargement and instead give primary attention to deepening the existing Community; the Maastricht Treaty, in fact, said almost nothing about Eastern Europe. The justification for this inward focus was that only a deeper EC could serve as the basis for a wider one. Now, however, with final ratification of the Maastricht Treaty and strong popular opposition to further deepening, enlargement has pushed its way to the top of the Community agenda. Enlargement has also been promoted by such key member states as Germany and Britain, although each for their own distinctly different reasons, and concern about rising Russian nationalism and the potential for instability in Eastern Europe. Nevertheless, as this book has pointed out, enlargement poses a host of difficult institutional, economic, and political problems and therefore represents a tremendous challenge to the Community. There can also be little doubt that as a result of enlargement the EU of the future will look very different from the one of today. Among other things, enlargement could prompt the Community to adopt more of a multi-speed or variable geometry approach to further integration.

Among the problems posed by enlargement is the EU's internal political balance, which has already been greatly affected by German unification and the fall of the iron curtain. The presence of a united and powerful Germany in the center of Europe has revived the German problem and fears of German independence and dominance. How to deal with this problem, either through deeper integration (as favored by France) or through a wider, less integrated Europe (as preferred by Britain) continues to be a key topic for debate. Also of major importance, the geopolitical changes since 1989 have affected the crucial Franco-German relationship. Germany has been among the primary winners of the end of the cold war, whereas France is generally considered a key loser. Enlargement of the Community eastward would only further enhance German power and influence by shifting eastward the EU's center of gravity both geographically and politically.

This shift would place Germany even more at the heart of the EU, whereas France would be in danger of being relegated to the periphery. Also, in a wider EU the Franco-German relationship could be undermined or replaced by increased German ties to Eastern European countries. Whether and how the Franco-German relationship can be preserved, along with the Community's internal political balance more generally, are key questions posed by the end of the cold war. How they are answered will be of primary importance for the future development of the EU.

Despite the strains generated by unification and the end of the cold war, the Franco-German relationship has thus far survived. As we have seen, this relationship brought the Maastricht Treaty to fruition; indeed, both capitals viewed it as a means of preserving close Franco-German ties in the altered geopolitical context of the New Europe. At the same time, Franco-German steadfastness and cooperation were a key source of stability for the Community during the turbulent days of 1992–1993 as it was rocked by both popular rejection of the Maastricht Treaty and currency crises. Absent Franco-German cooperation and determination full realization of the Maastricht Treaty's goals would be even more problematic than they currently are.

How the Franco-German relationship will fare in the future, however, remains uncertain, particularly in view of growing popular skepticism about the EU and European integration in both countries since December 1991. In both France and Germany, the basic purposes and value of integration are being reconsidered. For many French, the EU now seems much less a means for projecting French influence and containing Germany and more a trap leading to loss of national independence and German domination. Many Germans increasingly question why relations with France should continue to be given priority over pressing German economic and political interests in Eastern Europe. In both countries, but particularly in France, integration has contributed to a growing crisis of national identity.[1]

Equally uncertain is the attitude toward European integration of future generations of leaders in both Germany and France. A major objective of both Kohl and Mitterrand, as we have seen, was to set European unification on an "irreversible" course since both men were concerned about the commitment of their successors to this goal, as well as their ability to bring it about.[2] In this regard, some uneasiness was evident in Germany over the election of Jacques Chirac to succeed Mitterrand as the French president in May 1995. Not only had Chirac equivocated on European integration in the past, but also during his campaign he hinted that as president he might give a higher priority to the rejuvenation of French growth and employment than to the achievement of EMU.[3] At a first postelection meeting, however, Chirac went out of his way to assure Chancellor Kohl of France's continued commitment to the Maastricht goal of EMU.[4] In congratulating Chirac on his election, German president Roman Herzog informed the new president that not only would he be leading France into the next century and millennium but also that he would play an essential role in shaping "the future of the Franco-German partnership and thereby the fate of Europe for coming generations."[5]

One means of preserving the Franco-German partnership could be the adoption of a multispeed approach to future integration, in which these two countries form the nucleus of a deeper European economic and political union. The dynamics of the Franco-German relationship, in fact, could be one of the main factors promoting such an approach.

A third important way in which the end of the cold war has affected the EU is by altering its external political and security environment. For more than four decades, Western Europe was protected by the U.S.-led NATO alliance. In the first instance, this security system protected Europe against external aggression by the Soviet Union and its allies. It also, however, enhanced mutual confidence among Western European countries and helped them overcome traditional national rivalries and conflicts; in this fashion, the NATO system helped in the construction of a Western European "security community."[6] Also, since the United States took much of the responsibility and bore many of the costs for European security, EC countries did not have to develop their own security and defense institutions; in fact, the United States and NATO even discouraged their doing so. With the end of the cold war and a reduced U.S. security presence and role in Europe, however, there is now the need for an independent European security and defense capacity, as well as a more common approach to foreign policy. Not only must the EU take a much stronger role in regional security affairs, but also the advent of a more pluralistic New World Order both creates the space for and requires a more unified European voice on the global stage. Nevertheless, the challenge of building new institutions in such sovereignty-sensitive high politics areas is a considerable one. The costs of failing to do so, however, could be tremendous, including the possibility of renewed unilateralism, increased interstate rivalry, and geopolitical fragmentation.

Two Logics of Integration

In even broader terms, the geopolitical changes since 1989 have affected the EU by shifting the emphasis between the two primary logics of European integration, both of which have been in operation since the late 1940s. The first of these is the logic of interdependence and economic necessity. In general terms, integration has been necessary to enable relatively small European countries to survive and compete in an increasingly interdependent world economy dominated by large-market economies such as the United States and Japan. Furthermore, integration has enhanced the joint and individual capacities of European states to manage interdependence, the consequences of which—economic instability, environmental destruction, social uncertainty—are beyond the power of even larger national governments to control. In this manner, the sacrifice of some authority and policy independence to European institutions has enabled national governments to better perform the economic and social tasks required of democratic welfare states and has thereby actually bolstered, rather than undermined, the sovereignty and legitimacy of European nation-states. The experiences of the early 1990s indicate, however, that there may be limits on the extent to which integration can achieve this effect. In the process, however, European nation-states have been transformed, as has the exact meaning of national sovereignty, in that they have become increasingly dependent on integration for survival.

The second logic of integration is that of security and geopolitics. An original purpose of integration was to ensure that conflict and war would not endanger Western Europe again. To this end, the central interstate relationship of European integration has been that between France and Germany, the EU's two largest and most important powers. Indeed, one of the most significant achievements of postwar European integration has been the peaceful reconciliation of France and Germany and the maintenance of a rough balance of power, and cooperative relations, between these two former enemies. More generally, integration has been an important means for containing the power of a resurgent Germany and restoring a high level of mutual trust among Western European states. Although integration has been important for providing security within the Community, external security in the postwar decades was guaranteed by the U.S.-led NATO alliance. This arrangement not only decreased the need for, and even discouraged, European defense integration but also eliminated the possibility of renewed security rivalry between Western European states.

Both logics have been at work since the late 1940s, but their relative importance for European integration has changed over time. In the early postwar years, security considerations, in particular the need for Franco-German reconciliation, were a primary motivation behind the formation of the ECSC and the ill-fated attempt to create the EDC. By the late 1950s and the formation of the EEC, however, economic interests and necessity had become the driving force of integration. Moreover, the predominance of economics only grew throughout the following three decades, a period in which the regional security situation further stabilized and global interdependence continued to increase. This is not to say that security considerations disappeared altogether as a factor in European integration during this time. Nevertheless, integration after the mid-1950s focused mainly on economics or low politics questions, thus sustaining theoretical interpretations of integration that were based on an economic-functionalist logic.

After 1989, however, with the sudden collapse of communism in Eastern Europe and the rapid unification of Germany, security or "high politics" factors once again became predominant in the integration process.[7] Even though plans for EMU had been discussed and largely agreed on prior to the opening of the Berlin Wall, this issue now took on a much greater urgency, with monetary union viewed as a key means of containing a united Germany and guaranteeing continued German commitment to European integration. The need to act quickly to bind in or tie down the new German colossus was widely accepted by European governments, with the major exception of London, but it was a particularly important goal for France, arguably the primary loser of the end of the cold war. Germany also desired further integration as a means of assuaging the fears of its neighbors and stabilizing the security situation in post–cold war Europe. Among most European political elites, further integration was viewed as the only alternative to increased national rivalry and geopolitical fragmentation. More than any other factor, it was the security and geopolitical imperatives generated by the end of the cold war and German unification that were responsible for the Maastricht Treaty. This fact also helps explain how European leaders, in concluding the treaty, could get so far ahead of what both popular opinion and the market were prepared to accept.

With the dust from the Maastricht ratification crisis and accompanying currency upheavals now settling, it becomes apparent that both the economic and security imperatives that have driven European integration in the past are not only still present but also perhaps more vital than ever before. The world has not become any less interdependent, and recent turmoil in international currency markets has only reinforced the point that full EMU is necessary among those member states that can afford or are prepared for it. At the same time, building a stable new political-security order in Europe on the basis of the reordered status and power of key European states remains an overriding priority. In particular, Europe cannot afford a more powerful Germany to become detached from its supranational moorings and to perceive its interests in nationalistic or unilateral terms. As in the past, the EU will continue to be an important institutional means for mutually reconciling and balancing the relative interests and power of its member states. Beyond this, the EU must develop a more unified capacity and will as an external actor so that it can serve as a focal point for regional security and order in the New Europe and have a more influential voice in world affairs. At both the regional and global levels, greater unity will not only enhance the influence and effectiveness of Europe but will also reduce the temptation for individual member states to act unilaterally and thereby heighten the potential for increased interstate rivalry. On each of these levels—Community, regional, and global—the EU has an important role to play as a provider of security.

A Multispeed Europe?

As the EU prepares for the 1996 intergovernmental conference, the union is experiencing a profound crisis. The long-term implications of this crisis remain uncertain. It is entirely possible that the EU's current difficulties are only temporary and that once economic growth resumes and the European geopolitical situation stabilizes, the movement toward further integration will resume. In this case, the current crisis can be regarded as merely the latest downturn in what has historically been a cyclical process of European integration, with periods of crisis and stagnation, accompanied by excessive pessimism and malaise, alternating with periods of progress and vitality, attended by equally exaggerated optimism and overly inflated expectations. In fact, there may be a dialectical relationship between these episodes of crisis and advance. According to one historian of European integration, "The concept of crisis is central to the Community's experience," with such periods in the past often serving as catalysts for institutional innovation and further integration.[8]

A more positive view of the EU's future is supported by the fact that the basic economic and security imperatives motivating integration in the past are still present and important today, if not even more so. For this reason alone, further integration is likely. Nevertheless, integration will not be easy, and the EU has a number of major barriers to overcome on the road to economic and political union. Among these are the problems posed by significant differences of interest among EU member states concerning the pace, scope, and design of future integration. There are also the problems of the EU's democratic deficit, and the need to convince skeptical European publics of the need for and benefits of further integration.

If the EU overcomes these barriers, what will be the future design of European integration? The EU is unlikely to remain as it is today or to continue developing according to the pre-1989 model of integration. This model basically entailed a uniform movement toward greater integration. It also, despite frequent reaffirmation of the original goals of political union, was essentially an economic Community. In the future, however, in addition to further economic integration, greater political and security integration will be necessary. At the same time, different national levels of economic and political strength, as well as preparedness for further integration, will have to be recognized and taken into account in the EU's institutional development, even more so as the Community expands eastward. In other words, the future EU will have to become a Europe of variable geometry. This, in turn, means different countries or groups of countries moving toward further integration at different speeds.

The idea of a multispeed Europe is not particularly new. A two-speed model was first suggested by German chancellor Brandt in 1974, and this concept was later taken up by the Tindeman's committee on the future of European union.[9] In a 1975 final report, the Tindeman's committee suggested the possibility of a two-speed approach as a means for dealing with the varying economic abilities and political wills of member states to proceed with further integration. This idea was not well received by most member states, nor were similar notions of a two-tier, or variable geometry Europe or "Europe à la carte" that were also circulating at this time. Smaller and poorer countries feared being relegated to a second-class status under such schemes, while large countries objected to the loss of sovereignty these approaches would entail.[10]

The same factors that led the Tindeman's committee to consider a two-speed approach to further integration are present and relevant today; indeed, perhaps even more so. An expanding EU will become even more economically and politically diverse, thus making uniform integration impossible. At the same time, increased popular opposition to integration in many countries and the general politicization of EU affairs after 1991 will further constrain some member governments from agreeing to additional integration, particularly in politically sensitive areas such as money and defense. As a result, if further integration is to occur, it will have to be at a more differentiated pace.

In fact, there is ample precedent for this. Examples of a multispeed approach to integration already abound. Most notable is the EMS, which did not require members to join its exchange-rate mechanism unless they were both able and willing to do so. Once they did, there was the possibility of wider fluctuation bands to accommodate countries with weaker economies. Further examples of a multispeed approach are provided by the WEU and the Euro-Corps. There is also the Schengen Agreement, which as of mid-1995 had not been signed by all EU member states.[11] Each of these arrangements was developed outside the Treaty of Rome framework, which requires uniformity in the application of common rules and policies. This fact indicates, however, the extent to which European countries have been willing to be flexible and innovate to achieve greater integration.

A multispeed approach is also embedded in the Maastricht agreement on EMU, which allows some countries to proceed with monetary union if others are not yet ready, even as it specifies that all member states must be involved in the decisionmaking process. Furthermore, the multispeed principle is recognized by the opt-out given to Britain on EMU and the special exemptions from the Maastricht Treaty provided to Denmark at the December 1992 Edinburgh summit. Also, there is the separate Maastricht protocol on social policy, which allowed the other eleven member states to proceed without Britain in the development of common policies in this area.

Open discussion of a multispeed approach to integration was revived by the currency crises of 1992 and 1993, which highlighted the continued divergence of economic conditions among European countries and prompted increased speculation about a two-speed EMU. Also generating renewed interest in a multispeed approach was the popular backlash against Maastricht in many EU countries, indicating that some governments may not be able to secure the political consent of their citizens to further integration. In addition, there is the Community's impending enlargement into Eastern Europe, which will result in a further diversification of economic and political interests within the EU. In fact, one possibility that has been discussed as a response to the security needs of Eastern European countries is to admit them into the WEU, but not initially into the EU's economic and monetary arrangements.

At the heart of any version of the multispeed concept is the Franco-German relationship. European integration has served as the primary means for achieving reconciliation and partnership between these two countries in the postwar era. After the end of the cold war and German unification, this central purpose of European integration gained renewed emphasis and importance. As this book has shown, the desire to preserve this key bilateral partnership in the more uncertain geopolitical and security environment of the New Europe was a primary factor promoting the Maastricht Treaty. Similar considerations should lead these two countries to continue pushing the process of European integration forward, even if doing so results in a more open resort to a multispeed model. In fact, such an approach has long been favored by Germany as a means for dealing with British intransigence and the economic weakness of other member states. France has been somewhat more reluctant, fearing that a miniunion would not give it sufficient allies to counterbalance the power of a dominant Germany. In the new political and economic circumstances of the post–cold war era, however, French calculations of national interest and of how a multispeed approach to integration would serve this interest might well change.

The prospects for a multispeed Europe were boosted by the appearance in early September 1994 of a paper prepared by the parliamentary group of Germany's governing CDU/CSU.[12] The paper suggested a multispeed approach for the EU, with a hard core of countries moving ahead with EMU and further integration of foreign and defense policies. This step, according to the paper, should occur within the next five years, irrespective of the decisions on EMU taken in 1997 or 1999 under the terms of the Maastricht Treaty. At the same time, unlike the joint decisionmaking provided for in the Maastricht Treaty, in the CDU/CSU plan the core countries would proceed on their own, without the involvement of other EU members. Other countries would remain behind this core and could join at their own pace. The five countries that the CDU/CSU plan designated as part of the core were the ones most committed to, and prepared for, further integration: Germany, France, and the Benelux countries. In addition to the core, the plan provided for two other tiers of EU membership: the first consisting of present EU members, which would maintain the current level of integration, the second comprising Eastern European countries that would be more loosely integrated into the EU. The proposal suggested the year 2000 as the entry date for new Eastern European members.

Even though the CDU/CSU proposals focused on a core group of five countries, it also made clear that within this group was an inner core, consisting of the Franco-German partnership. According to the paper, Franco-German relations "must be raised to a new level if the historic process of European unification is not to peter out before it reaches its political goal."[13] As in the past, therefore, the Franco-German partnership would undergird European integration in the future. At the same time, the paper stated that European integration would continue to be the primary vehicle for bilateral cooperation.

In presenting the CDU/CSU paper, the party's parliamentary leader, Wolfgang Schäuble argued that "for a transitional period we must accept as the lesser evil that not all members will take part in every step of integration at the same time."[14] Where exactly the chancellor stood on the proposals was not clear. Kohl refrained from giving his public support to the plan, but it was generally assumed that the paper had his tacit approval. During a debate in the Bundestag on September 7, Kohl neither endorsed nor criticized the paper, saying that it was intended merely as an invitation to further discussion.[15] One person who was critical of the

CDU/CSU paper, however, was French prime minister Balladur; this despite the fact that the paper appeared to echo some of the views he had expressed only days earlier, when Balladur had claimed that he could support the concept of a multi-tiered Europe of "concentric circles."[16]

The CDU/CSU paper was immediately and vigorously criticized by the governments of EU member states that were not included in the hard core. The Italian Foreign Ministry released a statement claiming that the paper's ideas, if implemented, would "risk a breakup of Europe."[17] Also critical was British prime minister Major, who in a speech on September 7 at The Hague (The Netherlands) suggested an alternative vision of a variable geometry Europe: an à la carte Europe of different clubs with overlapping memberships rather than one of different groups or "classes."[18] The CDU/CSU paper also drew considerable fire within Germany. Among the critics were German foreign minster Klaus Kinkel—head of the FDP, the CDU/CSU's government coalition partner—and officials of the opposition SPD.[19] The commission was also officially critical, and at a meeting on September 10–11, EU foreign ministers were unanimous in condemning the CDU/CSU proposals.[20]

In all likelihood, the CDU/CSU paper was simply an initial attempt to influence the agenda and tone of the 1996 intergovernmental conference and was not meant as the basis for Germany's bargaining position at the conference. Certainly the paper has helped launch a much-needed public debate on the EU's future shape and direction. The paper could also be an attempt to exert pressure on Britain and other integration laggards in advance of the conference.

The floating of the core Europe idea seemed odd in view of declining public support for further integration in both France and Germany after the Maastricht Treaty. That such plans are nevertheless being discussed gives some indication, however, of the seriousness of these ideas and argues that they are more than simply a means of applying pressure to Britain and other reluctant Europeans. Further evidence of this was provided by a February 1995 announcement by Delors, previously a strong opponent of such schemes, that he now favored a multispeed approach led by France and Germany as the basis for further integration and that he viewed such a model as necessary for coping with the EU's eastward enlargement.[21] In June 1995, the CDU/CSU announced a set of follow-up proposals to its previous paper. Although this new paper avoided any explicit reference to the core Europe concept, it preserved the concept's essence in suggestions for further integration in the realm of foreign and security policy.[22]

Two Models for the Future

Two models for EU integration in the future thus appear possible. The first of these is the à la carte Europe, or Europe of multiple clubs. According to this model, EU member states, while all belonging to the Single Market, would be free to pick and choose from among a variety of other arrangements for closer economic and political cooperation. In addition to monetary and currency union, these would include arrangements in such areas as foreign policy, defense, immigration, and police and judicial affairs. These clubs would not be mutually exclusive, and their memberships could overlap. The key here would be that national participation in these clubs would be voluntary and not mandated by membership in the Single Market and other basic economic arrangements. At the same time, decisionmaking in these clubs would be on an intergovernmental basis, with an emphasis on avoiding the formation of a supranational political center with authority over member states. Such a scheme would obviously address the problems for integration created by varying levels of economic preparedness and political will among European states. It would also satisfy the interests of those opposed to the further erosion of national sovereignty in favor of European institutions. Not surprisingly, this model is strongly favored by the current Conservative government of Britain.

The second model for future EU integration is the Europe of multiple speeds, multiple tiers, or concentric circles. Whatever the name, the basic structure of this model is one of core and periphery. As with the first model, all EU member states would adhere to the Single Market and other basic economic arrangements. Beyond this, however, a smaller group of countries, those both economically ready and politically willing, would proceed with further economic and political integration. Other countries would be assigned to one or more associated categories of membership, each distinguished by a certain level of integration above and beyond the Single Market. Once they had progressed economically to a certain point, these countries would then be eligible to join the core group. Decisionmaking in this inner core would not necessarily be federal, but greater use of weighted majority voting would undoubtedly lead to a further blurring of the boundaries between national and EU authority. The countries most commonly viewed as candidates for this inner core are the original EEC six—Germany, France, the Benelux countries, and Italy—along with Austria, although there are many questions about Italy's ability to qualify economically for this core group.

Of the two models, the core-periphery one is the most likely to define the future institutional development of the EU because this model best fits the needs and interests of the Community's two most important states, France and Germany, and because it is the most realistic in political and security terms. Regarding the former, neither France nor Germany can afford to see the project of European integration fail, and political elites in both countries feel that a lack of continued progress would inevitably lead to increased fragmentation and interstate rivalry in Europe. Both states have already invested far too much in the success of the European project, and neither could survive its collapse. Only such considerations can explain the various contingency plans devised by French and German authorities in 1992–1993 in the event that the Maastricht Treaty was not ratified; these plans reportedly involved the two countries going it alone into EMU if necessary. Given the economic and political weight of France and Germany, it is hard to imagine how a decision to forge ahead with the formation of a core Europe could be ignored by others and not have a decisive impact on the future structure of the EU. Developing the domestic political support for this plan remains a key problem, but five decades of integration have so transformed popular perspectives of national interest and destiny that this problem would not be insurmountable.

The second factor supporting a core-periphery model is that the dictates of international politics and security require a center, without which disorder and instability are likely to follow. Although integration has substantially transformed the nature of European international politics, it has not obviated the need for a concentration of political power and authority as the basis for order. Even if this fundamental axiom of politics was overlooked in Western Europe during the cold war, in which order was largely externally imposed by superpower alliances, it cannot be disregarded any longer now that one pole of power has collapsed and the other is in the process of disengaging from Europe. A key problem with the multiple clubs model is that it allows for no political center but is instead based on a modified form of balance of power among independent states, a dynamic that has not worked very well for Europe in the past. Alternatively, this model presumes either the fundamental transformation of human nature and interstate behavior or the continued role of the United States as guarantor of European security. Neither is very likely, making the further self-organization of Europe in political and security terms more necessary. At any rate, even if something resembling a multiple clubs EU did come into existence, it would probably evolve into the core-periphery model since the small group of countries participating in most of the important clubs would be the very same ones usually regarded as potential members of a core Europe.

Nonetheless, saying that something is necessary and/or likely does not mean it will happen. Solutions must be found to the main problems generated by a core-periphery Europe: the institutionalized stratification of EU member states and the potential for growing marginalization of the periphery. In fact, such center-periphery dynamics could touch off a process of disintegration in the periphery and even a breakup of some existing nation-states. These may be the inevitable outcomes, however, of the construction of a New Europe.

Notes

1. On the French identity crisis, see Stanley Hoffmann, "Thoughts on the French Nation Today," *Daedalus* 122 (Summer 1993):63–79.

2. See, for instance, the comment of Chancellor Kohl quoted in *Der Spiegel*, September 28, 1992, p. 18.

3. On German concern about Chirac, see *Economist*, May 6, 1995, pp. 49–50.

4. *New York Times*, 22 May 1995, p. A3.

5. *Deutschland Nachrichten*, May 12, 1995, p. 1.

6. On the concept of security community, see Karl W. Deutsch, *Political Community at the International Level: Problems of Definition and Measurement* (Garden City, N.Y.:

Doubleday, 1954); Karl W. Deutsch et al., *Political Community and the North Atlantic Area* (Princeton: Princeton University Press, 1957).

7. A similar argument is made by Ole Waever, "Identity, Integration, and Security: Solving the Sovereignty Puzzle in E.U. Studies," *Journal of International Affairs* 48, 2 (Winter 1995):389–431.

8. Desmond Dinan, "The European Community, 1978–93," *Annals of the American Academy of Political and Social Science* 531 (January 1994):14. On the cyclical theory of European integration, see "Back to the Drawing Board" (Survey of the European Community), *Economist,* July 3, 1993, p. 5; Stanley Hoffmann, "Europe's Identity Crisis," *Daedalus* 123 (Spring 1994):2–4. For a dialectical interpretation of EU integration, see Dorette Corbey, "Dialectical Functionalism: Stagnation as a Booster of European Integration," *International Organization* 49, 2 (Spring 1995):253–284.

9. Juliet Lodge, "Preface: The Challenge of the Future," in Juliet Lodge, ed., *The European Community and the Challenge of the Future,* 2d ed. (New York: St. Martin's Press, 1993), p. xxiii.

10. On the Tindeman's report see Desmond Dinan, *Ever Closer Union? An Introduction to the European Community* (Boulder: Lynne Rienner, 1994), p. 94. For fuller exploration of these integration concepts, see Helen Wallace, *Europe: The Challenge of Diversity* (Boston: Routledge, 1985), pp. 29–49.

11. On the existing multispeed arrangements in Europe, see Hugh Miall, *Shaping a New European Order* (London: RIIA, 1994), pp. 88–89. On the Schengen Agreement, see Juliet Lodge, "Internal Security and Judicial Cooperation," in Lodge, ed., *The European Community and the Challenge of the Future,* pp. 321–323. See also Alan Butt Philip, "European Immigration Policy: Phantom, Fantasy, or Fact?" *West European Politics* 17 (April 1994):168–191.

12. The text of the CDU/CSU paper is reprinted in *Blätter für deutsche und internationale Politik* 39, 16 (October 1994):1271–1280. For a description of the CDU/CSU paper, see *New York Times,* September 4, 1994, p. A4; *Economist,* September 10, 1994, pp. 14, 21–23; *The Week in Germany,* September 9, 1994, pp. 1–2.

13. Quote cited in *Economist,* September, 10, 1994, p. 14.

14. *New York Times,* September 4, 1994, p. A4.

15. Ibid.; *The Week in Germany,* September 9, 1994, pp. 1–2.

16. On Balladur's critical response to the CDU/CSU paper, see *New York Times,* December 4, 1994, p. A6. On his concentric circles idea, see *New York Times,* September 4, 1994, p. A4; *Economist,* September 10, 1994, p. 14. The text of the August 30 interview in which Balladur made his concentric circles remarks is reprinted in *Europa-Archiv* 49, 18 (September 15, 1994):D544–547.

17. *New York Times,* September 4, 1994, p. A4.

18. *Economist,* September 10, 1994, pp. 14–15.

19. *New York Times,* September 4, 1994, p. A4; *Economist,* September 10, 1994, p. 21. For a number of articles debating the CDU/CSU's core Europe idea, see *Die Neue Gesellschaft/Frankfurter Hefte* 12 (December 1994).

20. *Deutschland Nachrichten,* September 16, 1994, p. 2.

21. *Financial Times,* February 24, 1995, p. 2.

22. *Economist,* June 17, 1995, p. 56.

Selected Bibliography

Theory

Groom, A.J.R., and Paul Taylor. *Functionalism: Theory and Practice in International Relations.* New York: Crane Roussak, 1975.

Haas, Ernst. *The Obsolescence of Integration Theory.* Berkeley and Los Angeles: University of California Press, 1975.

———. *The Uniting of Europe.* Stanford: Stanford University Press, 1958.

Lindberg, Leon. *The Political Dynamics of European Integration.* Stanford: Stanford University Press, 1963.

Lindberg, Leon, and Stuart Scheingold. *Europe's Would-Be Polity.* Englewood Cliffs, N.J.: Prentice-Hall, 1970.

Taylor, Paul. *The Limits of European Integration.* London: Croom Helm, 1983.

General EU and History

Adams, William James, ed. *Singular Europe: Economy and Polity of the European Community After 1992.* Ann Arbor: University of Michigan Press, 1992.

Cafruny, Alan, and Glenda G. Rosenthal, eds. *The State of the European Community,* vol 2; *The Maastricht Debates and Beyond.* Boulder: Lynne Rienner, 1993.

Dinan, Desmond. *Ever Closer Union? An Introduction to the European Community.* Boulder: Lynne Rienner, 1994.

Duff, Andrew, John Pinder, and Roy Pryce, eds. *Maastricht and Beyond: Building the European Union.* London: Routledge, 1994.

George, Stephen. *Politics and Policy in the European Community.* 2d ed. New York: Oxford University Press, 1991.

Hoffmann, Stanley. *The European Sisyphus: Essays on Europe, 1964–1994.* Boulder: Westview Press, 1995.

Keohane, Robert O., and Stanley Hoffmann, eds. *The New European Community: Decisionmaking and Institutional Change.* Boulder: Westview Press, 1991.

Lodge, Juliet, ed. *The European Community and the Challenge of the Future.* 2d ed. New York: St. Martin's Press, 1993.

Nugent, Neill. *The Government and Politics of the European Union.* 3d ed. Durham, N.C.: Duke University Press, 1994.

Pinder, John. *European Community: The Building of a Union.* New York: Oxford University Press, 1991.

Ross, George. *Jacques Delors and European Integration.* New York: Oxford University Press, 1995.

Sbragia, Alberta M., ed. *Euro-Politics: Institutions and Policymaking in the "New" European Community.* Washington, D.C.: Brookings Institution, 1992.

Smith, Dale L., and James Lee Ray, eds. *The 1992 Project and the Future of Integration in Europe.* New York: M. E. Sharpe, 1993.

Urwin, Derek W. *The Community of Europe: A History of European Integration Since 1945.* 2d ed. London: Longman, 1991.

Wallace, William, ed. *The Dynamics of European Integration.* London: Pinter, 1990.

German Unification and European Integration

Kurz, Heinz D., ed. *United Germany and the New Europe.* Aldershot, England: Edward Elgar, 1993.

Lankowski, Carl, ed. *Germany and the European Community: Beyond Hegemony and Containment?* New York: St. Martin's Press, 1993.

Lippert, Barbara et al. *German Unification and EC Integration: German and British Perspectives.* London: Royal Institute of International Affairs, 1993.

Merkl, Peter H. *German Unification in the European Context.* State College: Penn State University Press, 1993.

Stares, Paul B., ed. *The New Germany and the New Europe.* Washington, D.C.: Brookings Institution, 1992.

France and Germany

Friend, Julius W. *The Linchpin: Franco-German Relations, 1950–1990.* New York: Praeger, 1991.

Gordon, Philip H. *France, Germany, and the Western Alliance.* Boulder: Westview Press, 1995.

McCarthy, Patrick, ed. *France-Germany, 1983–93: The Struggle to Cooperate.* New York: St. Martin's Press, 1993.

Simonian, Haig. *The Privileged Partnership: Franco-German Relations and the European Community, 1969–1984.* Oxford: Clarendon Press, 1985.

Willis, Roy. *France, Germany and the New Europe.* 2d ed. Stanford: Stanford University Press, 1968.

Economic and Monetary Union

Guerrieri, Paolo, and Piercarlo Padoan, eds. *The Political Economy of European Integration.* New York: Harvester Wheatsheaf, 1989.

Ludlow, Peter. *The Making of the European Monetary System.* London: Butterworth, 1982.

Nölling, Wilhelm. *Monetary Policy in Europe After Maastricht.* New York: St. Martin's Press, 1993.

Padoa-Schioppa, Tommaso. *The Road to Monetary Union in Europe: The Emperor, the Kings, and the Genies.* Oxford: Clarendon Press, 1994.

Tsoukalis, Loukas. *The New European Economy. The Politics and Economics of European Integration.* 2d ed. Oxford: Oxford University Press, 1993.

European Political Union

Feld, Werner. *The Future of European Security and Defense Policy.* Boulder: Lynne Rienner, 1993.

Laursen, Finn, and Sophie Vanhoonacker, eds. *The Intergovernmental Conference on Political Union: Institutional Reforms, New Policies, and International Identity of the European Community.* Dordrecht, The Netherlands: Martinus Nijhoff, 1992.

Nuttall, Simon. *European Political Cooperation.* Oxford: Clarendon Press, 1992.

Rummel, Reinhardt, ed. *Toward Political Union: Planning a Common Foreign and Security Policy.* Boulder: Westview Press, 1992.

Enlargement and Eastern Europe

Michalski, Anna, and Helen Wallace. *The European Community: The Challenge of Enlargement.* London: Royal Institute of International Affairs, 1992.

Pinder, John. *The European Community and Eastern Europe.* London: Royal Institute of International Affairs, 1991.

Wallace, Helen, ed. *The Wider Western Europe: Reshaping the EC/EFTA Relationship.* London: Royal Institute of International Affairs, 1991.

About the Book and Author

Exploring the politics of European integration, Michael Baun argues that the end of the cold war and German unification have created a new set of geopolitical realities in Europe that have profoundly affected the nature and dynamics of European union. His primary focus is the "high politics" of European integration after 1989, especially the role of the Franco-German relationship in the Maastricht Treaty process.

Acknowledging the important roots of the treaty in economic and institutional developments prior to 1989, Baun argues that Maastricht principally can be understood as a response by the EU and its member states to German unification and the end of the cold war. In making this argument, he departs from more conventional neofunctionalist or institutionalist interpretations of European integration.

After providing the historical background of developments before 1989, Baun weighs the decision to launch parallel intergovernmental conferences on monetary and political union in 1990 and describes in detail the negotiations and treaty outcomes in each of these areas. He then examines the difficult ratification of the Maastricht treaty in 1992–1993, in the face of growing popular opposition and economic and monetary instability. The book concludes with an analysis of the future prospects for European union in the post-Maastricht era, as the EU approaches its next major intergovernmental conference in 1996.

Michael J. Baun is assistant professor of political science at Georgia State University.

Index